# State Formation in Palestine

The crisis-ridden progress in Palestinian state formation since the signing of the Oslo Agreements raises important questions about reform priorities and the future prospects of constructing a viable Palestinian state. Were the obstacles to progress primarily due to poor governance and poor leadership on the Palestinian side, how far have corruption and the weakness of democracy in the Palestinian Authority been responsible, and what were the effects of the economic and political relationships between Israel and the emerging Palestinian state? This book examines these key questions, and challenges the widely prevalent view that the Palestinian Authority collapsed because of its internal governance failures, its lack of commitment to democracy, and its failure to control corruption.

It argues that the analytical framework of "good governance" is not appropriate for assessing state performance in developing countries, and that it is especially inappropriate in conflict and post-conflict situations. Instead, an alternative framework is proposed for assessing state performance in a context of economic and social transformation. This is then applied in detail to different aspects of state formation in Palestine to show that while there were indeed internal failures of governance, the institutional architecture set up by the Oslo agreements established an asymmetric Israeli control over the emerging Palestinian state and this was responsible for many of the most serious failures of governance.

This architecture is based on Israel's insistence on security first, and since this is not likely to change soon, the analysis has important implications for the prospects of Palestinian state formation.

**Mushtaq Husain Khan** is Senior Lecturer in Economics and Associate Dean (Research) in the Faculty of Law and Social Sciences, the School of Oriental and African Studies, University of London. He has written extensively on the economics of governance, corruption, clientelism, rent-seeking and state failure.

**George Giacaman** is co-founder and Director of Muwatin, the Palestinian Institute for the Study of Democracy (Ramallah)

**Inge Amundsen** is a political scientist and a Research Director at the Chr. Michelsen Institute in Bergen, Norway.

## The RoutledgeCurzon Political Economy of the Middle East and North Africa Series

Hassan Hakimian,
*Cass Business School, City University, London*

### Editorial board

**Jacques Charmes**
University of Versailles Saint Quentin en Yvelines, France

**David Cobham**
University of St Andrews, UK

**Nu'man Kanafani**
The Royal Veterinary and Agricultural University, Denmark

**Massoud Karshenas**
SOAS, University of London, UK

**Jeffrey B. Nugent**
University of Southern California, USA

**Jennifer Olmsted**
Sonoma State University, California, USA

**Karen Pfeifer**
Smith College, Northampton, Massachusetts, USA

**Wassim Shahin**
The Lebanese American University (LAU), Byblos, Lebanon

**Subidey Togan**
Bilkent University, Ankara, Turkey

### Titles in the series

**Trade Policy and Economic Integration in the Middle East and North Africa**
Economic Boundaries in Flux
*Edited by Hassan Hakimian and Jeffrey B. Nugent*

**State Formation in Palestine**
Viability and Governance during a Social Transformation
*Edited by Mushtaq Husain Khan*

# State Formation in Palestine

Viability and governance during a
social transformation

Edited by

**Mushtaq Husain Khan**

**with**

**George Giacaman and Inge Amundsen**

RoutledgeCurzon
Taylor & Francis Group

LONDON AND NEW YORK

First published 2004
RoutledgeCurzon
11 New Fetter Lane, London EC4P 4EE

Simultaneously published in the USA and Canada
by RoutledgeCurzon
29 West 35th Street, New York, NY 10001

*RoutledgeCurzon is an imprint of the Taylor & Francis Group*

Typeset in Times
by Taylor & Francis Books Ltd
Printed and bound in Great Britain
by TJ International Ltd, Padstow, Cornwall

*British Library Cataloguing in Publication Data*
A catalogue record for this book is available from the British Library

*Library of Congress Cataloging in Publication Data*
A catalog record for this book has been requested

ISBN 0–415–33802–6 (hbk)
ISBN 0–415–33801–8 (pbk)

# Contents

# Illustrations

# Contributors

**Inge Amundsen** is a political scientist and a Research Director at the Chr. Michelsen Institute in Bergen, Norway. He has published on state failure, corruption and democratization in a number of African countries.

**Basem Ezbidi** is associate researcher at MUWATIN, the Palestinian Institute for the Study of Democracy (Ramallah), and Assistant Professor of political science at Najah University in Nablus (West Bank). He has published on political culture, Islamist political movements and political theory.

**Odd-Helge Fjeldstad** is an economist and researcher based at the Chr. Michelsen Institute at Bergen, Norway. He has published on corruption, decentralization, taxation and state failure, with a specialization in African countries.

**George Giacaman** is co-founder and Director of Muwatin, the Palestinian Institute for the Study of Democracy (Ramallah) and is a faculty member in the Department of Philosophy and the MA programme in Democracy and Human Rights at Birzeit University (West Bank). He has published on Palestinian state formation and transition to democracy, and contemporary Western and Islamic philosophy.

**Sari Hanafi** is associate researcher at MUWATIN, the Palestinian Institute for the Study of Democracy (Ramallah), and is Director of Shaml, the Palestinian Refugee and Diaspora Centre (Ramallah). He has published on Palestinian refugee networks, relationships between the Palestinian Diaspora and Palestine, issues facing returnees, NGOs, and conflict resolution in the post-war period.

**Jamil Hilal** is associate researcher at MUWATIN, the Palestinian Institute for the Study of Democracy (Ramallah). He is a senior research fellow associated with the Law Institute and the Development Studies Programme at Birzeit University (West Bank), and is a member of the Palestinian Poverty Commission. He has published (in Arabic and English) on Palestinian society and politics.

**Mushtaq Husain Khan** is Senior Lecturer in Economics and Associate Dean (Research) in the Faculty of Law and Social Sciences, at SOAS, the School of Oriental and African Studies, University of London. He has published on the economics of governance, corruption, clientelism, rent-seeking, state failure, institutional economics and land reform in developing countries.

**Mohamed M. Nasr** is associate researcher at MUWATIN, the Palestinian Institute for the Study of Democracy (Ramallah), and Associate Professor of Economics at Birzeit University, (West Bank). He has published on industrial economics and economic development issues in the region.

**Linda Tabar** is associate researcher at MUWATIN, the Palestinian Institute for the Study of Democracy (Ramallah), and is currently finishing a PhD at SOAS, the School of Oriental and African Studies, University of London.

**Adel Zagha** is associate researcher at MUWATIN, the Palestinian Institute for the Study of Democracy (Ramallah), and Assistant Professor of Economics and Dean of the Faculty of Commerce and Economics at Birzeit University (West Bank). He has published on issues of foreign aid and economic development in Palestine, permanent status trade relations between Palestine and Israel, and monetary and fiscal measures for stimulating capital formation in developing countries.

**Husam Zomlot** is an economist who has worked for UNSCOM in Palestine and for a number of Arabic language newspapers and is currently completing a PhD in Economics at SOAS, the School of Oriental and African Studies, University of London. He is also counsellor for political affairs at the Palestinian General Delegation to the United Kingdom.

# Abbreviations

| | |
|---|---|
| BOI | Bank of Israel |
| CAC | Joint Civil Affairs Co-ordination and Co-operation Committee |
| CET | common external tariff |
| GS | Gaza Strip |
| ICA | Israeli Controlled Areas |
| ITD | Income Tax Department |
| JEC | Joint Economic Committee |
| NIS | New Israeli Shekel |
| OEIP | Oslo Extended Interim Period |
| PA | Palestinian Authority |
| PCBS | Palestinian Central Bureau of Statistics |
| PCSC | Palestinian Commercial Services Company |
| PEP | Paris Economic Protocol |
| PIF | Palestinian Investment Fund |
| PLC | Palestinian Legislative Council |
| PLO | Palestine Liberation Organization |
| PMAD | Palestinian Public Monitoring and Audit Department |
| PNA | Palestinian National Authority |
| PNGOs | Palestinian non-govermental organizations |
| PRA | Palestinian Revenue Authority |
| PTF | Peace Technology Fund |
| TAP | Tripartite Action Plan |
| WB | West Bank |
| WBG | West Bank and Gaza |
| WBGS | West Bank and Gaza Strip |

# Acknowledgements

The research project was supported by grants from the Royal Norwegian Ministry of Foreign Affairs, and NORAD (The Norwegian Agency for Development Cooperation), which financed an ongoing cooperation between the CMI (the Chr. Michelsen Institute) and MUWATIN (the Palestinian Institute for the Study of Democracy). MUWATIN and its wonderful staff provided the coordination and logistics in Palestine and SOAS (the School of Oriental and African Studies, University of London) provided logistical support in London. Particular thanks are due to May Jayyusi at Muwatin for her unstinting support and to Asma Khan in London for her meticulous editing.

# Introduction

## State formation in Palestine

*Mushtaq Husain Khan*

### Achievements, constraints and prospects for the future

The historic significance of the Oslo Agreement signed by the Palestinian Liberation Organization (PLO) and Israel in 1993 was that this was the first time that Israel formally recognized, even if only in part, the national aspirations of the Palestinian people. Many Palestinians believed that Israel had implicitly accepted the necessity of creating a fully fledged Palestinian state on 1967 borders. But the exercise eventually ended in the failure of Camp David and the commencement of the Second *Intifada* of 2000. Our analysis of Palestinian state formation in the period after 1994 identifies a number of key external and internal factors that contributed to the eventual failure. The Road Map announced in 2003 retained many of these damaging elements, without enjoying the goodwill or the relative political stability that made Oslo appear so promising at the time. Thus, the impasse reached in 2000 raises questions of great importance for the future. Was the failure due to poor Palestinian governance, poor leadership on one or both sides, or the economic and political relationships that Israel sought to construct with the emerging Palestinian state under the aegis of Oslo? In particular, what role did the quality of *governance* as measured by corruption, rent-seeking and the weakness of democracy within the Palestinian Authority play in the eventual crisis? These questions are not just important for the historical record; they are critical for assessing the prospects of constructing a viable Palestinian state in the future.

The Palestinian Authority (the PA, often also referred to as the Palestinian National Authority or PNA) was established in 1994.[1] It had the unenviable task of *first* ensuring security for Israel while, in the interim period, it only controlled a number of non-contiguous population centres in the occupied territories, with authority over health, education, social services and tourism, the power to raise direct taxes and to elect a representative council. The PNA did not control its external borders, it lacked territorial contiguity, and it lacked meaningful sovereignty over its own land, water, minerals, airspace or even access to the sea. Yet, it had many of the symbols and trappings of a state (such as passports, stamps, car number plates, an international airport, ministries, police and security forces, and other public institutions)[2]. In substance, however, it was actually a limited self-government with very limited administrative, security and legislative powers over *limited* areas in the West Bank and Gaza Strip (WBG). The Israeli occupation continued over East Jerusalem, some 60 per cent of the area of the West Bank, and just over 25 per cent of the area of the Gaza Strip. Israeli settlements remained atop every strategic hilltop and vital aquifer in the West Bank, breaking up the PNA's territories into a series of non-contiguous and water-scarce plots. Nevertheless, the PNA was more than a municipal government because it was established following the three agreements signed between the PLO and Israel between September 1993 and September 1995, as an interim measure, awaiting the results of final status negotiations.[3] Its supporters believed it to be the future Palestinian state in embryonic form, which would take over as Israel withdrew, as they believed it must, from all the territories it occupied in 1967 in line with UN Resolutions 242 and 338. In mid 1999, the population of the WBG was estimated at 3,019,704, including East Jerusalem.[4] The majority of this Palestinian population in the occupied areas came under the jurisdiction of the PNA, with the exception of East Jerusalem and areas that remained under Israeli control.[5]

The amount of land the Palestinians would eventually get was left for final status negotiations, as were all the difficult questions including the status of East Jerusalem, the refugees, and the Jewish settlements in the occupied territories. The Palestinians believed that by signing the Agreements, Israel had accepted that it would have to withdraw to the internationally recognized 1967 borders. But even if it did, the Palestinians would still barely be getting 22 per cent of historic Palestine. Even this best-case scenario, and the process through which it was to be achieved, was highly controversial from the Palestinian perspective. The international sponsors of the PNA recognized this, since they prioritized assistance to the Authority to immediately set up a massive Palestinian internal security force. But while the Authority acquired the power to police its population, it lacked powers to police its borders and negotiate independent trade agreements; it did not have its own currency and it could not define citizenship. As a result, its economic survival and its relationship with the outside world were controlled by Israel in ways that often worsened the already vulnerable situation of many Palestinians. This superstructure needs to be explicitly recognized in any objective attempt to evaluate governance under the PNA or to identify areas of weakness where reform priorities should be directed.

While the PNA lacked many of the fundamental characteristics of a state, the fact that it could legitimately exercise violence to maintain social order within the territories it controlled gave it a state-like quality. Moreover, Palestinians perceived many of its political and economic interventions as the actions of their emerging state. At the same time, from the outset, there was an internal Palestinian critique of the PNA's quality of governance, coming from across the Palestinian political spectrum. These critiques pointed out a number of areas of concern, including a widespread perception of corruption, of human rights abuses in arrests and interrogations, the lack of attention given to developing democratic procedures, and of the emergence of monopolies and cartels that were distorting the market against the interests of consumers and small producers. These internal Palestinian critiques were pointing out the slow progress towards the *goals* of the Palestinian state formation process from a Palestinian perspective. In contrast, a related critique of the Authority began to emerge from the 'good governance' school and the related neo-patrimonial framework that identified a number of these same characteristics as *causes* of economic stagnation and political crisis. There is no question that the problems of corruption and weak democracy in the PNA were real and undesirable. The question is rather about the causes and consequence of these problems, so that the most important factors can be prioritized for policy. We will argue that both the good governance and neo-patrimonial frameworks are seriously inadequate for assessing the achievements and failures of governance under the PNA, or for identifying the lessons to be learnt for the future.

Our argument is therefore both about methods of analysis and about assessing the historical evidence. On the method of analysis, we question the usefulness of the *good governance* and *neo-patrimonial* frameworks in the context of developing countries, and particularly in contexts of conflict, such as the Palestinian one. We argue that to evaluate the problems of governance in such contexts requires a framework that takes account of the fact that developing states face challenges that are quite different from the service-delivery tasks appropriate for advanced country states. States in developing countries are frequently and necessarily engaged in reconstructing their societies and economies and thereby overseeing far-reaching processes of *social transformation*. In particular, processes of creating a capitalist sector are always intensely contested, and there are inevitably winners and losers. In contexts such as that of Palestine, we also have intense colonial-type conflicts between a colonial power and a colonized population. To assess governance in these developmental contexts, we propose an alternative framework derived from the experience of economic and social transformation in developing countries. This framework focuses on the 'transformation' capacities of states and the potential of developing these capacities. It provides a very different set of criteria for assessing areas of strength and weakness in the Palestinian administration. It is likely to be of wider interest in the Middle East, and in other developing countries. We then use this framework to assess the historical evidence of Palestinian state formation.

Chapter 1 by Khan sets out the analytical and empirical approaches that are developed in this book. It begins by questioning the appropriateness of the good governance and neo-patrimonial approaches applied to developing countries. These models are based on an underlying mainstream economics model where the existence of 'rents' signals economic inefficiency. 'Rent' is a term used by economists to describe incomes that are higher than those possible in a competitive market. In most cases, rents therefore refer to politically generated incomes, since political intervention is the most obvious way in which 'above normal' incomes are generated. Rents include monopoly profits, and subsidies and transfers of all types, where political power is used to create privileged incomes for some. 'Good governance', in the mainstream political economy tradition, is achieved if institutional structures prevent the emergence of rents and the associated rent-seeking activities. Anti-corruption strategies and the support for democracy have an *instrumental* value in this analysis. Corruption is illegal rent-seeking, where the state is bribed to create or maintain privileged incomes, or to allocate privileged resources in particular ways. Anti-corruption strategies are expected to reduce this illegal rent-seeking. It is also theoretically assumed that it will become more difficult to create rents if we have a democracy, because rents by definition always benefit a minority. The good governance argument is that to have a vibrant market economy, governance reforms have to tackle corruption, establish democracy, and liberalize the economy at the same time. The neo-patrimonial argument is closely related. It argues that rents are widespread in developing countries because of pre-modern and personalized political institutions and cultures. These allow unaccountable leaders to create rents for themselves and their clients, with the same damaging economic and political consequences.

In contrast to these theories, we argue that an examination of the historical evidence of economic transformation in developing countries tells us that rents are pervasive in all developing countries, *and they have to be*. While some rents are damaging, many other rents are essential for organizing the economic transformation that creates a capitalist economy, and for political stabilization. In conflict and post-conflict situations, the importance of rents for managing political stabilization is even more marked. It follows that in developing and conflict societies we have to examine the determinants of different *types* of rents. Compared to the attractive simplicity of the good governance agenda that tries to achieve a rent-free competitive market, with relatively simple institutional and political reforms, the real world demands are more complex. From this perspective, the task of state-building and of reform is indeed to attack the institutional and political factors that induce the creation of damaging rents. But at the same time, and no less importantly, reform has to promote institutions and political arrangements that allow the creation and management of rents that are essential for economic transformation and political stabilization.

Accelerating *economic* development requires interventions and rent-creation that accelerates the emergence of a viable capitalist class, and supports and regulates its development. States also have to carry out significant redistributions to maintain *political* stability, often having to use patron–client networks to achieve stabilization. This too requires significant rent-creation and rent-management capacities. In Palestine, there were additional limits on what the 'state' could do that were set by external powers. These external constraints ensured that important rents were controlled by external powers, and this significantly affected the way in which PNA institutions operated. We argue that some of these external constraints played a critical role in blocking state formation in Palestine, and this has important implications for state formation strategies in the future.

We apply this framework to the Palestinian context to identify the strengths and weaknesses of the Palestinian quasi-state set up in 1994. Our method is to start with an investigation of the dominant types of rents that characterized the Palestinian economy and polity. What were the major resource flows and rents that describe the activities of the quasi-state? This information helps us to identify some of the main characteristics and capacities of the PNA, as well as identifying some of the directions in which it was likely to evolve. Some of the most important resources that were critical for the survival of the Palestinian quasi-state were controlled by Israel as a deliberate feature of the security architecture negotiated under Oslo. The bulk of Palestinian fiscal revenues was collected and transferred to the Palestinians by Israel; Palestinian trade was controlled by Israel in ways that allowed Israeli trading monopolies to extract rents from Palestinian consumers, and Palestinian labour movements, to Israel and even within the Palestinian territories, were rigorously controlled. These restrictions meant that resources that were critical for the survival of the Palestinian quasi-state were transferred to it in the form of rents controlled by Israel, and this leads us to argue that Israel's intention was to create a *client state*. Although neither side used this term for obvious reasons, the Palestinian leadership implicitly accepted the necessity of these Israeli controls over the economy for an indefinite period. It was clear to them that they had no option but to accept these conditions and prove that they could deliver security to Israel's satisfaction.

But to assess the viability of the client-state strategy, we need to ask why Israel wanted to maintain these types of controls over the emerging Palestinian state, and this too is discussed further in Chapter 1 by Khan. Security behind recognized international borders does not necessarily require a client state in a neighbouring country, particularly given the military balance of power between Israel and the Palestinians. One possibility is that Israel foresaw the permanent presence of Jewish settlements throughout the Palestinian territories. Ensuring the security of a myriad of enclaves would make it necessary to have a client state on a permanent basis in Palestine. Or even worse, perhaps Israel's political classes believed that a Palestinian state would not solve the 'Palestinian problem' from their perspective, since the problem of the refugees and of Israel's internal Palestinians would remain. If this was the concern, Israel's long-term strategic interests might have demanded the creation of an *unviable* or dependent client state, which could be relied on to assist in the long-run management of other aspects of the Palestinian problem. If so, the two sides may have had very inconsistent expectations about the type of Palestinian state that was to be constructed. While we do not know precisely *why* Israel insisted on developing and maintaining the controls that we describe as the client-state system of rents, we do know that it did (and this system is the subject of Chapter 3 by Zagha and Zomlot).

Even though Israel insisted on retaining control over critical Palestinian rents, we argue (in Chapter 1 by Khan) that these arrangements may nevertheless have allowed substantial Palestinian economic growth, but only if Israel had allowed rapid economic integration of the Palestinian territories with the Israeli economy. Of course, this would not be possible if the Israeli intention was to create an unviable state in the first place. But if the client-state controls were simply to ensure Israel's security, Palestinian viability and security could also have been ensured. Given its control over a range of rents critical for the survival of the Palestinian quasi-state, Israeli strategies of ensuring compliance by its client state could in theory have ranged from *integrationist* strategies at one pole to *asymmetric containment* at the other. As the terms suggest, an integrationist strategy would aim to create *incentives* for compliance by rapidly deepening the economic integration of the Palestinian and Israeli economies across all fronts. In contrast, asymmetric containment would create large *penalties* for non-compliance by maintaining and enhancing an asymmetric vulnerability of one side to achieve the security aims of the other. We argue that while Israeli policy statements initially suggested a commitment to integrationist policies, their policies on the ground could only be described as asymmetric containment. The retention by Israel of strategic points of control all over the occupied territories, and the rapid construction of a system of checkpoints within the WBG were the critical components of this system of asymmetric containment. This is one reason why disagreements over small amounts of territory have been so important in final status negotiations. Palestinian negotiators frequently pointed out that in a prison, the prisoners control 95 per cent of the space. The 5 per cent they do not control make it a prison. It appears that Israel was unwilling to give up either the client-state system or its system of maintaining asymmetric containment within the client state. We argue that many of the most important governance failures in the Palestinian territories were directly connected with the management of such a client state.

It is in this context that the other rents and interventions of the PNA have to be assessed. Apart from the rents created by external powers, the Authority created, allocated and extracted its own rents. Some of these rents were undoubtedly damaging rents. These included predatory extortions and monopoly profits for privileged individuals. Clearly there were some embryonic predatory characteristics within the client state, and if these activities had considerably expanded, the client state could have collapsed into a full-fledged *predatory state*. While many of the factors supporting the further development of predatory rents were internal to Palestinian society, external containment also played an important part. The more constrained economic development becomes because of containment, the more likely it is that a political leadership will engage in short-term predation rather than attempt long-term development. At the same time, the Palestinian quasi-state also had to manage considerable redistributive transfers to maintain political stability, particularly by creating jobs in the public sector and in the security forces. These transfers were also rents, and there was a danger that the emerging state might lose control over these rents. If so, these rents might have become the subject of factional competition, with powerful factions organizing to capture these rents. If this had happened, Palestine may have become similar to many developing countries that suffer from *fragmented clientelism*, where the state loses control over developmental allocations, and political stability is threatened by the intense competition over redistributive rents. We discuss the conditions under which this could happen in Palestine and conclude that while it was a possibility, the conditions pushing the client state to collapse into a fragmented clientelist state were relatively weak.

Finally, and given the context perhaps most surprisingly, there were examples of developmental rents and rent-management capacities in the Authority. These embryonic *developmental characteristics* of the emerging state were supported and promoted by the PNA leadership, which was strongly motivated by economic nationalism, and which had access to a large group of expatriate Palestinian capitalists who could be potential developmental partners of the state. These circumstances created opportunities of accelerating capitalist development that are not available to most developing-country states. The Authority tried to take full advantage of this, but given its limited fiscal and legal powers, it often used unorthodox methods that appeared to violate good governance criteria. Thus, monopolies and market power were often created for investors to attract critical investments into a conflict zone. In other cases, Palestinian trading monopolies were created that prevented the loss of some monopoly profits to Israeli trading monopolies, and these enhanced the fiscal viability of the Authority. The Authority also displayed a strong capacity to maintain internal political stability in a difficult context. It managed rent transfers for stabilization without letting the allocation of these rents get out of control. Thus, there were some limited, but extremely important, developmental rent-management capacities of the client state. If the client-state status could have been overturned and full sovereignty attained, and if policy-makers had been able to identify and strengthen these capacities, the outcome might have been quite promising for Palestinian development.

In Chapter 2 by Hilal and Khan, the conditions supporting the development of each of these sets of state characteristics and capacities are extensively discussed. This chapter draws on other chapters and presents both a historical analysis of state formation in Palestine as well as an evaluation of policy options. Our analysis identifies a number of different constraints that have to be addressed if there is to be viable progress in the future not only towards state formation but also towards sustainable reductions in corruption or progress in democratization. Palestinian popular aspirations were to achieve rapid *outcomes* in terms of statehood, democracy and a corruption-free society. These aspirations for outcomes have to be distinguished sharply from the analysis of the good governance and neo-patrimonial frameworks that identify democracy and the reduction of corruption as instrumental *preconditions* for the formation of a viable state. Our reading of the historical evidence suggests that the achievement of sustainable democracy and low corruption are themselves *dependent* on the construction of viable and dynamic economies and states. Long-run state viability has, historically, not been dependent on initial levels of corruption or democracy, but rather on the ability or otherwise of their states to push through developmental transformations. This has been a critical precondition for reducing corruption and entrenching democracy in sustainable ways.

To assess whether Palestinian demands for democracy and good governance are going to be furthered by the growing external pressure in pushing good governance reforms as *preconditions* for progress, we need to ask whether these reforms are likely to enhance the developmental and transformation capacities of the Palestinian state. In Chapter 2 by Hilal and Khan, we note that following the failure of the Camp David talks and the beginning of the Second *Intifada* in 2000, a number of governance reforms were imposed on the PNA that enhanced transparency and weakened the centralization of power in the hands of the executive. Far from increasing the chances of successful state formation along the two-state route, our analysis suggests that these reforms may have a negative effect on sustainable state formation given that the external constraints have not been addressed and are not likely to be addressed in the near future. Weakening the Palestinian executive in such a context may have the effect of reducing rather than enhancing the viability of a future quasi-state.

In terms of policy, our analysis suggests that observations of governance failures in Palestine (such as corruption, rent-creation, or weak democratic processes) fall into three categories. First, many of the most damaging governance failures under the PNA were directly caused or encouraged by the framework of control that Israel insisted on and that was deliberately created under Oslo and related agreements as a necessary part of a particular route of state formation. For instance, executive centralization was a design feature of the quasi-state created under Oslo, and was required to ensure the security-first conditions that Israel insisted on. Many governance failures followed directly from this constitutional arrangement. Similarly, much of the corruption at borders and checkpoints was directly the product of a complex system of restrictions. Another example is the way in which Israel paid part of the Palestinian tax revenues it collected into special accounts controlled by the Palestinian presidency. These arrangements assisted both sides to further objectives that could not be achieved with transparency, but they also manifested themselves as serious failures of governance. A second category of governance failures had genuinely internal causes and had straightforward negative effects. These failures could and should have been the focus of reform policies. Thus, some aspects of arbitrariness in decision-making were clearly dysfunctional. There was also evidence of predatory behaviour associated with a lack of accountability within the authority, particularly at lower levels of the security apparatus.

But a third category of *apparent* governance failures was particularly interesting because these 'failures' described the PNA's responses to external constraints and its attempts to break out of these constraints. These responses were governance failures from the perspective of the good governance framework. But, paradoxically, they were reasonably efficient developmental responses that improved economic and political outcomes *given the alternatives available*. For instance, the PNA's allocation and management of contracts, and its creation of some monopolies created and managed high returns for investors in a way that maintained high rates of productive investment in a conflict-zone. Expatriate Palestinian investors had to be compensated not only because of the risk of conflict, but also because there was no guarantee that the territories would not be taken back by Israel, and their 'property rights' lost. The Authority demonstrated some surprising capacities in recognizing and managing these incentives, and managed to maintain high rates of private investment in an otherwise unfavourable environment. In many cases, it also ensured that these investments remained productive. In addition, redistribution to maintain political stability was also effectively managed from the centre, which did not lose control, say to warlords or to fragmented clientelism. In achieving these things, the authority often had to override theoretical good governance criteria. The importance of these capacities is not recognized in the good governance framework. Consequently, uncritically applying that framework to drive policy may result in a significant destruction of vital state capacities. Identifying these distinctions between types of governance problems is important for prioritizing areas of reform. They are equally important for locating the external institutional and political issues beyond the internal governance ones that need to be addressed if an emerging Palestinian state is to be viable.

The possibility that the emerging Palestinian state could have developed in a number of different directions is not surprising. It was at best an embryonic state, and its critical relationships with Israel and its own internal constituencies were still being negotiated. While it did have some serious governance problems, only some of these were entirely due to its internal failures, many more were related to the peculiar security and rent-transfer arrangements that the PNA had little power to change. Most importantly, it also had areas of positive developmental potential and it displayed some significant developmental rent-management capacities that should have been further encouraged and developed. The task of future policy must be to identify and strengthen these tendencies, and this must remain a major challenge for the future. While the PNA's shortcomings in instituting democracy and controlling corruption were very real, our analysis questions the *causality* suggested by the new consensus. We are not sure that progress in directly pushing democratization and anti-corruption, however desirable in itself, would necessarily have aided state viability in this context. On the contrary, progress in democracy and the ability to address issues of corruption were significantly blocked by the failure to sustain a rapid developmental transformation, and this in turn was constrained by the higher level institutional architecture governing the route to state formation and relationships with Israel.

Addressing the relationship of the emerging Palestinian state with Israel is therefore of fundamental importance in any discussion of Palestinian state formation and viability. In particular, we have to ask whether Israel really has an interest in allowing a viable sovereign Palestinian state to emerge, or is it only interested in a client state. And even if it is only the latter, is it going to allow an integrationist client state or demand a client state subject to asymmetric containment. If Israel wants both a client state *and* asymmetric containment, a two-state solution is not likely to be viable at all. A client state with integration *may* be viable, and would require the development of some appropriate state capacities. A fully sovereign Palestinian state is the most desirable outcome. Given the incipient developmental capacities observed in the PNA, there is a possibility that by strengthening some of these early rent-management capacities, a sovereign Palestinian state may achieve a rapid social transformation and thereby remain reasonably viable. This in itself is an important policy conclusion. Unfortunately, in terms of what is on offer, the actual possibilities are exactly the reverse of the desirable ones. Only a client state with asymmetric containment was on offer at Camp David, and is still on offer from the Israeli government. Neither the Road Map, nor the informal Geneva Accords signed by some unofficial Palestinians and Israelis in 2003, move beyond these limitations of Oslo. All the indications are that Israel intends to retain the capacity to inflict asymmetric pain on Palestinians through the control mechanisms associated with the presence of a significant number of settlements. The only difference is that even less territory was on offer after 2000. A client state with integration was ruled out by Israel in the early stages of the Oslo period. It is unlikely that this route will be re-opened in the near future given the demographic dangers for Israel if economic integration deepens. But a truly sovereign Palestinian state has not been on offer at any time, and it is difficult to see how this can emerge from the 'security-first' route that Israel insists on. The security-first route rules out Palestinian sovereignty for an indefinite period. Till security is achieved, and this may take years, and security may never be deemed to be satisfactory, Palestinians under the security-first route will have to live under a client state. And if the Israeli motivation for insisting on a client state is not just driven by security, but also by other considerations such as protecting the settlements or broader concerns with other aspects of the Palestinian struggle, the client state may turn out to be a permanent state of affairs. While Israeli motivations are not the subject of this book, an awareness of the implications of Israeli strategies is critical for understanding the viability of the two-state solution and of the governance failures that are likely to emerge in a Palestinian state. The vulnerability of Palestinian state formation to these Israeli motivations, and the dependence of Palestinian internal governance options on Israeli strategies is one of the critical conclusions of Chapter 2 by Hilal and Khan.

Chapter 3 by Zagha and Zomlot examines the economic relationship between Israel and the Palestinian territories under the PNA during the Oslo interim period. These relationships were enshrined in the Paris Economic Protocol and its one-sided interpretation by Israel. We argue that these relationships defined a client state, and one based on asymmetric containment rather than economic integration. Thus, this chapter records the evidence and provides the background to arguments in other parts of the book. Chapter 4 by Amundsen and Ezbidi looks at the operation of political institutions under the PNA and points out significant areas of concern. While the previous chapters look at governance in the broader context of the challenge of transformation and the constraints set by the client-state architecture and asymmetric containment by Israel, this chapter focuses on how PNA governance appeared from below to Palestinians. It identifies areas of concern that would need to be addressed if a sovereign Palestinian state were to be achieved. Chapter 5 by Nasr examines the controversial subject of the Palestinian monopolies. It elaborates the points made in the chapters by Khan, and Hilal and Khan, about the need to distinguish between different types of monopolies and different motivations driving the creation of monopolies during this period. Some Palestinian monopolies were indeed damaging, others were rational and possibly even efficient responses to containment or to the problem of attracting investment into a conflict zone with no final settlement in sight. Chapter 6 by Fjeldstad and Zagha examines the tax administration system of the PNA. This again highlights the limitations on state formation set by the client-state architecture. The bulk of the PNA's revenues were collected by Israel, and Chapter 6 outlines the mechanisms that allowed this, and its consequences. Finally, Chapter 7 by Hanafi and Tabar discusses the evolution of the Palestinian non-governmental organization sector during the PNA period. This was an important sector in terms of resource flows but it played a quiescent role in state formation, and this chapter examines why.

## Notes

1    Its internationally recognized name is the Palestinian Authority or PA, but many Palestinians refer to their Authority as the PNA, a name that they believe reflects

the claim of the Authority to be their future state in embryonic form. On the other hand, other Palestinians argue that the Authority does not represent the full national aspirations of the Palestinian people. We make no judgement about the merits of the different arguments, and refer to the Authority in both ways.

2    Much of this was mainly symbolic, for instance, the passports were effectively travel documents and the stamps were not internationally recognized. Foreigners entering Palestine through Gaza International Airport had to go through Israeli rather than Palestinian immigration checks.

3    The Oslo Accord signed on 13 September 1993 between the PLO and Israel was a 'Declaration of Principles'. This was followed by the 'Agreement on Interim Self-Rule' signed on 4 May 1994 that established Palestinian self-rule in Gaza and Jericho. The last main agreement was signed in Washington on 28 September 1995 and was called the 'Israeli–Palestinian Interim Agreement on the West Bank and Gaza Strip' and this established the structure of the Palestinian Authority.

4    The population of WBG including East Jerusalem was 2,895,683 at the end of 1997 (Palestinian Central Bureau of Statistics (PCBS) Population Census 1997). The 1999 population estimates are also from PCBS.

5    The occupied territories were divided into a patchwork of territories designated A, B and C. In zone A the Palestinian Authority alone was responsible for security, in zone B security was jointly controlled by Israel, but in zone C Israel alone was responsible for security. The Palestinian population in zones A and B thus came under the Palestinian Authority. This arrangement continued until the Israeli re-occupation of March 2002, when Israel took over security control in all areas.

# 1 Evaluating the emerging Palestinian state

## 'Good governance' versus 'transformation potential'

*Mushtaq Husain Khan*

In assessing the governance capacities and areas of weakness of the Palestinian state, we have to remember that we are evaluating a developing-country state that potentially shared all the challenges of economic development faced by other developing country states. But moreover, the 'quasi-state' that was set up in 1994 to administer parts of the occupied Palestinian territories lacked most of the powers of a conventional developing country state. Apart from lacking control over borders or possessing contiguous territory, the PNA also lacked an adequate fiscal base and was dependent on tax remittances of customs and income taxes collected by Israel from Palestinians. Its trade relationships with the outside world were dependent on Israel with which it remained in a customs union. Its economic survival therefore depended on transfers from Israel of taxes collected from Palestinians and on aid from donors. The movements of goods and people to the outside world and even within its own territories had to go through multiple Israeli controlled checkpoints that could be opened or closed depending on the satisfactory performance of the PNA from the Israeli perspective of delivering security (see Chapter 3 by Zagha and Zomlot). On the Palestinian side, Oslo and the subsequent accords were premised on a huge gamble by the PLO, and later by the PNA. Their leadership hoped that rapid progress could be achieved, based on these agreements, to lead to a sovereign Palestinian state on the entire occupied WBG (*including* East Jerusalem), that a just solution to the question of Palestinian refugees would be found, and that there would be rapid economic progress under Palestinian sovereignty. Only then would it be able to undercut support for rejectionist political positions within the Palestinian community and guarantee its own political survival.

State formation under these conditions required a high degree of executive centralization. This was widely recognized and built into the governance architecture created for the PNA under the Oslo Agreements. Much of the observed maladministration and some of the evidence of corruption flowed directly from the construction of this architecture. It is important to remember that this architecture was essential for the 'security-first' route that Israel insisted on, and nothing else was on offer to the Palestinians in their attempt to construct a two-state solution. Nevertheless, the Palestinian president operating this centralized system enjoyed widespread legitimacy within the WBG Palestinian constituency. This offered a unique historical opportunity to make painful decisions provided clear achievements towards rapid statehood could be demonstrated to the Palestinian public. But in fact, progress on this route came to a grinding halt with the outbreak of the Second *Intifada* following the breakdown of final status negotiations at Camp David in July 2000. As the *Intifada* advanced and Israeli military and political reactions intensified, the project that motivated the establishment of the PNA became increasingly vulnerable. Inevitably, the *Intifada* and Israeli reactions to it will lead to a fundamental re-thinking of strategies on both sides, and what may have been possible in the Oslo phase may not be possible later on. In any case, the causes behind this dramatic reversal have to be properly understood, even if only to identify more accurately the hurdles on the way.

Table 1.1 gives a picture of the economic performance of the Palestinian territories during this period. Clearly, the period in question was very short and the data has a margin of error. But it is good enough to indicate the broad outlines of economic performance. Compared to other middle-income developing countries, economic growth in the Palestinian territories was remarkably high before the blockade that was imposed on the economy after the beginning of the Second *Intifada* in 2000. These high growth rates, and the high investment rates sustaining them, are particularly remarkable given the great uncertainty about the future of the territories. Immediately after the creation of the PNA in 1994, growth rates were low, partly because of administrative disruptions but largely because Israel immediately set about establishing internal borders and checkpoints to control Palestinian population movements and the transit of goods. However, by 1997 real gross domestic product (GDP) growth became strongly positive. By this time, the PNA had established much of its administrative apparatus. Moreover, by then Israel had also set up its checkpoints and internal borders, and it began to allow more Palestinian labour movements, but now with the possibility of shutting off entire Palestinian areas not only from Israel but also from each other at very short notice. Private investments in the Palestinian territories also picked up sharply after 1997, indicating that the PNA had acquired the capacity and credibility to induce expatriate Palestinians to begin investing in the territories. The share of industry, broadly defined, remained constant at around 20 per cent of GDP over 1994–2000. Given the rapid growth of GDP during this period, this indicates that growth rates for industry were just as high.

Throughout this period, the Palestinian territories remained heavily aid dependent, with 18 per cent of GDP coming from aid in 1994. However, as GDP grew, the share of aid declined sharply to around 10 per cent of GDP by the end of the period, and this possibly explains the decline in *public* investment over this period, which was heavily financed by aid.[1] In 1999, the

*Table 1.1* The economy of the Palestinian territories 1994–2002

| | 1994 | 1995 | 1996 | 1997 | 1998 | 1999 | 2000 | 2001 (est) | 2002 (est) |
|---|---|---|---|---|---|---|---|---|---|
| *Real GDP growth rate* | 8.5 | 6.1 | 2.5 | 12.2 | 11.8 | 8.9 | -5.4 | -15.0 | -14.5 |
| *Real GNI growth rate* | 0.9 | 8.5 | 0.8 | 12.4 | 16.3 | 8.4 | -6.8 | -16.2 | -16.4 |
| *Share of industry in GDP (%)* | 21.8 | 21.7 | 19.8 | 19.9 | 20.0 | 19.1 | 20.7 | na | na |
| *Share of private fixed investment in GDP (%)* | 26.5 | 21.8 | 26.3 | 25.3 | 26.4 | 31.7 | 25.0 | 20.1 | 16.6 |
| *Share of public fixed investment in GDP (%)* | 6.6 | 9.5 | 6.6 | 6.5 | 6.4 | 7.0 | 5.4 | 6.1 | 3.5 |
| *Aid as proportion of GDP (%)* | 18 | 17.6 | 15 | 14 | 10 | 11 | 12 | na | na |
| *Unemployment rate* | 14.8 | 18.2 | 23.8 | 20.3 | 14.4 | 11.8 | 14.1 | 25.5 | 31.1 |

The difference between gross domestic product (GDP) and gross national income (GNI) is that the latter includes the income of Palestinians working in other countries, in particular, Israel. Industry includes mining, manufacturing, electricity, water and public enterprises. Figures not available are reported as 'na'.

Source: IMF (2003): 20-25 (for recent estimates of disbursed aid), Tables 2.1, 2.2, 24; Valdivieso *et al.* (2001): Table 1.1, World Bank (2000, 2001).

per capita GDP (at current prices) for WBG (excluding East Jerusalem) was estimated at $1,641 ($1,851 for the West Bank excluding East Jerusalem and $1,339 for the Gaza Strip).[2] Clearly there were serious economic problems but Palestine was potentially not the typical basket-case economy that often emerges out of long-running conflict situations. In particular, the evidence on *private* investment and GDP growth, once the administration had stabi-lized, are not unimpressive for a high-conflict zone. Service-delivery by the authority in key areas of health and education had its critics and suffered from resource scarcities, but performance was comparable to or better than in countries at similar levels of development (as assessed by a task force commissioned by the US Council on Foreign Relations 1999: 5). All of these achievements, however limited, came to an abrupt halt in 2000. The Israeli control over the borders of non-contiguous Palestinian enclaves and many of their inner roads explains the massive and immediate impact of Israeli closure measures following the Second *Intifada*. The subsequent years mark a clear break with the previous period. The administrative structure of the PNA was seriously degraded, with direct attacks on its physical infrastructure. Not surprisingly, the private investments that had buoyed the economy also collapsed as the territories were closed off.

Even when the economy was rapidly growing in the late 1990s, there were many observations of internal maladministration, petty and not-so-petty corruption, and very slow progress in the deepening of democracy. Questions began to be asked about the institutional and governance reforms that had to be addressed if the PNA was to achieve better economic performance and greater political viability. The good governance approach is one of a number of approaches that try to answer this question by comparing developing country states with an abstract model of a liberal democratic state as it is supposed to work in an advanced capitalist economy. The observed differences between actual governance and theoretical good governance are used to *explain* backwardness or poor economic performance in the developing country. While the *good governance model* is based on neo-liberal political and economic theory, its conclusions and criticisms have gained wide currency because these appear to be supported by other analytical methodologies as well. The neo-patrimonial model, based on extensions of Weberian sociology, reaches similar policy conclusions about the importance of democracy and corruption. Both approaches provide a ready-made critique of what went wrong in the PNA. Since evidence of corruption, monopolies, centralized power, and slow progress towards democratization could be readily found within the PNA, the good governance and neo-patrimonial models suggest that these factors played an important role in impeding Palestinian progress towards viable statehood.

There are two fundamental problems with the good governance and related neo-patrimonial approaches. First, at a general level, the causality implied in these models, running from anti-corruption, democracy and liberalization to economic prosperity, is contrary to a significant body of historical evidence (Khan 2004, 2002b). The theory and evidence underpinning the good governance model and our alternative framework for assessing the role of the state during processes of *social transformation* are discussed in the next two sections. The social transformation framework suggests that there can be no disagreement about the desirability of democracy or a corruption-free society as *goals*, there is considerable doubt about whether policy to push either agenda as a *means* of accelerating development is likely to be effective in the typical developmental context. It is not even clear that these reforms can be implemented at all in the absence of transformation being accelerated through appropriate policies.

A second problem with any attempt to apply the good governance frameworks in the Palestinian context is that the PNA was a unique type of quasi-state that lacked almost all the powers and territorial sovereignty of a normal state. The expectation that it should achieve democracy and good governance *before* it had achieved statehood is even more implausible as a demand. Moreover, even the limited powers that it had under the Oslo Agreements included deliberately designed anti-democratic features and structures that created incentives for corruption. These characteristics were the result of the peculiar economic and security concerns of Israel that the Oslo framework was trying to operate within. It is important to remember that the Oslo Agreements allowed Israel to maintain its settlements and extend controls over the movement of goods and people *within* the Palestinian territories and between the territories and Israel without giving the PNA almost any of the powers of a sovereign state. The PNA did not control a contiguous territory, it had almost no fiscal autonomy, and it did not control its own borders, including internal borders between enclaves. These arrangements made executive centralization and corruption not just possible but almost *inevitable* if the 'state' was to operate at all, and in the early years, Israel and the external sponsors of the peace process participated heavily in setting up these structures. As Joseph Saba, the former head of the World Bank's West Bank and Gaza division put it: 'You set up gates, and you set up gatekeepers on each side of the gate, and history tells us that gatekeepers charge tolls' (Lagerquist 2003: 26). Palestinian traders had to set up elaborate systems of influence and often of bribery involving Israeli customs and other officials simply to be able to trade on a day-to-day basis. Similarly, Oslo quite deliberately set up strong executive and security institutions in the PNA to push through a peace process that was likely to face strong, often violent, internal dissent within the Palestinian territories. This too is not surprising when we recognize the enormous historic compromise the Palestinians were asked to make by giving up all claims on 78 per cent of historic Palestine in exchange for an uncertain promise to get an unknown fraction of the remainder. And during this interim period, there were no promises about the eventual status of Jerusalem, of refugees, or the degree of sovereignty that was eventually going to be achieved.

An application of abstract good governance criteria to judge the emerging Palestinian state is therefore doubly misleading and can give a seriously distorted impression of what went wrong on the way to statehood. In contrast to the good governance and neo-patrimonial approaches, the social transformation perspective argues that confusing means with ends is dangerous, particularly in conflict situations and in situations like that in Palestine where the 'state' faced powerful externally determined institutional, political and economic constraints. In these contexts, it is important to focus instead on identifying and developing the state capacities that are required to achieve a rapid transformation of society in the direction of greater economic and political viability. A naïve good governance or neo-patrimonial approach may be misleading or worse. They may be misleading if they lead policy-makers to believe that attempts to tackle in a general way problems of corruption and democracy would have yielded, or will yield in the future, the economic and political results that are desired. But they may be worse if intentionally or otherwise they write off a state-building exercise that may actually have worked, and which failed for reasons that international policy-makers have no desire or ability to address.

The first section of this chapter discusses the thinking behind the good governance agenda with its roots in neoclassical economics and liberal politics, and the related neo-patrimonial model, which reaches similar policy conclusions from a neo-Weberian perspective. In the second section, we examine an alternative framework for looking at the role of the state during processes of social transformation. This approach focuses on the importance of different types of 'rents'. It argues that while some rents are damaging, others are critical for accelerating development and maintaining political stability. In this alternative approach, the importance of analysing corruption and rent-seeking is to identify critical areas where state capacity has to be improved with the aim of accelerating a viable and developmental social transformation. In the third section, we discuss the Palestinian evidence on rents and rent-seeking in the context of our framework and identify the major types of rents and rent-seeking that were in evidence over this period. In the fourth section, we argue that these rents were consistent with a number of different incipient state capacities and characteristics. Since the viability of the Palestinian quasi-state was initially subject to Israeli control through fiscal, trade and other mechanisms, we describe these rent-management arrangements as a client state. We then argue that within this client state, a number of contrary state characteristics and capacities were observable in incipient form. These included some predatory characteristics, some characteristics of a fragmented clientelist state, and some developmental characteristics. In the final section, we discuss the methodology that we will use in the rest of the book for analysing the likelihood of these different outcomes materializing, and the conditions under which this might happen.

## The liberal state as a benchmark for reform

To arrive at an appropriate theoretical framework for assessing the Palestinian quasi-state, we will first critically examine the appropriateness of the good governance framework applied to developing countries, and in particular to Palestine. In this section, we examine in turn the good governance framework and the related neo-patrimonial framework, before discussing our alternative framework in the next section.

### The good governance framework

The good governance agenda emerged out of a confluence of neoclassical free-market economics and the 'new' political economy. It established a set of plausible and apparently policy-relevant interconnections between democracy, anti-corruption policies and the establishment of a free-market economy from which prosperity is supposed to follow. These relationships are summarized in Figure 1.1. The first and most critical claim in the good governance model comes from neoclassical economics that argues that the achievement of economic prosperity requires a competitive market economy, defined by free entry and exit. This is shown in step (i) of the good governance argument in Figure 1.1. The underlying logic is that if the market is competitive, only those who can satisfy consumer demand at the lowest cost can survive, and this ensures that welfare is maximized. To maintain competition, the role of the state is only to protect property rights, maintain free-markets, and provide a small number of essential public goods that cannot be efficiently provided by the private sector. The way to check whether a state is maintaining competitive markets is to see if it allows any 'rents' to exist in the economy. *Individuals or firms earn rents if they can earn a higher return in a specific activity than they could in their next-best opportunity.* In liberal economic theory, excess incomes would never exist in the absence of some political intervention in the market. So, a commonsensical definition of a rent is that it is a politically generated income, which would not exist without some specific rights, subsidies or transfers that were artificially maintained through a political process. Monopoly profits, subsidies, transfers, unnecessary job creation in the public sector are all examples of rent-creation. Conversely, the theory says that the absence of rents means that the market is fully competitive and this ensures the maximization of prosperity and therefore of social welfare (see Khan 2000a for a detailed analysis of rents).

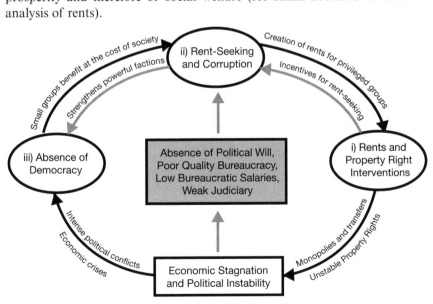

*Figure 1.1* State failure in the good governance framework

A wide variety of state interventions can create these damaging types of rents. For instance, states can give monopoly rights to favoured companies to import particular products. They can prevent competition over the award of public construction contracts, thereby creating monopoly rents for favoured contractors. They can subsidize inefficient industries, creating rents for them through transfers. They can create artificial jobs for favoured groups; another case of transfer rents. In the simplest case, the state can transfer resources legally or illegally to unproductive groups, creating rents for these recipients. In each of these cases of damaging rents, the state-created rent lowers economic efficiency as measured by a lower net output for society as a whole. Moreover, to create these rents, states have to create new property rights, disrupt existing property rights or transfer property rights. Disrupting property rights further lowers incentives to invest in that society. *The first principle of the good governance agenda is therefore that states should protect rent-free competitive markets, and by extension, stable property rights.*

The second step in the good governance model is to explain why, if rents are so damaging for the economy, states persistently create them. The explanation provided is that individuals who want to benefit from rents drive the rent-creation. They spend resources to 'influence' or 'capture' the state and this activity creates rents. *Rent-seeking is the expenditure of resources to influence or capture the state in order to acquire or retain rents.* This is step (ii) in Figure 1.1. While rent-seeking creates rents, rent-seeking is in turn more likely if rents already exist and more can be created. As a result, there is a two-way relationship between (i) and (ii): rents and rent-seeking reinforce each other. Corruption is illegal rent-seeking, where the rent-seeker breaks the law by bribing a public official to get a benefit that is by definition a rent. But much rent-seeking consists of legal activities that aim to influence public officials for the benefit of the rent-seeker.

*Legal rent-seeking* includes expenditures on lobbying, legal contributions to political parties, the time spent on these activities, and so on. These are clearly an important part of any legitimate political process, but in economic terms, legal rent-seeking has the same costs as any other type of rent-seeking. *Illegal rent-seeking* includes corruption of different types. Corruption is an illegal exchange between a public official and an individual or firm, where in exchange for a bribe, a public official provides a benefit not otherwise available to the briber (by definition a rent). Corruption includes the bribing of public officials, illegal funding of parties and political movements, and other illegal forms of influencing activity. The bribe is the rent-seeking expenditure, which if successful, 'buys' rents of different types. Outright expropriation or extortion can also be classified as a variant of illegal rent-seeking. Here a public official threatens to create illegal rents for himself or a client (extortion is essentially an illegal transfer) and to achieve or stop this, the official and/or the affected individuals spend resources on rent-seeking. The official spends resources to achieve coercive power to capture the illegal rent while affected individuals spend resources to restrict this power or to bribe the official to take less.

Finally, there is a grey area of *quasi-legal rent-seeking*, which may not be formally illegal, but which is not legally sanctioned either. Examples of this type of rent-seeking in developing countries include the use of traditional and personalized sources of power and influence. These often work through *patron–client networks* that give well-connected individuals privileged access to the state and to its resources. To maintain their power to influence the state and capture rents, patrons spend resources to maintain their networks. This includes providing resources for clients in times of need, finding them jobs, and so on. The cost of doing this is the rent-seeking cost for the patron, and this allows the patron to maintain his political power based on his clients, and use this to bargain with the state for more rents. Although there are clear *economic* similarities, there are clearly *moral* and *political* differences between legal and illegal rent-seeking, since unchecked corruption can over time destroy the legitimacy of a state. But even these differences are ones of degree, since legal rent-seeking can also be immoral in its privileging of some groups, and too much of it can easily damage the political legitimacy of the state.

In the good governance framework, the effects of all types of rent-seeking are *always* negative because rent-seeking has a two-fold negative effect summarized in Figure 1.2. First, rent-seeking expenditures (whether legal, lobbying type expenditures or illegal corruption and bribery) are always a social cost because these are unproductive expenditures. This is shown in the arrow marked A in Figure 1.2. Second, in return for these

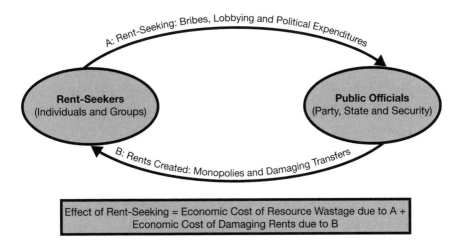

*Figure 1.2*  The effects of rent-seeking in liberal market models

expenditures, the state creates rents for rent-seekers, shown by the arrow marked B in Figure 1.2. These rents have *additional* negative effects on the economy because rents are also damaging for the economy, according to liberal market economics. Thus, because both sides of the exchange in Figure 1.2, A and B, are negative for society, A + B adds up to a significant negative effect (or cost). This is the outcome of *all* rent-seeking, which includes corruption, lobbying and other forms. This analysis of rent-seeking was developed in a series of articles beginning with Krueger (1974), Posner (1975), Buchanan, Tollison and Tullock (1980) and Colander (1984). The subsequent literature on corruption was heavily influenced by this analysis. For a critical survey of the literature on corruption, see Andvig *et al.* (2000) and Bardhan (1997). A key policy position follows. *The second principle of the liberal state is that all types of rent-seeking have to be prevented.* In particular, the illegal and semi-legal types of rent-seeking, namely corruption and clientelism, are the most pernicious, since they are difficult to detect, and they corrode confidence in modern institutions and in the state.

The third and final element of the good governance model is to explain why rent-seeking with its negative effects continues to persist. The answer provided is that although rents impoverish society, they obviously enrich the few who are the beneficiaries. Hence, for rent-seeking to continue, the majority must be unable to stop the damage caused to them by powerful minorities. This is step (iii) in the good governance model shown in Figure 1.1. The absence of democracy allows small groups to monopolize access to the state and engage in rent-seeking. Rent-seeking in turn consolidates the power of privileged groups, further undermining democracy. Once again, the relationship between (ii) and (iii) runs both ways. *Thus, the third principle of good governance is that democracy and accountability must be promoted to ensure that minorities are not able to further their interests at the expense of the majority.* The claim that the absence of democracy allows minorities to seek rents was developed by the 'new institutional economics', in particular by North (1990) and Olson (1997, 2000).

The interlocking relationships suggested by the good governance model imply that societies can be locked into either a good or a bad political–economic equilibrium. In a 'bad' equilibrium, the absence of democracy supports substantial rent-seeking, which in turn allows the creation of lots of damaging rents and the economic and political crisis that follows ensures that democracy never develops. In a good equilibrium, democracy ensures that rent-seeking and corruption are low, as a result there are few rents, markets are competitive and economic prosperity and political stability follow, which in turn ensures that democracy remains stable. An important consequence of the good governance analysis is therefore that improvements in economic and political performance can only be achieved if *parallel* moves are made on all of these fronts. Economic liberalization, effective measures against corruption and rent-seeking, moves to deepen democracy and civil society participation, each have to be *simultaneously* pushed to break out of the equilibrium of poor performance.

### The neo-patrimonial analysis

One reason why the good governance framework has received wide support across academic and policy circles is that its conclusions are broadly supported by a number of other approaches assessing the performance of developing country states. In particular, the *neo-patrimonial* analysis of corruption and clientelism in developing countries identifies very similar problems and policy responses. Eisenstadt (1973) and Médard (various works, summarized in 2002) developed this analysis, based on their work in African countries. The neo-patrimonial analysis identifies a number of characteristics that differentiate African states from advanced European ones, and on this basis, it attempts to provide an explanation of poor economic and political performance in Africa.

The main lines of argument in the neo-patrimonial model are summarized in Figure 1.3. The key characteristic of the neo-patrimonial state is the personalization of power. This in turn is a product of the absence of democracy and of political accountability. The state is the 'property' of the leader who rules with the help of his clients. This has a number of important political effects. One result is that formal rules (laws) are less important than informal rules based on the use of power. Second, the leader and his clients operating through patron–client networks dominate politics. Third, corruption is systemic, operating at all levels of the state since there is no check on the venality of the supreme power. The effects of this arbitrary and unchecked power are that the economy is characterized by politically driven accumulation by the leader and his clients and the economy is, as a result, totally debilitated. Médard's analysis distinguishes between different countries in Africa and points out many subtle differences between them, but overall they are all variants of a neo-patrimonial type of state that is the

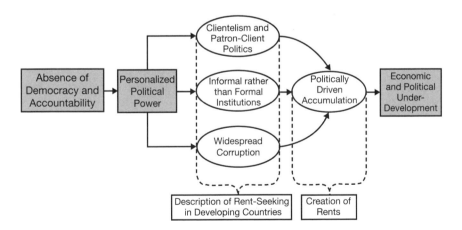

*Figure 1.3* The neo-patrimonial model

antithesis of a modern bureaucratic state. In particular, the political interventions of the neo-patrimonial state in the economy, and its interventions
in property rights through systemic corruption and outright expropriation
lead to economic backwardness.

Although its analytical roots are different from the neo-liberal model
discussed earlier, there are striking underlying similarities in the way the role of
markets and states is understood. As Figure 1.3 also shows, the neo-patrimonial model's emphasis on clientelism and corruption describes nothing other
than the dominant forms of rent-seeking in a developing country context. This
is identified as a problem because what follows is politically driven accumulation that disrupts the logic of the market. Disrupting the 'market' by politically
driven interventions that create special benefits for some groups is, by definition, the creation of rents. Thus, the underlying economic analysis of the
neo-patrimonial and good governance models is surprisingly similar. So are the
policy conclusions. Both agree that development requires a separation of the
state from the economy. Neo-patrimonial theorists like Médard do not believe
this can be achieved through liberalization in the first place, since liberalization
on its own can squeeze the state and make it even more predatory. This is
similar to the position taken by many neo-liberal good governance theorists
who argue that without political reform, liberalization cannot be implemented.
And as with the latter, the neo-patrimonial model argues that the separation of
state from society is to be achieved through the promotion of democracy,
accountability and pluralism. These will assist in checking the state's ability to
act arbitrarily, implicitly inhibiting its ability to create rents.

In this sense, the implicit analytical links in the neo-patrimonial analysis
are quite consistent with the causal links derived from rent-seeking theories
that inform the good governance analysis summarized in Figure 1.1. There
is an even more fundamental similarity in the *sequencing* of reforms. They
both identify as a policy goal the need to *first* establish a modern state with
a formal set of rules governing it. This state has to have an impersonal and
non-corrupt professional bureaucracy that does not politically interfere in
the market, and it has to have checks and balances limiting executive power
through an effective democracy. Once all this is in place, a (rent-free)
competitive market economy will follow and will lead to economic and
political progress. Unfortunately, no evidence is provided from recent history
to show that this sequence of reforms has ever worked to accelerate a developmental transition. Before we discuss the relevance of these approaches for
assessing the Palestinian quasi-state, we need to consider the adequacy of
the good governance framework and the related neo-patrimonial framework
in comparative historical terms.

## The role of the state in transformation processes

The *good governance* model and the related *neo-patrimonial* model are not
only superficially plausible, the correlation they suggest between variables

such as democracy and a corruption-free society on the one hand and economic development on the other is highly desirable from a humanist or progressive perspective. Unfortunately, the historical evidence suggests a more complex reality. While a correlation between these variables can indeed be found in the historical data, the *causality* between the variables is much more problematic. The statistical correlation that is observed in cross-country regressions shows that countries with lower corruption and greater democracy do indeed have greater wealth and higher growth rates (for instance, Hall and Jones 1999; Kauffman, Kraay and Zoido-Lobatón 1999; Johnson, Kaufman and Zoido-Lobatón 1998; Clague *et al.* 1997; World Bank 1997; Knack and Keefer 1997, 1995; Barro 1996; Mauro 1995). But these correlations do not establish *causality* (Khan 2004). Developing countries are by definition poor and most have low growth rates. Most of them also have relatively high corruption and weak democracies, or authoritarian regimes. On the other hand, most advanced countries have the reverse characteristics. It is not surprising that when we correlate these variables, we find that rich countries are less corrupt and more democratic. But are rich countries rich *because* they first instituted democracy and reduced corruption or do they have viable democracies and low corruption *because* they first became rich and are now already developed? Examining *sequence* is the only way to test for causation: did advanced countries *first* achieve democracy

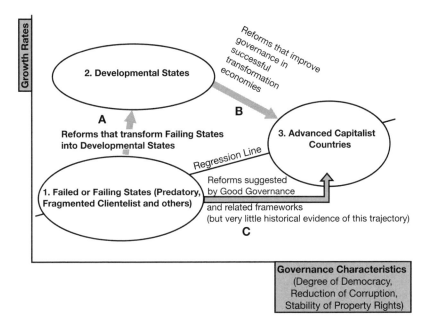

*Figure 1.4* Good governance, state capacities and the capitalist transformation

and the reduction of corruption and *then* become rich or is it the other way around? The historical evidence, as opposed to correlation analysis, suggests that the deepening of democracy and the lowering of corruption were long historical processes that made serious progress in the early capitalist countries well after their industrial revolutions.

Most developing countries are located in group 1 in Figure 1.4, with poor governance characteristics and low growth rates. These failed or failing states can in turn be classified in various ways: predatory, fragmented clientelist and so on. In contrast, advanced countries are mostly in group 3, with good governance characteristics and somewhat higher growth rates. Countries in group 1 obviously want to reach group 3 but how do they get there? The correlation summarized in the regression line suggests that the appropriate policy is to follow the good governance prescription and improve the governance characteristics identified in these models; this will enable a country to go from group 1 to group 3. These are the reforms shown by arrow C in Figure 1.4. The problem is that we have no historical evidence of any country achieving a transition to advanced country status by following the reforms suggested. The recent examples that we have of countries moving from group 1 to group 3 are the transitions to capitalism in a small number of developing countries over the last 50 years. These include countries like South Korea, Taiwan, Malaysia, Thailand and now China, which are at different stages of a transition from group 1 to group 3. But in terms of the sequencing of 'good governance' characteristics, they seem to be following the arrows marked A and B rather than the arrow marked C. If developing countries have any lessons to learn, clearly they have to look carefully at these recent cases of successful transition and not primarily at countries that became capitalist centuries ago and are already very rich. The evidence of historical transitions thus shows that the sequence of reforms that led these countries to successful capitalist development contradicts both the good governance and neo-patrimonial policy prescriptions (for a discussion of some of the evidence see Khan 2004, 2002b; Woo-Cumings 1999; Aoki, Kim and Okuno-Fujiwara 1997; Wade 1990; Amsden 1989).

During their high-growth transition periods, these developmental countries were located in the region marked group 2. They scored badly in terms of democracy, corruption, stability of property rights and other 'good governance' characteristics. Contrary to the neo-patrimonial analysis, they also suffered from a confusion of formal and informal rules. Political power was highly centralized and could be used to override formal rules, they had regimes that relied on variants of clientelism and patron–client networks for maintaining regime stability, and all of them extensively used political power for accelerating accumulation by emerging capitalist groups. Clearly, these countries are the ones that are most relevant for understanding the *sequence* involved in successful development. Some of the more advanced of these successful developing countries subsequently made slow but sustainable progress in reducing corruption and deepening democracy, the trajectory shown by arrow **B** in Figure 1.4.

This history suggests that the most important task for developing countries is to identify the reforms shown in arrow **A**, which could transform failing states into developmental ones. This involves developing the capacities of states to push developmental changes in their society, a process we have described as the capitalist transformation. Success has depended on identifying and then sustaining and strengthening these developmental characteristics of states. The important point is that historically, developing these transformation capacities has *not* necessarily involved a *prior* reduction of corruption, clientelism, patron–client networks, the centralization of power, the instability of property rights or any of the features identified in the good governance and neo-patrimonial models. Nevertheless, it *has* involved wide-ranging changes in institutions, policies and politics that enhanced specific state capacities to push developmental changes, manage necessary rents and destroy damaging rents. Indirectly, this had the effect of changing the *types* of corruption, clientelism and rent-seeking that were prevalent even if the aggregate amount did not immediately go down significantly. We argue that the critical role of the state in development can be better understood by distinguishing between different types of rents and rent-seeking (including differences in the types of corruption and patron–client networks), and this enables us to distinguish successful transformations from the others.

There are, of course, high-growth cases like Indonesia where the state failed to deepen democracy and reduce corruption fast enough and as a result suffered a precipitous collapse of legitimacy during an economic crisis. Clearly while sustained economic development is *necessary* for the sustainable deepening of democracy and the achievement of lower corruption, it is not *sufficient*. The trajectory shown in arrow B is by no means automatic and does require institutional and political attention, but these are only likely to be viable if the conditions for viable growth have already been achieved. This sequence and prioritization is markedly different from that proposed by the good governance and neo-patrimonial models, where the reform priorities are shown by the arrow marked C in Figure 1.4. Here, the sequence is to *first* achieve the good governance characteristics of a liberal-democratic state, and then the expectation is that higher growth will be realized. But to repeat, there is no evidence that such a strategy has worked in the past (Khan 2004).

Even cross-country correlations, for all their shortcomings, show that the relationships between good governance characteristics and economic performance are quite complex. For instance, it is *not* the case that democracy is always associated with lower corruption even when we pool advanced and developing countries. The effect of democracy on lower corruption is found in some studies to be very weak and if it operates at all, it does so with a time lag of *several decades*. This suggests that the main determinant of lower corruption may be economic development, since only countries that grow reasonably fast can sustain democracy over decades (Treisman 2000). Burkhart and Lewis-Beck (1994) also find that rises in per capita incomes *precede* the emergence of democracy and not the other way round, suggesting that economic development may be a precondition for democracy, rather than democracy being a precondition for economic development.

Let us be clear though about what this historical evidence is telling us. It is *not* saying that we should not be worried about corruption or democracy. Instead it is saying that to attack these problems we have to ensure that the conditions for rapid development are achieved. This requires targeting damaging rents and rent-seeking that can have extremely negative effects on growth. On the other hand, it requires an *enhancement* of state capacities to create and manage necessary rents, both for political stabilization and for accelerating the emergence of capitalists and regulating their incentives. It follows that the rent-free market is not a very useful benchmark for judging the efficiency of a transformation economy. The challenge for policy-makers is to be able to identify damaging monopolies, transfers to unproductive groups and other damaging rents, with their associated rent-seeking and corruption, and to tackle the causes of these rents vigorously. On the other hand, if the capacity of the state to create and manage the rents necessary for political stabilization or the rents necessary for accelerating the capitalist transformation are removed, far from more rapid development, we may instead see a collapse. In the case of a conflict economy, where rents may also be used as a mechanism through which one country or group attempts to exert influence over another, there is an added and critical dimension of the problem that affects our assessment of the efficiency or otherwise of other rents.

We will argue that when we look at the redistributive rents, monopolies and other transfers that the PNA was involved in creating and managing, we observe a complex picture. Some of these rents were indeed damaging and if their scope increased over time, the future Palestinian state would be doomed to remain in group 1 in Figure 1.4, with other poorly performing developing country states. However, we will argue that many rents managed by the PNA were dynamic rents that gave the emerging Palestinian economy *some* of the characteristics of group 2 countries. Given the very limited formal powers of the quasi-state, the adverse external constraints, and the context of extreme uncertainty about the future, these developmental characteristics of the PNA were quite remarkable. But given the high growth-rates achieved in Palestine under the PNA, shown in Table 1.1, it should not be surprising to discover that the PNA had some developmental rent-management capacities. If a Palestinian transition to a group 3 country is to be accelerated, these incipient powers and capacities of the fledgling quasi-state would need to be developed in the future. Before we look at some of the specific features of the Palestinian quasi-state, we will identify some of the general issues that transformation states have had to address.

### Property rights and rents

The foundation of the good governance model, shown in point (i) in Figure 1.1, is that a rent-free economy with stable property rights is the most efficient market structure for development. This is a fundamental proposition of liberal economic theory, but it has significant shortcomings when applied to developing countries. Economic development is not just a process of making 'the market' work better. Development historically has involved the emergence and growth of a *capitalist* sector. Even in the most volatile and vulnerable contexts, the creation of a viable capitalist sector is usually a critical requirement for achieving economic, and therefore political viability. Far from requiring the stability of property rights and the absence of rents, development is a period of momentous changes in the structure of property rights. It involves the emergence of new classes through processes that involve the creation and management of substantial rents as well as disruptions of pre-capitalist property rights. Far from state withdrawal from the market being a necessary condition for a successful capitalist transition, the historical evidence suggests that it is necessary for the state to intervene to accelerate the emergence of capitalists and assist and discipline them in the acquisition of technological capacity. By definition, this requires state support for 'politically driven accumulation', contrary to the neo-patrimonial model (Figure 1.3). The relevant state capacity in these contexts is its ability to carry out the appropriate social transformations, its ability to allocate rents to emerging capitalists, discipline them if they do not perform, and to use rents to maintain social stability at acceptable levels (Amsden 1989; Wade 1990; Aoki, Kim and Okuno-Fujiwara 1997; Woo-Cumings 1999; Khan 2004).

Before a capitalist economy has become dominant, the accumulation that drives the emergence of capitalism has usually required state assistance to transfer resources to the emerging capitalist sector from non-capitalist sectors and activities. These types of accumulation classically have been referred to as *primitive accumulation*. Primitive accumulation is common when pre-capitalist production systems have become unviable but a viable capitalism has not yet emerged. Stabilizing the pre-existing but economically unviable pre-capitalist rights is not possible, nor is capitalism likely to emerge rapidly through the operation of a market in such a context. Examples of non-market transfers of rights that have played a critical role in the transition to capitalism have included compulsory land reform (in South Korea, Taiwan and China) and transfers of assets to emerging capitalists through state-owned or controlled banking systems (South Korea, Malaysia, and many other developing countries). They have included state-supported seizures of natural resources, and in particular of land, by emerging capitalists (in Thailand in the 1980s, during the English Enclosures of the seventeenth to nineteenth centuries, and during the westward expansion of the United States of America into Indian territories till well into the nineteenth century). They have also included more subtle mechanisms such as exchange rate controls that have been used to transfer resources from peasant agriculture to emerging industrial capitalists (in most developing countries). This is not an exhaustive list, but it reminds us that state actions during rapid transformations typically have not been to *stabilize* pre-existing allocations of resources, but more often to directly or indirectly change that allocation, if necessary by radically disrupting prior property rights systems (Khan 2002b). It also tells us that politically driven accumulation and the rent-seeking associated with it is unavoidable during this period of development.

Yet, it is also clear that in many cases the result of such interventions in property rights has only been destructive. Unstable property rights have often been associated with predation and plunder. Unfortunately, this is the more usual story in the typical developing country where state officials and their clients capture resources, subsidies and credit to enrich themselves, and they do not go on to become productive capitalists. Nevertheless, the difference between dynamic and collapsing developing countries is *not* that in the dynamic countries property rights were stable, and politically driven accumulation did not occur. Rather the difference was a subtler one. In the dynamic group, the transformation of property rights rapidly took these societies in the direction of viable and dynamic capitalist economies. Ensuring this required different combinations of conditions, but most often, it required a state that could discipline primitive accumulation and ensure that those who were enriching themselves remained productive. Over a period, this resulted in growth and development that in turn allowed a deepening of democracy and the achievement of greater accountability. The problem in most non-dynamic developing countries is that property rights are transferred to unproductive classes and groups who do not graduate to become productive capitalists for a variety of reasons, including the failure of the state to adequately assist or discipline them. In these more typical cases, economic and political development is stifled. But it would be wrong to argue that development would be faster if these countries could stabilize property rights and prevent their states from intervening. There is no example in history where stabilizing pre-capitalist rights accelerated the transition to capitalism.

The good governance and neo-patrimonial frameworks are also wrong to argue that successful development requires the absence of rents. In fact, economic theory recognizes that many rents are essential for the efficient operation of a market economy (Stiglitz 1996; Aoki, Kim and Okuno-Fujiwara 1997). The problem is that 'good' rents can very easily become 'bad' rents and effective *rent-management capacities* of the state are critical for success. For instance, redistributive rents are essential for achieving political stabilization, even though they can have disincentive effects on those who are taxed. Properly managed, the benefits of stabilization can more than compensate for these costs. However, in other cases redistributive rents can impose costs that are greater than the benefit of the political stability that is achieved: and in the worst cases, redistribution can even result in *lower* political stability! Similarly, 'developmental' rents for capitalists can create incentives for the generation of information, and for risk-taking and innovation (Khan 2000a). For instance, patent laws, competition laws, and taxes and subsidies can create rents for innovators and risk-takers in ways that improve economic performance. But here too, mismanaging these rents can do more harm than good. Rents for risk-takers that last too long simply convert them into monopolists. The aim of rent-regulation is to create incentives, say for innovation, but also to ensure that these rents do not last for so long that they become monopoly rents. In advanced countries, there are sophisticated institutions such as competition regulators and courts that exercise judgement in eliminating wasteful monopoly rents while protecting rents that create incentives for national innovation and risk-taking.

In developing countries, the need for making considered judgements about the social value of different rents is even greater, but the capacity for making such judgements is much less developed. Ironically, the economic models of free-market economics have prevented international agencies from providing support to developing countries to develop these critical rent-management capacities. Rents are important in all developing countries to encourage emerging capitalists and assist them to acquire entrepreneurial and technological skills, but they are particularly important in conflict societies like Palestine where capitalists would not otherwise be sufficiently attracted (Aoki, Kim and Okuno-Fujiwara 1997; Khan 2000a). Of course, many other rents, like monopoly rents, are indeed harmful, and states must have the capacity to identify and remove them. Thus, economic theory tells us that different types of rents can be beneficial or damaging for society. But even the potentially beneficial rents have to be managed and regulated if they are to have a beneficial effect.

In advanced countries, the redistribution of income that is required for political stabilization is usually organized in a transparent way through the budget. States in developing countries also have to maintain social and political stability, but the absence of sufficient budgetary resources often means that political stabilization works through the allocation of resources to critical clients within patron–client networks. By definition, the resources for such targeted redistribution necessary for stabilization does not come from the budget. Clientelism is thus a way of achieving political stability in a context of resource scarcity. The distribution of rents to clients through patron–client networks can take a variety of forms, ranging from job creation in public enterprises to outright subsidies. If the same degree of political stability had to be achieved through general fiscal transfers, broader categories of recipients would have to be identified that included the politically critical individuals and factions as a subset. Clearly, much greater fiscal resources would be required to achieve this.

The historical evidence from developing countries suggests that clientelism is only likely to end when states have the fiscal resources to maintain political stability through general transfers, in other words, when a substantial degree of economic development has already been achieved. Not surprisingly, and in contrast to the claims of the neo-patrimonial model, we find variants of patron–client networks in *all* developing countries, including the high-growth ones, before they eventually make a transition to political management through transparent fiscal redistributions. The difference between dynamic developing country states and the others is not that the former did not engage in clientelism while the latter did. Rather, in the dynamic countries, states possessed the ability to discipline and control their clients to ensure that a rapid capitalist transformation took place. In non-developmental states, the clients of the state are unproductive, just as the neo-patrimonial model argues, and the state lacks the capacity and eventually the inclination to do anything about it. Thus in contrast to point (i) in the good governance model in Figure 1.1, *the transformation approach recognizes that property right interventions are necessarily widespread in all developing countries; in addition some types of rents are critical for growth and political viability while others are indeed damaging.*

### Rent-seeking and corruption

If we move to point (ii) of the good governance model outlined in Figure 1.1, rent-seeking theory *is* correct in its claim that if rents exist, so will rent-seeking. Individuals and groups will spend resources to capture or retain rents. If many types of rents are essential for the social transformation, we should expect a considerable amount of rent-seeking to be characteristic of this period. Indeed this is what we observe in every developing country without exception. Since rents in some countries can be mostly damaging and in other countries mostly growth-enhancing, rent-seeking can be associated with both growth and stagnation. This overturns the link made in step (ii) of the good governance logic in Figure 1.1 that suggests that rent-seeking and corruption are always associated with poor economic outcomes. The neo-patrimonial model in Figure 1.3 also associates systemic corruption with poor performance, and this model too is challenged by our observation that extensive rents and political interventions are necessary in *all* developing countries. In fact, even advanced countries have massive rent-seeking as part of the institutional structure of their democracies. The only difference between advanced and developing countries is that in the former a bigger part of overall rent-seeking is legal, having become institutionalized in the form of many different forms of lobbying, political contributions to parties, legal costs, entertainment accounts and so on. In contrast, in developing countries, a bigger share of rent-seeking takes the form of corruption or expenditures on patron–client networks. Part of this difference is due to

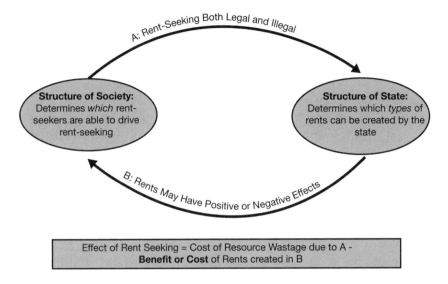

*Figure 1.5* Rent-seeking in the real world

an inadequate institutionalization of rent-seeking, which is difficult to achieve before a reasonably stable economic structure has emerged.

The most important point that follows from our analysis is that the *types* of rents that are being created through processes of rent-seeking and corruption are critically important. This is the main difference between countries, not the presence or absence of rent-seeking, since the latter is widespread in *every* society. This is shown in Figure 1.5, which can be contrasted with the liberal market perspective summarized in Figure 1.2. While rent-seeking and corruption always have a cost, they may be associated with rents that are critical for growth and social transformation. In these cases, the overall effect of A + B in Figure 1.5 can be positive even in the presence of significant costs due to rent-seeking and corruption. In contrast to the good governance proposition that all corruption and rent-seeking have to be attacked, in point (ii) in Figure 1.1, the policy conclusions of the transformation approach are more complex. *Given the impossibility of ruling out all rents, the task for policy must be to prevent the creation of damaging rents, and the types of corruption associated with these, while enhancing the state's capacity to create and manage developmental rents. There will inevitably be rent-seeking associated with developmental rents, and here policy should seek to legalize and regulate this rent-seeking.* This approach directs our attention to the factors determining the *types* of rents that are demanded and created in different societies rather than the impossible 'good governance' task of trying to create a rent-free market economy.

The neo-liberal policy conclusion that ending corruption at any cost is a *precondition* for progress is based on the assumption that a no-rent economy is both possible and desirable in a developing economy. In contrast, the social transformation perspective suggests that the fight against corruption has to distinguish between the corruption associated with damaging rents and the corruption associated with essential rents. In the former case, anti-corruption can aim to get rid of both the corruption and the rents associated with it. But in the latter case, anti-corruption strategies have to be very careful to target only the corruption, while *strengthening* the capacity of the state to create and manage these rents. A simplistic anti-corruption strategy that damaged the capacity of the state to create and manage developmental rents could do more harm than good. The long-term goal for these rents would be to legalize and regulate the associated rent-seeking, rather than get rid of the rents.

### Democracy and rent-seeking

Finally, step (iii) in the good governance model in Figure 1.1 claims that democracy limits the rent-creating interventions of the state, and the absence of democracy is also the key driver of the neo-patrimonial model in Figure 1.3. This argument too is theoretically and empirically weak. Democracy is supposed to be desirable *because* it makes politically driven interventions in the economy (in other words rent-creation) more difficult. But we have already seen that some rent-creation and politically driven accumulation may be both necessary and desirable during the transformation period and beyond. Moreover, if democracy reduced corruption, developing country democracies like India would have less corruption than non-democratic developing countries. The evidence does not even support this conclusion (see Treisman 2000). And if democracy reduced rent-seeking in general, we would expect advanced countries with mature democracies to suffer the least from rent-seeking. But in fact, advanced country democracies suffer from massive, though mostly legal rent-seeking, in the form of lobbying, contributions to political parties, expenditures on consultancies and so on. In advanced countries, popular majorities do not succeed in preventing rent-seeking by minority interests in agriculture, or the oil and arms industries, for example. The obvious explanation is that in democracies, minorities find it easier to organize compared to majorities particularly when the minorities are smaller and richer than the majority. In fact, it is widely recognized that stable democracies suffer from very extensive rent-seeking driven by well-organized vested-interest groups (for instance, Olson 1982).

Far from democracy being a bastion against rent-seeking, it would be more accurate to describe democracy as a form of *institutionalized rent-seeking*, where rules are defined for different groups to seek rents through the political process. The historical evidence is that democracy becomes truly viable when productive and growth-enhancing groups become big enough and organized enough to use democracy to protect and promote their interests (Moore 1991; Rueschemeyer, Stephens and Stephens 1992). Meaningful democracy also requires substantial fiscal resources such that legitimate demands for redistribution can be met legally through fiscal redistributions (Khan 2002a). These conditions too are unlikely to be met before substantial development has already occurred. Without them, democracy is likely either to remain vulnerable, as it is in most developing countries, or to break down entirely if unproductive groups are large, powerful or organized enough to democratically capture political power.

In advanced capitalist countries, we find that the rents created through the democratic process are usually not totally debilitating for a number of reasons. One reason is that when capitalism has become the dominant sector in the economy, long-term growth in the incomes and welfare of all classes and groups, including those who are not capitalists, depends on the growth of the capitalist sector. Hurting the capitalist sector impacts rapidly on virtually everyone and this prevents other groups creating rents that hurt the capitalist sector too much. Since the well-being of the state also depends on the health of the capitalist sector, advanced country states have regulatory structures that can discriminate between acceptable and damaging rents. Thus, instead of democracy *preventing* rent-seeking in advanced capitalist countries, we find a large amount of rent-seeking that is nevertheless (on the whole) consistent with dominant capitalist interests and economic growth (Khan 2002a).

In contrast, the link between democracy and development is more problematic in developing countries. Developing countries, whether or not they have democracy, are not, by definition, dominated by capitalism. Rent-creation that damages capitalist growth has a negligible effect on most people because the capitalist sector is itself negligible. By definition, the politically powerful groups and factions driving politics in developing countries are not yet dominated by capitalists. As a result, democracy in developing countries does not provide any institutional guarantee that rents that may damage the emergence of capitalism will not be created, but neither does authoritarianism. In general, the outcome of the political process, whether democratic or authoritarian, is much more open in developing countries in terms of the types of rents that are created. The outcome can sometimes be a predominance of productive rents but often it can be a predominance of damaging rents and destructive property right interventions. The implication is that democracy cannot be an instrumental variable in developing countries despite the claim in point (iii) of the good governance approach in Figure 1.1 or the neo-patrimonial model of Figure 1.3. *In the social transformation approach, democracy is supported as an end in itself; the viability of democracy depends on getting other institutional and political conditions right so that the rents created through the democratic process are value-enhancing and the state has the institutional and political capacity to manage these rents.*

## Characterizing the emerging Palestinian state

In this section, we will review what the evidence tells us about the dominant types of rents and rent-seeking in Palestine under the PNA. This in turn will help us to say something about the transformation capacities of the state. Over the period we are looking at, we find that there is no clear dominance of some types of rents over others. This is obviously because an identifiable type of Palestinian state hardly existed. Instead, a number of quite different types of rents and rent-seeking could be observed in *emergent* form in the Palestinian quasi-state, and under different circumstances, each of a number of different constellations of rents and rent-seeking *may* have consolidated to become the dominant ones. To help our analysis, we identify four 'types' of state that could have consolidated in Palestine, each defined by the combination of a particular constellation of rents. These state types are purely descriptive and are defined by the predominance of certain types of rents. Our focus is also restricted to Palestinian territories over this period, and these state types are not necessarily relevant for other cases. We begin by reviewing the types of rents and rent-seeking that were observed in Palestine over this period, and the political processes with which they were associated.

### Rents in the Palestinian context

Many rents in the Palestinian context were directly the result of the specific arrangements set up by the Oslo Agreements. But other rent-management problems were more like those faced by all developing country states. Some rents were intrinsic to the promotion of capitalists and the attraction of new technologies and investments. As in other developing countries, these rents could play a dynamic role, but under quite likely conditions, they could also become very damaging and reduce growth. And finally, some redistributive rents were critical for political stabilization and were recognized as such by external donors. These rents too, have in some contexts played a useful role in stabilizing the polity, and at other times have gone out of control and caused a lot of damage. Looking at some of these rents helps to identify the critical issues of rent-management in the Palestinian context and the conditions assisting or blocking a potentially successful transformation in Palestine.

### Monopolies

There are a number of reasons why we would expect to have seen some degree of monopolistic market power in the Palestinian economy. First, economies of scale can make many firms "natural monopolies" in a small economy like that of Palestine. The most efficient way of producing often involves companies that are so big relative to the economy that one or two can dominate the market. These firms are then able to raise prices and earn monopoly profits. Services like telecommunications, or utilities like electricity and water (if the Palestinian economy were allowed to develop its own utility supplies) are very likely to be natural monopolies in a small economy. But large firms in these sectors may still be the most efficient alternative provided an efficient regulatory structure ensures that profits are not excessive and the most efficient managers are selected. For regulation to be effective, regulators would have to have the capacity to assess performance, as well as have the political power to impose penalties if managers proved to be inefficient. Thus, enhancing efficiency does not always dictate the destruction of natural monopolies, but always requires their effective regulation.

A second factor that made monopolies quite likely in the Palestinian economy was the nature of the trade and import conditions imposed by Israel under the aegis of Oslo. These conditions ensured that virtually all imports into the Palestinian territories had to take place through Israel (the monopolies are discussed further in Chapter 2 by Hilal and Khan, and Chapter 5 by Nasr). Israel's control of borders allowed it to protect its own domestic monopolies in critical commodities like cement and petroleum. For instance, in the case of cement, the Nesher Company of Israel was an effective cement monopoly in the greater Israeli market that included the Palestinian territories. The Oslo Agreements and the Paris Economic Protocol allowed the Palestinians to import limited quantities of specified commodities from non-Israeli sources, but in practice, these imports could be obstructed by Israeli customs and security checks. If Israeli border guards decided to open every bag of cement to hunt for weapons, the imports allowed to the Palestinians from outside Israel could be disrupted at any time. On the other hand, importing cement from Israel meant allowing an Israeli monopoly to extract rents from Palestinian consumers.

While the PNA could not bypass Israel's control of its borders, it did have the power to prevent access by Israeli companies to Palestinian markets. The outcome that eventually emerged was a Palestinian cement monopoly that bought cement at world prices from Nesher and sold it on to Palestinians at or even slightly above the Israeli price. This arrangement allowed the Israeli monopoly to retain monopoly pricing within the Israeli customs union while the PNA could earn margins that contributed to its own survival given the very limited tax revenues it could collect from other sources (Lagerquist 2003). Given these circumstances, how should we evaluate the implications of the trading monopolies set up by the PNA? On the one hand, they probably did *not* make matters much worse for Palestinian consumers given that Israeli monopolies existed anyway, and attempts to import from third countries would very probably be impeded by Israel. On the other hand, the Palestinian trading monopolies allowed the Palestinian Authority to capture some of the rents that would otherwise have passed to Israel. Assessing the social efficiency of these monopolies thus requires an explicit consideration of the trade and fiscal agreements that the PNA had to sign with Israel as part of the Oslo Agreements (Chapter 2 by Hilal and Khan).

A third issue with respect to the role of monopolies in Palestine is related to the problem of attracting investment into a conflict zone. The rights of investors in Palestine were uncertain given that the end game in terms of the eventual Palestinian state was itself hardly clear. Much more than the infant industry struggling to learn new technologies in the typical developing country, investors in a conflict zone like Palestine require temporary rents to induce them to invest anything at all. The PNA's problem was that it did not have the resources to offer any direct inducements to new investors, particularly expatriate Palestinian investors who were taking big risks to invest in the emerging state. We will see in the chapters in this volume by Hilal and Khan, and by Nasr, that one of the ways in which the PNA attracted new investors was to offer them temporary monopolies, or at least substantial market power in key sectors like telecommunications by limiting entry in favour of critical investors.

Was this a socially damaging strategy? The answer depends on an assessment of the viable alternatives. On the one hand, market power in these sectors did mean higher prices for consumers. Indeed that was the intent, thereby giving investors sufficient rents to attract them to Palestine. On the other hand, the economy collectively benefited from investments and technologies that might otherwise not have been attracted at all. Far from being a simple story, this evidence suggests that there were contradictory forces at work within the Palestinian state, with at least some conditions supporting rent-allocation in ways that maintained economic dynamism and political stabilization. Expatriate investors were attracted, and at least in some cases, the more efficient were systematically preferred. Thus while some monopolistic arrangements were clearly restrictive practices in the classic textbook sense, a number of apparently monopolistic arrangements may not have been as damaging as they appear at first sight. Indeed, in creating and managing these monopolies, the PNA displayed some nascent developmental capacities, and an intelligent policy of engagement would have sought to strengthen these nascent state capacities.

*Redistributive (transfer) rents*

Redistribution is a necessary part of social stabilization in every society. In the conflict situation in which the PNA found itself, it is not surprising that *substantial* redistributive rents were politically necessary to stabilize the polity by accommodating critical constituencies. But more than 60 per cent of the PNA's revenues depended on taxes collected in the first instance by Israel from Palestinians and then transferred to the PNA, and aid accounted for around 10 per cent of GDP over this period (Chapter 6 by Fjeldstad and Zagha). This excessive fiscal vulnerability of the PNA gave considerable potential leverage to those responsible for clearing the transfers required for its day-to-day survival. The symbiotic interest of both the Israeli and the Palestinian side in being able to allocate these rents in ways that furthered their interests resulted in some unexpected 'institutional' arrangements. For instance, the Israeli government paid part of the official tax remittances owed to the PNA into accounts outside the Palestinian Ministry of Finance that were directly controlled by Arafat and his financial advisor, Muhammad Rashid (Lagerquist 2003; IMF 2003: 88).

Since Israel colluded for many years in these arrangements, until after the beginning of the Second *Intifada*, we can conclude that these arrangements were initially advantageous for both sides. On the one hand, the situation allowed Israel to withhold transfers at will without having to formally justify this, thereby maximizing its leverage over Arafat and the PNA. At the same time, Arafat's executive maximized its freedom of allocation over these resources and was able to use them for political stabilization in ways that might be difficult in a fully accountable system. While the existence of these accounts was well known from the outset, Israel only began to mobilize international concern with Arafat's special accounts when it became clear during the Second *Intifada* that Arafat had refused to construct the type of client state that was on offer from Israel (Hilal and Khan discuss the special accounts at greater length in Chapter 2).

The executive in turn used a large part of its vulnerable fiscal resources to create jobs to stabilize the polity. The explosion of employment in the public sector and in the security agencies followed from these political concerns. This kind of job creation effectively creates redistributive rents for critical constituencies. The challenge is to evaluate how damaging these redistributive rents were, by examining their cost in terms of economic inefficiency as against the political stabilization they achieved. If the economic inefficiency of these transfers is to be outweighed by the benefits of political stabilization, the state has to be able to control effectively the type and allocation of these redistributive rents. If powerful clients can force the creation of a growing number of damaging redistributive rents, economic inefficiency can rapidly escalate and the political stability that is purchased can be illusory (Khan 2000b). In our investigation of the Palestinian context, (Chapter 2 by Hilal and Khan) we find that individual Palestinian factions were not strong enough to veto the executive's allocation of redistributive rents. In other words, even though as in every developing country much redistribution was necessary for stability, in the Palestinian case the executive retained the ability to determine the type and allocation of these redistributive rents. This makes the Palestinian case potentially different from some of the more serious cases of state failure in developing countries.

A second redistributive imperative in developing countries is the need to make resources available to emerging capitalists to accelerate the emergence of capitalism from essentially pre-capitalist societies. Accelerating the development of the productive sector often involves giving tax breaks, subsidies, subsidized credit or other inducements to emerging capitalists as part of a strategy of promoting capitalism. The pay-off from such a strategy depends on the state's regulatory framework and whether it can ensure that these privileged individuals deliver growth. In the Palestinian case, the very limited state powers under the Oslo Agreements meant that the resources available for direct redistribution to emerging capitalists were extremely limited. There were some tax breaks for investors that are examined in Chapter 6 on taxation by Fjeldstad and Zagha. But the most important incentive for potential investors came from the creation of effective partial monopolies in the way discussed earlier, and examined here in the chapters by Hilal and Khan (Chapter 2) and Nasr (Chapter 5).

Finally, some of the redistribution that happened could only be described as predatory. This consisted of forced transfers from small traders and merchants to security officials, customs and tax officials and others, in ways familiar to most developing countries. Examples of such predatory behaviour were, however, less widespread in Palestine than in equivalent developing countries elsewhere in the world. But to the extent that these processes were going on, they were clearly very damaging. It is important to point out that we are not suggesting that the Palestinian Authority necessarily created any of these rents as the outcome of a deliberate plan or careful foresight. Indeed that is rarely the case in any country. On the contrary, we argue that a number of structural, political, institutional and external factors have to be taken into account to explain the specific patterns of rent-creation. In promoting the capacity of the state to manage developmental rents and limit damaging rents, these factors need to become targets of policy.

### Corruption and rent-seeking in Palestine

The theory of rent-seeking suggests that each of the important types of rents observed in the Palestinian context might be associated with a specific process of rent-seeking or corruption. Beginning with the most damaging types of rents and rent-seeking, there was undoubtedly evidence in Palestine of rent-seeking associated with straightforward predatory *extortion*. Extortion in Palestine was mostly a low-level activity by officials managing a highly restrictive network of security. The rent-seeking expenditures associated with these predatory activities were resources spent by officials to get into positions that allowed them to extort, and expenditures by citizens to evade extortion. Fischer, Said and Valdivieso (2001: 73) estimate that for trade with the outside world, Israeli security restrictions directly resulted in Palestinian businesses facing costs that were 30 to 45 per cent higher than those faced by equivalent Israeli companies. Israeli customs and security officials thus had the power to financially destroy Palestinian traders by delaying their goods at borders. This gave them not only powers of occasional extortion but also ultimately the power to ensure that Palestinian traders would cooperate with Israeli economic and political interests. Thus, it was often cheaper for Palestinians to engage in corruption to bypass Israeli restrictions, or to pay Israelis to import or release goods through security points and thereby earn easy margins. Similar security checks and checkpoints had to be maintained on the Palestinian side, though the restrictions were relatively less onerous. Nevertheless, similar exactions on the Palestinian side inevitably happened. Most journalistic reports refer to relatively small though systematic exactions by Palestinian officials at borders and crossings, or tolls collected by security personnel. There is no clear evidence that the Palestinian security forces operating within the Palestinian territories were significantly more corrupt or extractive than the Israeli military government that preceded them, and no evidence that Palestinian security forces carried out outright looting as Israeli troops did in Palestinian areas during Operation Defensive Shield in 2002 (Lagerquist 2003).

Since the Israelis were an occupying force and could therefore get away with high levels of looting and extortion, it would be more relevant to compare extortion by Palestinian security forces with the experience of internal extortion in other developing countries. While such judgements inevitably have to be impressionistic rather than quantitative, the Palestinian territories suffered relatively little from extreme forms of extortion, for instance by warlords linked to crime. Nevertheless, since any restrictions that generate this type of extortion and corruption are themselves damaging for the economy, there can be no disagreement that the removal or reduction of these extractions is highly desirable. But clearly a significant reduction in this type of extortion would be contingent on restructuring the system of checkpoints and gatekeepers, and extortion is unlikely to be significantly reduced by reforming the Palestinian security forces alone.

The much bigger transfers associated with political stabilization created their own structures of rent-seeking and influence-buying. These rent-seeking activities included, most importantly, the PNA's investments in security to assure external powers to release PNA resources on time, and the establishment of personalized networks between Palestinian officials and critically placed individuals in the Israeli administration to negotiate and facilitate the transfers. While it is easy to understand the functional necessity for these special accounts given the external constraints, there was obviously the possibility of misuse and misappropriation by rent-seekers with access to the executive. Indeed, we might expect that since the PNA had resources that were going to be used for political stabilization, there would have been some, maybe even substantial amounts of rent-seeking by political factions seeking to get a share of these rents. All of these types of rent-seeking were the result of the systemic presence of rents that were available to the executive for political stabilization as part of the design of the Oslo architecture and the necessity of at least some of these expenditures during a period of contested state formation. Thus, it is *not* the case that rent-seeking or corruption was *driving* the creation of these rents in any simple sense. On the contrary, the rent-seeking and corruption associated with these rents were the *result* of specific rents that were created and managed as a necessary part of the Oslo Agreements.

Nevertheless, these rent-seeking expenditures, for instance in maintaining patron–client networks, had a clear social cost. But the net effect of the rents distributed by the PNA for political stabilization was not necessarily negative. Much of these redistributive rents were used for job creation in the security services. The direct effect of many of these rents was very likely negative because sectors such as security were not high priority in terms of social needs, and they allowed the employment of individuals who were not best qualified for specific service-delivery sectors. Nevertheless, to the extent that this employment-generation achieved political stability, it had a positive economic effect in the form of faster development, greater investments and so on, compared to the alternative of social disruption by disaffected groups. The net effect of such stabilization rents may be positive or negative depending on the allocation and management of such rents, and the net positive effect may be big enough to also outweigh the rent-seeking costs in terms of the costs of maintaining patron–client networks, corruption, and so on. These judgements are difficult to quantify precisely, but before 2000, a significant degree of political stabilization *was* achieved by the PNA through these mechanisms, and this did create a context for considerable external investments despite the overall context of uncertainty and conflict with Israel.

Finally, we have seen that a number of rents have historically been critical for *economic* development, and the PNA was involved in the creation and management of some of these developmental rents. With these rents too, there is bound to be some associated rent-seeking and even corruption. However, if (as in the East Asian countries) a developmental state can allocate these rents efficiently, then even though corruption is always undesirable, some amount of corruption can co-exist with rapid development. As the economy becomes more developed and a capitalist class entrenches, some of this corruption is rapidly converted into legal influence-buying in the form of lobbying and political contributions, and the more damaging aspects of this corruption can be outlawed. The real problem emerges when a state lacks the capacity to create growth-enhancing rents. In these cases, states end up supporting inefficient industries and growth-reducing transfers. The corruption that is associated with *these* rents effectively allows inefficient capitalists to buy themselves protection, or maintain their damaging monopoly profits or subsidies, and the overall effect can be massively negative (Khan 1996a, b). Thus while the focus on corruption is important, its significance is to enable us to identify the causes preventing states from playing a dynamic transformation role. A state with high transformation capacities could perform well with some degree of corruption, but it would obviously perform even better if corruption could be reduced. But a state that lacks transformation capacities would not necessarily perform much better if it got rid of all corruption. Most seriously, if a badly constructed reform aiming to reduce corruption and increase account-ability damaged the limited capacities of such a state to create and manage developmental rents, the results could paradoxically be very negative. In the chapter by Hilal and Khan, we will consider whether some of the post-2000 governance reforms that were pushed through in the PNA under external pressure may have had just such damaging effects.

## Democracy in Palestine

Quite apart from the general problems of deepening democracy in devel-oping countries, Palestine and the PNA faced some special problems over this period. This is because the PNA was clearly *not* set up through the Oslo Agreements primarily to deliver democracy to Palestinians. Its primary objective was to negotiate the territorial and constitutional limits of a Palestinian quasi-state in the context of an extreme asymmetry of power and resources vis-à-vis Israel. To get anything at all, it had to demonstrate its ability to deliver security to Israel on terms determined by the latter. In turn, this meant that from the beginning, there were serious conflicts between the immediate democratic rights of the Palestinian opponents of this particular 'peace process' and the imperative of maintaining security. The implications were well understood and widely reported from the outset by human rights organizations.

A particular problem for the operation of democracy in the Authority was that it had to allocate Israeli controlled fiscal resources to achieve polit-ical stabilization and security. For these redistributive rents to be allocated transparently, we have to ask if it might have been possible to institution-alize and legalize the transfers necessary for political stabilization in the Palestinian context. Transparent and democratic regulation of these rents in such a context would be highly desirable but would not be simple. The public regulation of these transfers would require the prior existence of a majority in Palestine that agreed about the aims that were to be achieved through political stabilization. For instance, it would have to agree that it was proper and necessary for these transfers to be ultimately controlled by Israel during the interim period and perhaps beyond, with Israel retaining the fiscal and political capacity to halt these transfers if Israeli aims were not being achieved. It would then have to agree to monitor the use of these funds controlled by Israel to maintain Palestinian political stability to achieve Israeli aims of security without knowing in advance the nature of the Palestinian state that Israel would eventually allow. A constituency with such a sympathetic understanding of the security concerns of the occupying power is unlikely to have been broadly enough based in Palestine to have allowed a democratic government to be constructed that could openly carry out the necessary regulation of these political transfers. Moreover, as we have argued earlier, the possibility of open democratic transfers assumes that fiscal resources are sufficient to satisfy enough demands legitimately to maintain stability. It is unlikely that Palestinian fiscal capacity, even with a full transfer of tax-collecting powers to the PNA, would have been sufficient to achieve stability through generalized transfers given the widespread economic deprivation and political dissatisfaction with the terms of the two-state solution. This fiscal constraint is an important imperative driving patron–client politics in developing countries. By definition, patron–client politics involves secret transfers to critical groups rather than open transfers to all deserving groups. These considerations warn us not to be overly optimistic that democratization of control over tax revenues would be sufficient to achieve the allocation of resources required in conflict and transformation contexts.

If it was not the *intention* of the Oslo Agreements to immediately create a liberal-democratic state in Palestine, it makes little sense to criticize the PNA leadership for not delivering a satisfactory democracy before the 'peace process' had delivered a state. In addition, even in a more typical developing country where a sovereign state already exists, it is not clear that a democratic state can be entrenched without addressing the problem of how to create a viable and dynamic economy. If we reject the simplistic good governance or neo-patrimonial models, rapid democratization would not *in itself* have addressed the problem of social and economic transformation, without which the conditions for sustaining democracy and making it viable would not have been attained.

Clearly, progress in democratization under the PNA was too slow. But how is progress to be accelerated? Here there is room for genuine disagreements about the extent to which the pace of democratization was held back by a lack of 'democratic will' on the part of the Palestinian leadership, as opposed to structural constraints, in particular the institutional and economic arrangements underpinning the peace process. In Chapter 2 by Hilal and Khan, we argue that economic development and political stabilization were primarily constrained by the nature of the institutions set up by the Olso agreements and by the external strategies and constraints imposed by Israel. In turn, this made progress in democratization very difficult to sustain. Given these internal and external constraints, far from the concentration of executive power being dysfunctional, centralization arguably maintained the viability of the PNA, by allowing the executive to create rents and transfers that stabilized the economy and polity in very difficult circumstances. It is likely that a weaker executive would have led to an earlier collapse of the PNA due to its inability to maintain even limited stability and security.

In the aftermath of the Second *Intifada*, the US-sponsored Road Map demanded a decentralization of power within the Palestinian Authority and the creation of checks and balances on the powers of the executive as a precondition of further progress. It is not clear why checking the executive will necessarily deliver democracy that is more meaningful for the

Palestinian people. Moreover, it is far from clear that a weaker executive will be able to manage rent-allocation for economic and political stabilization even to the extent of the previous administration. While the Palestinian public was dissatisfied with the degree of democracy that it enjoyed, and progress towards statehood was indeed stalled, it does not follow that the weakness of democracy was the *cause* of the stalled peace process. Correlation does not establish causation. Democracy in Palestine, as elsewhere in the developing world, is an end in itself. Democracy of any particular type does not *necessarily* play a functional role in terms of promoting the viability of transformation economies or reaching territorial compromises with a colonial power. Rather, democracy needs to be entrenched by ensuring rapid economic growth and the construction of a viable polity. Over the longer term, the democratic aspirations of the Palestinian people were more likely to have been furthered by strengthening the capacity of the Palestinian quasi-state to manage developmental strategies in the context of a viable state. Indeed a full-blooded Palestinian democracy may have made the 'security-first' route to statehood much more difficult if not impossible. Since this was self-evident to Israel in 1994, one can question why Israel and its external allies have put so much emphasis on the 'democratization' of the PNA after 2000. It is possible that Israel began to believe that a divided and weak Palestinian leadership would be easier to negotiate with. But if the Palestinian executive were actually to be weakened, this would be a Pyrrhic victory for the Israelis. A Palestinian leadership that was weak enough to accept impossible Israeli terms is likely to be too weak to impose any such 'solution' on its unwilling population.

## Four routes of state formation

The rents observed in the Palestinian economy suggest that the effects and implications of externally controlled rents dominated the operation of the quasi-state. We described such a state as a client state. At the same time, other rents observed in the Palestinian context suggested a number of different state characteristics that existed in incipient form in the PNA. Some of the observed rents were compatible with aspects of a predatory state, others with a fragmented clientelist state, and others with a developmental state. If the client state was an interim rather than a permanent phenomenon, the PNA could have progressed along one of these possible routes, depending on which rents and rent-management capacities became more dominant over time. Table 1.2 lists the rents and rent-management features that are consistent with each of these state types, and summarizes the evidence discussed so far.

In the rest of this section, we discuss the client state and its two variants – the integrationist and asymmetric containment client states. Since these variants have very different implications for Palestinian state viability, and therefore for internal governance improvements, we discuss the viability of

*Table 1.2* Rents, rent-seeking and state characteristics in the Palestinian context

| | Client state | Predatory state characteristics | Fragmented clientelist state characteristics | Developmental state characteristics |
|---|---|---|---|---|
| *Rents defining each type of state* | Transfers to the PNA conditional on political compliance for downward transfer to internal factions | Economically damaging monopolies; Extortion by PNA officials | Monopolies and transfers for faction leaders *who can veto* rent-reallocations | Transfers to capitalists *conditional* on performance; Clientelist transfers to maintain stability |
| *Associated forms of rent-seeking* | Resources spent by officials to maintain security control; Corruption by officials managing rent-allocation for political stabilization | Corruption/ lobbying to get monopolies; Expenditures by state to maintain its coercive apparatus | Extensive expenditures on maintaining factions; Kickbacks to state leaders from factional leaders | Lobbying by emerging capitalists and kickbacks to state leaders; Expenditures by state to maintain centralized power |
| *Expected economic outcomes* | Moderate growth with *integration stategy*; Poor/vulnerable growth with *asymmetric containment* | Poor economic growth | Poor to moderate economic growth | Moderate to very high economic growth |
| *Evidence in Palestinian context* | Extensive evidence of client-state rents and of an Israeli attempt to achieve *asymmetric containment* in Palestine | Moderate evidence of predatory rents but some monopoly creation could have alternative explanations | Moderate evidence of factional allocation but weak evidence that faction leaders could veto rent-allocations | Moderate evidence of developmental rents but limited state capacity in regulating rents |

these state types at length. We also discuss Israel's possible strategic calculations in wanting a client state, and eventually a particular variant of a client state in Palestine. These strategic concerns are important for assessing the feasibility of the state formation process as a whole. We then discuss the incipient predatory, fragmented clientelist and developmental characteristics of the quasi-state, and the significance of these observations.

### Client-state characteristics

As we have already observed, the rents transferred by external powers to ensure political compliance by the PNA played an important role in the security-first route to Palestinian statehood. If these externally controlled rents had institutionalized into a long-term arrangement for determining the economic and social policy of the Palestinian state, this would amount to a consolidation of a Palestinian *client state*. The client-state outcome is specific to the Palestinian state-formation experience, and the conditions underpinning it flow from the peculiar security concerns of Israel. Since Israel believed that it was unlikely that a sovereign Palestinian state would put the security of Israel at the top of its agenda, it insisted on controlling a range of rents that were critical for the survival of the emerging Palestinian state. The Oslo Agreements institutionalized the dependence of the PNA on rent flows controlled by Israel and the donors during the interim period (see Chapter 3 by Zagha and Zomlot as well as Chapter 2 by Hilal and Khan). Many of the Palestinian critics of the PNA identified the way in which Israel sought to control rents that were critical for the Palestinian economy, and the way in which the PNA appeared to acquiesce to this control, as evidence of an operating or emerging client state. In the eyes of these critics, the donor community contributed to the construction of a client state by also making aid to the PNA conditional on Palestinian participation in a peace process that gave priority to Israel's security requirements. Although neither side would describe these arrangements as a 'client state', we will use this term to describe the external rent-control aspects of the Oslo Agreement. The facts of externally controlled transfers and other mechanisms of control are not in dispute (see Chapter 3 by Zagha and Zomlot, and Chapter 6 by Fjeldstad and Zagha). The question is only about the effects of this dependence, and whether these were transitional or permanent characteristics of the emerging state.

Transfers from an outside power can only ensure compliance by a client in conjunction with other policies. Compliance can in theory be induced by two quite different strategies. At one extreme, transfers could be linked to the implementation of policies that achieved the goals of the dominant power but which were greatly *beneficial* for the client as well. Some constituencies in the client state may resist these policies in the short run, and conditional rent-transfers from the dominant power could assist the implementation of mutually beneficial policies by creating immediate *incentives* for compliance. Once these policies were in place, external control of rents would no longer be necessary because co-existence would be mutually beneficial and there would be endogenous incentives for compliance on both sides. At the other extreme, if the goals of the dominant power could not be achieved through policies that benefited the client, transfers combined with policies that maintained the vulnerability of the client could ensure compliance. If the economy of the client were vulnerable, the threat to withdraw transfers and to otherwise damage the economy of the client would threaten regime survival and would therefore ensure compliance. In principle, each of these polar strategies could ensure that the external control of transfers and other control powers would have the effect of ensuring compliance, but with very different consequences for the client. The economic and political implications of a client state consolidating in Palestine would therefore depend critically on where Israeli strategies were located along this spectrum.

The best client-state scenario (from the Palestinian perspective) would clearly be one where Israel attempted to ensure compliance through policies that over time created endogenous *incentives* for compliance. The most obvious policy of this type in the Israel–Palestine context would be an Israeli push for the full integration of the two economies. Such an *integrationist strategy* would involve a rapid, or at least a steady increase in investment and capital flows from Israel into the Palestinian territories and an equivalent reduction of restrictions on the movements of labour of all skill categories in the other direction. From a Palestinian perspective, while integration is not necessarily the *best* strategy for ensuring the rapid development of the Palestinian economy, it is a reasonably attractive one. It is not the best because integration may slow down the development of a Palestinian national capitalism. Nevertheless, the Palestinian economy would clearly benefit from freer access to the labour and capital markets of the more advanced Israeli economy. It would allow accelerated capitalist development in the Palestinian territories, but one that would be dominated by Israeli capitalists for a very considerable time. Moreover, given the long history of conflict, economic development alone may not have satisfied Palestinian demands for justice and redress. Occasional acts of violence on both sides could be expected. Nevertheless, as integration deepened, a Palestinian client state would have neither the interest nor the ability to challenge Israeli interests, and eventually control of its fiscal resources would no longer be necessary. Thus while the long-term success of an integrationist strategy was not guaranteed, it had a good chance of success. But a minimum precondition for its success was that the Palestinian quasi-state should be able to offer rapid economic development for broad sections of its population, and to demonstrate to its people that prosperity depended on compliance with the security priorities of Israel. An *integrationist client-state strategy* might have satisfied these conditions.

Although some Israeli policy statements suggested that the Israeli strategy was indeed one of constructing an integrationist client state (see for instance, Peres 1993), in fact moves towards economic integration were at best halting. We argue (Chapter 2 by Hilal and Khan, and Chapter 3 by Zagha and Zomlot) that contrary to expectations, Israel rapidly strengthened the mechanisms of control that existed before Oslo, and introduced new mechanisms of control deep inside the Palestinian territories that significantly increased the vulnerability of the Palestinian economy. The failure to deepen integration and indeed its reversal in many respects cannot be explained by security threats because the reversal began at the very outset, at a time when there was widespread support for the Oslo route on both sides. However, it is possible to make sense of Israel's retreat from this route if we remember that along with security, Israel had another fundamental objective, and that was to maintain its identity as a Zionist state. As the European Union (EU) model shows, in the long run the political separation of closely integrated economies makes less and less sense. It may have been the fear that ever closer economic integration may in a distant future lead to political integration that ruled out strong support for an integrationist strategy in Israel (see DellaPergola 2001 for an analysis of the demographic data and its implications for the viability of Israel).

If the integrationist approach failed to make progress for this or for any other reason, leverage over a Palestinian client state would have to be maintained by other means. The worst scenario of a client state from a Palestinian perspective would be one where Israel did not allow economic integration, but attempted to create an economic context where the suspension of transfers would amount to a severe *penalty* for non-compliance. Instead of integration, an Israeli capacity to periodically close down movements of labour and goods in large parts of the Palestinian economy would also ensure that Israeli control over PNA rent transfers would provide significant leverage over the client state. But to do this without also hurting the Israeli economy, integration would have to be highly selective to maximize the asymmetric impact of closures. We describe this as a strategy of *asymmetric containment*. By ensuring that the Palestinian economy could be hurt in an asymmetric way by Israeli decisions, the Israeli state ensured that the Palestinian economy remained in a state of sustained vulnerability. A suspension of transfers would then greatly magnify Israel's economic and political influence. Arguably, compliance would follow. Indeed, following this strategy, if the Palestinian economy were to become more self-sufficient, the threat of rent-withdrawal would work less well for ensuring compliance.

Many aspects of Israeli policy during this period are consistent with a strategy of *asymmetric containment*. Even before the Oslo Agreements, only unskilled Palestinians could find employment in Israel, and they could be excluded at short notice without significant cost to the Israeli economy. This did not change after Oslo, contrary to the requirements of deepening economic integration. On the contrary, the Palestinian labour market became much *more* vulnerable. Israel rapidly institutionalized what began as a temporary system of checkpoints and prohibited areas. This allowed it to disrupt movements of goods and people *within* the Palestinian territories, and potentially to isolate Palestinians within particular villages and towns. In addition to formalizing and deepening existing methods of control, Israel established extensive controls over Palestinian trade and diplomatic relationships with the outside world as part of the Oslo Agreements. This made Palestinian consumers and producers much more vulnerable than if they had been purchasing imported products directly from Israelis, as they had been before Oslo.

The effects of this system of control assisted in the 'de-development' of the Palestinian economy (Roy 2001). Our notion of asymmetric containment suggests that de-development may have been to some extent an *intended* consequence of Israeli policies. Palestinian economic vulnerability ensured that control over critical Palestinian rents gave Israel greater leverage to ensure compliance in security and other issues. To make matters worse for the Palestinians, it would be much more difficult to guarantee Israeli security with asymmetric containment since Palestinians would now face much greater hardships. Compared to an integrationist client state, a client state that accepted containment would have to use much greater repression on its own people. In our assessment (Hilal and Khan, Zagha and Zomlot, this volume), Israeli strategies on the ground were closer to the *asymmetric containment* end of possible compliance strategies. There were some investments in Palestinian territories by Israelis over this period (for instance in the Jericho casino and in some indirect shareholdings), but significantly, there was no loosening of restrictions on labour movements. In fact, controls over labour movements became *much more* restrictive during this period, as did controls over movements of goods. The degree of restriction has to be measured not just by looking at the aggregate movements of labour and goods, but by looking at the system of control that allowed Israel to stop movements on a daily basis *inside* the Palestinian territories, as well as to and from the outside world.

While the Palestinian leadership clearly accepted some version of a client state as the only deal on offer in the interim period, for their own survival they refused to accept a client state based on asymmetric containment as a long-term possibility. However, it soon became apparent that this was the only client state that was on offer in the interim period and beyond, creating profound obstacles for the Oslo road-map. Many of the conflicts between the Palestinian leadership and the Israelis during the Oslo period, and particularly towards the end of this period, reveal a growing tension between Israeli attempts to enforce a system of compliance based on asymmetric containment and Palestinian attempts to break out by following independent developmental strategies.

### Israeli objectives and the feasibility of its client-state strategy

A number of deeper questions are raised by these observations. It is easy to explain why Israel wanted and still wants a two-state solution. The demographic balance has already shifted to the point that a Zionist state in historic Palestine (that is 1948 Israel and the occupied territories) is no longer viable. But why did Israel want to have a client state in the occupied territories that would now become the truncated state of Palestine? And why did it then impose asymmetric containment on it? These are fundamental questions with enormous implications for the future viability of a Palestinian state. After all, Israel could simply have withdrawn to the internationally recognized 1967 borders and allowed full sovereignty to the new state. We can only reflect on a number of possible answers to these questions since fully satisfactory answers would require a separate project on Israeli political economy. The simplest but least plausible possibility is that Israel felt threatened by a fully sovereign Palestinian state if it simply withdrew to its 1948 borders, and it therefore needed to have security guarantees by retaining controls over the foreign and defence policies of the new state. This may appear to be plausible but it is actually extremely unlikely that Israel had anything to fear militarily from the fledgling Palestinian state.

A more plausible possibility is that powerful groups in Israel would not give up the large number of settlements (with roughly a quarter of a million settlers) in the Palestinian territories that they saw as Jewish territories by divine right. If so, full separation would not be feasible and Israeli security would now definitely require a client Palestinian state. Palestinians would have to accept a number of non-contiguous territories as a 'state' and they would have to accept a permanent Israeli presence in strategic and economically valuable locations within their 'state', such as settlements sitting atop all the critical water sources. In such a context, Palestinian security cooperation would be required on an ongoing basis to protect the settlements (Judt 2003). This is plausible, but if the survival of Zionism behind 1948 borders only required action against the settlers, we would have expected to see greater efforts, at least by Labour, to prepare the grounds for removing them. But instead of any concerted attempts to withdraw settlements, *both* Labour and Likud built *new* settlements and expanded existing ones after the signing of the Oslo Agreements. So, if the impossibility of withdrawing settlements drove Israel to a client-state strategy, it was not because the establishment that signed the Oslo Agreements discovered that it could not get rid of the settlers, but rather it appeared that it did not even intend to remove them.

This suggests a third possibility that the problem facing the Israeli state may have been even more intractable than that of removing the settlers. The actions of both Labour and Likud suggest that a broad swathe of the Israeli political class did not see the creation of a sovereign Palestinian state as a solution to the 'Palestinian problem'. A possible explanation of such an attitude could be that the Israeli political class could see that even after the creation of a Palestinian state, a significant Palestinian minority would remain in Israel with Israeli citizenship. This Israeli Palestinian minority was already around 20 per cent of the Israeli population at the time of the Oslo Agreements, and its faster growth was expected to steadily increase this percentage in the decades ahead. There was also the issue of the refugees. Many of them were unlikely to give up their historic struggle to gain the right of return, irrespective of any agreements signed by their leaders. This can explain why the Israeli political class may have felt that Israel as a Zionist state would always have to live with a 'Palestinian problem', and the exercise of power over the Palestinians was going to be a permanent part of Israel's survival strategy as it had always been in the past (see for instance, Shlaim

2000). If so, it would make perfect sense to concede at best a client Palestinian state that may in the future assist in the ongoing management of the bigger problem.

If a client state for the Palestinians made sense for Israel, why did it also want to impose asymmetric containment on this state? The answer to this would depend on why we think Israel wanted a client state in the first place. If the client-state strategy had been driven primarily by security fears, and the need to have some degree of influence over security expenditures and security arrangements in the Palestinian state, a client state with integration would be eminently feasible. Indeed, the relatively low level of violence in the period immediately following Oslo suggests that security cooperation between the two sides was initially quite good. Moreover, remarkable optimism and calm on both sides characterized the immediate post-Oslo period. Clearly, the problem was not the policing capacity or even the determination of the quasi-state to deliver security. If integration could rapidly increase the incentives to comply, why was the integrationist strategy not more forcefully pursued, and why did asymmetric containment increasingly become the dominant strategy? To find a plausible explanation we have to remember that Israel was not just concerned about security, but security *and* demography. If the possibility of sharing sovereignty with a non-Jewish majority in any form and at any time, even in the distant future, is ruled out, so is economic integration, since the latter is likely to lead in the end to some forms of political integration. Thus even if the initial concern was purely one of security (whether security within 1948 borders or security for the intractable settlers as well) demographic concerns would still rule out an integrationist strategy. If the initial concern was one of security *and* keeping all options open regarding a much bigger demographic challenge that included Palestinians within Israel and the refugees, then integration was even more forcefully ruled out, even though a client state would still be desperately required. While a number of factors were clearly jointly at play, this complex set of options may help to explain why Israel wanted to achieve both a client state *and* one that was based on asymmetric containment.

What was amazing about the historical opportunity that was opened up by Oslo was that on the Palestinian side, the Palestinian leadership accepted the necessity of at least a temporary form of 'client' status for the emerging Palestinian state (defined as external control over critical rents and decisions). It was clear to the Palestinian leadership that at best what was on offer as the outcome of the Oslo Agreements was not only a territorial compromise from the perspective of historic Palestine, but also an acceptance of an Israeli veto over many important decisions of their 'state', which would therefore be less than sovereign. For instance, it was clear that any future Palestinian state would have limited military and foreign policy freedoms compared to other states and cooperation with Israel on security was not going to be optional at least in the immediate future. By signing the Oslo Agreements, Arafat and his leadership implicitly accepted these limits. Perhaps surprisingly, there was initially strong internal support for a compromise along these lines within the WBG Palestinians, and this provided Arafat with his political constituency.

Nevertheless, within these limits, Arafat and his constituency had some clearly defined minimum requirements. Some of these requirements are well known and were articulated during the Camp David talks on the final settlement. On the issue of territory, it was clear that after relinquishing the 78 per cent of Palestine on which Israel had been established in 1948, the Palestinian state would have to include all of the territory occupied in 1967 (including East Jerusalem), with minor border adjustments on the basis of exchanging territory where necessary. On the issue of the refugees, the PNA knew that no solution would work if Israel did not admit that ethnic cleansing took place in 1948. It followed that Israel had to recognize in some form the right of return that is enshrined in international law, but with flexibility in its implementation. What is critical is that while Arafat demanded 'true independence and full sovereignty: the right to control our own airspace, water resources, and borders; to develop our economy; to have normal commercial relations with our neighbours, and to travel freely'[3], these demands were not articulated to include military and foreign policy independence, or to exclude security cooperation. In other words, the PNA deferred to Israeli security concerns in ways that *de facto* amounted to reduced sovereignty during the interim period and beyond.

The compromise that Arafat and his constituency were willing to make was to accept a state that had all the trappings of sovereignty but which allowed Israel to have a say in all matters that could be related to security. Such a state clearly would not have full sovereignty in all respects. *But this compromise on sovereignty could only remain politically viable if the emerging state could provide the PNA's internal constituency with substantial new economic opportunities.* The rents that Israel and the donors controlled could have assisted in attaining these economic and political objectives provided Israeli policies allowed rapidly expanding economic opportunities for all sections of the Palestinian people, including skilled professionals, Palestinian capitalists as well as unskilled workers. In theory, an integrationist strategy may have allowed this. However, as the strategy of asymmetric containment became clearer, the aspirations of both sides became increasingly inconsistent. The PNA's political viability was directly affected because its leadership had to generate growth through special privileges for expatriate investors that alienated important sections of its own population, and at the same time, the degree of 'policing' required to maintain a client state with asymmetric containment proved to be ever increasing in its required severity. These considerations have enormous significance for Palestinian state formation strategies of the future. If an integrationist client state is not possible for the Israelis, and an asymmetric containment state for the Palestinians, then a client state is effectively ruled out. The question then becomes whether Israel can ever concede a fully sovereign Palestinian state on 1967 borders even though this does not solve its bigger 'Palestinian problem', and may even shrink a number of options in dealing with other aspects of the 'problem'. If not, the Oslo experience tells us that the two-state solution is not likely to proceed much further.

### Predatory state characteristics

We have seen that there was evidence of some amount of extortion by PNA officials and of many damaging monopoly rents. For instance, the monopoly rents created by setting up trading monopolies, or the alleged extraction of tax resources into secret accounts controlled by the leadership could easily have become predatory rents. There was also evidence of lower-level extortion by PNA security staff from small businesses and others. Rents are predatory if leaders extract resources from society, and the extraction leaves society worse off than it would otherwise have been. The latter qualification is important because in our definition predation is not determined by the legality of the resource extraction but its economic effects. Resource extraction by the state happens in all states. In developed countries most of the resource extraction is legal in the form of taxes, but in developing countries, a greater part comes from grey activities or is illegal. To judge whether rent extraction in any context is predatory, we focus on the damage done to society, compared to viable alternatives where these rents could be avoided or allocated in a better way. When we look at many of the apparently predatory PNA rents from this perspective, only the examples of direct extortions from businesses are unequivocally predatory rents. Some of the Palestinian trading monopolies could have been beneficial for the Palestinian economy compared to the alternative of not having them, given the specific context of Israeli monopolies and Israeli control over external borders. Similarly, some of the kickbacks going into secret or special accounts may have been necessitated by the imperative of maintaining security and flexibility in a context of fiscal control by the colonial power. At the same time, some of these resources could easily be misappropriated and used to enrich the leadership at the expense of society *given what could be achieved under these constraints*. The judgement of when rents in a difficult transformation and conflict context become predatory is therefore a difficult one, and one over which there can be genuine disagreement.

### Fragmented clientelist state characteristics

Redistributive transfers, as well as the creation of monopolies for powerful faction leaders would also be consistent with aspects of an emerging *fragmented clientelist state*, but only if we can also find evidence that the recipient factions had the power to *veto* attempts at rent re-allocation by the state. The qualification is important since *all* states have to create some redistributive rents to maintain political stability. The PNA too was clearly distributing rent to critical client factions during this period. For instance, there was a rapid growth in employment in the state sector as thousands of individuals were absorbed into administrative jobs, particularly in the various security services. When public sector jobs are created without any proportionate service delivery purpose, these jobs primarily deliver rents to those who are employed. Was this simply political stabilization or was there evidence that powerful Palestinian factions had sufficient power to demand rent allocations of a type and extent that they themselves determined? In our next chapter by Hilal and Khan, we examine these possibilities and find very little evidence over this period that client factions could veto rent re-allocations in Palestine.

### Developmental state characteristics

Some of the rents created by the Palestinian state had potentially positive effects for economic development and political stabilization. The conditions and capacities required for a developmental state need to be carefully identi-fied because the range of rents such a state creates can be *superficially* similar to those created by predatory or fragmented clientelist states. For instance, a developmental state could create temporary monopoly rents, but in this case, it would be to attract investment and encourage risk-taking, and these rents would be managed to achieve these goals. A developmental state could also create transfers and redistributive rents to accelerate the emer-gence of capitalists and to maintain political stability, but these transfers would be managed so that their efficiency costs were controlled, and the net effect was an acceleration of developmental transformations.

To test if rent-management in the Palestinian context displayed any *devel-opmental state* characteristics, we should look for evidence of rent allocations that maintained political stability and provided *conditional* support to emerging capitalists. A developmental state would have to have a much greater degree of sovereignty than was allowed to the PNA under the Oslo Agreements. Nevertheless, although this is not widely recognized, there were elements in the rent-allocation organized by the PNA that were consis-tent with a nascent developmental state. The scale was inevitably small given the powerful external constraints facing the state, and the short time period before the first normal period of development ended in 2000. But there is evidence that the PNA used rents to attract expatriate Palestinian capitalists who had substantial investment funds and entrepreneurial experience. Many *did* invest in Palestine under the PNA despite the extreme uncertainty regarding the future of the Palestinian state formation experiment. The PNA also displayed some ability to correct mistakes in the allocation of rents, re-allocating rents to those who might be more efficient (and who could therefore offer bigger benefits to the PNA over time). The ability to override factional interests and to correct misallocations of rents despite factional opposition is a characteristic of developmental states that distinguishes them from fragmented clientelist ones, and enables them to ensure that rents remain growth-promoting.

Since the rents and rent-management capacities underpinning all of our incipient 'state types' could be found to some extent in the Palestinian territories under the PNA, our task is the more difficult one of identifying the conditions under which each may have become more dominant. State failure in our approach is explained not by the absence of conditions recognized as good governance characteristics. Rather it is explained by the weakness of conditions under which a developmental state with transformation capacities could have emerged, capable of dealing with the problems of transformation in the Palestinian context. Conversely, conditions that strengthened the possibility of one of the less dynamic types of state consolidating, in particular a predatory, fragmented clientelist or a client state based on asymmetric containment would result in a decline in state viability and possibly signal impending state failure.

## A methodology for assessing state performance

The *types* of rents a state supports and its rent-management capacities depend in turn on underlying institutional, political and other conditions. The institutional structure of states is clearly important since this can directly determine its rent-management capacities. The political context is also critical, in particular because the distribution of power between groups and classes can determine which groups are likely to succeed in getting the rents that favour them. Other variables that are likely to play a role in determining the dominant types of rents include external conditions, particularly in small states and states in conflict where rents may be controlled by external powers. Initial conditions are also important, of which the most important for our purposes is the prior degree of development of capitalism. This may determine the types of rents that are feasible since some rents, such as rents to accelerate technology acquisition, require a minimum level of prior capitalist development. Figure 1.6 shows the four key sets of conditions that we will look at in explaining the prevalence of different types of rents and rent-management capacities.

First, the prior degree of development of capitalism and the organizational strength of capitalists are important variables determining rent-outcomes. The relative power of different factions of capitalists and their power relative to other social groups can determine the types of rents that are created and how effectively the state can discipline and manage these rents. Second, and related to this is the distribution of organizational power in the broader society. The relative power of different groups and classes can explain their ability to demand rents of different types. A third

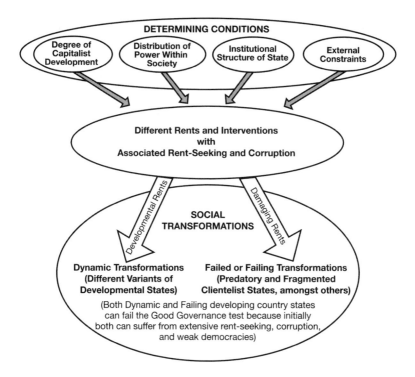

*Figure 1.6* Conditions determining rents and rent-seeking in social transformations

determinant of types of rents is the institutional structure of the state, and this refers to both economic and political institutions. But instead of presuming that democratic, decentralized or any other institutional structure results in better rent-management capacities, our approach is to establish the effects of a particular institutional structure, *given the overall context defined by other conditions*. Thus, it is quite possible for democratic institutions, for instance, to sometimes support value-enhancing rents, and at other times to support value-reducing rents. Similarly, the effect of the centralization of decision-making has to be examined in a specific context. At a general level, all we can say is that the centralization of some critical state powers is important for the functioning of any state. In particular the ability of the central executive to coordinate the activities of different state agencies is critical if developmental rents are to be created as opposed to redistributive rents that only benefit particular groups. The leadership in a coordinated state is less likely to benefit from damaging redistribution, because while some constituents gain, others lose out, and the support base for the state is not necessarily increased. In contrast, an institutionally fragmented state is more likely to support damaging redistributive rents because each agency can hope to benefit from redistribution to *its* constituents, without caring for the loss of other constituents unconnected to it (Okuno-Fujiwara 1997; Shleifer and Vishny 1993). Effective institutional centralization in turn requires a corresponding distribution of political power that supports it since the implementation of state decisions requires both institutional and political capacities (Khan 1995). Finally, external conditions also have to be taken seriously, particularly in the case of small countries and in conflict situations. Indeed, in the Palestinian case, external conditions were of paramount importance.

Each of these sets of conditions clearly keeps changing over time. Moreover, growth or stagnation can itself feed back to change these conditions, for instance by weakening or strengthening particular classes or by allowing state capacity in particular areas to be improved, or constraining it to collapse further. These feedbacks can in turn result in vicious or virtuous

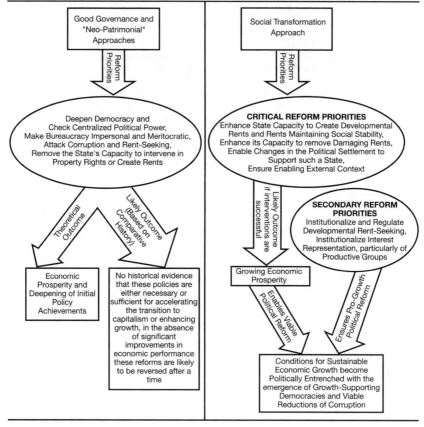

*Figure 1.7* Policy sequencing in the good governance, neo-patrimonial and social transformation approaches

cycles involving state capacity and economic performance. We can now summarize the main differences in the policy implications of the good governance or neo-patrimonial approaches on the one hand, and our historical approach on the other that aims to identify critical state capacities in a comparative context. The left-hand column of Figure 1.7 shows the well-known reform priorities of the good governance and neo-patrimonial models, and the right-hand column contrasts these with our analysis based on a comparative analysis of social transformation. The good governance and neo-patrimonial approaches claim that democratization, anti-corruption strategies and liberalization are *preconditions* for development because achieving them will ensure that economic growth takes off and political viability is achieved. The economic growth that is supposed to follow then ensures that these initial reforms are sustained and deepened. In contrast, we argue that comparative history does not provide much evidence that developing countries became advanced capitalist countries by following such strategies. Theory and evidence are at best weak and equivocal on the necessity or sufficiency of these policies for accelerating growth. In the Palestinian context, an uncritical application of good governance or neo-patrimonial models can be doubly problematic in that it can divert the frustration with the slow progress and relatively poor performance of state formation to problems that while real, were not primarily responsible for the results.

The right-hand column in Figure 1.7 shows in contrast the policy implications of the social transformation approach described in this chapter. Here the primary policy emphasis is to achieve the institutional, political and external conditions that assist the creation and effective management of developmental rents, including the rents necessary for maintaining political stability; while reducing the rents that are damaging for growth and rapid social transformation. If these necessary conditions for viable development can be put in place, the next tier of policy priorities would be to try and legalize the types of rent-seeking that support growth-enhancing rents so that the corruption associated with these rents can be reduced, or replaced with legal forms of rent-seeking. The historical evidence suggests that satisfactory reductions in corruption are only likely to be achieved once a broad-based capitalist class has developed that is no longer dependent on primitive accumulation and can legitimately bargain over the allocation of growth-enhancing rents. The growing prosperity of the economy in turn allows sustainable extensions of democracy since more and more of the rents required for political stabilization can be converted into formal fiscal transfers.

If capitalist development and the deepening of political institutions take place in parallel, the emerging capitalist system can become politically entrenched through democracy. On the other hand, a failure of these second tier reforms can mean that even high-growth emerging economies can face a political crisis at some point. But since the Palestinian economy during our period could hardly be described as having achieved the necessary conditions for viable economic development in the long term, focusing on the secondary reforms necessary for politically entrenching a dynamic capitalist economy would not necessarily ensure viability in this context. These reform priorities can be particularly misleading if they take attention away from the fundamental constraints that prevented the construction of a viable Palestinian state. Indeed, we have suggested that some of the apparent governance failures of the PNA were in fact rent-management strategies that attempted to enhance the economic and political viability of the state in a context of containment. If reform removed these capacities without addressing the problems they were responding to, the emergence of a viable state may become *less* likely. In the next chapter by Hilal and Khan, we use the methodology developed in this chapter to explore these possibilities.

## Notes

1  Consolidated figures for aid flows to the Palestinian territories have not yet been collated. Figures here are estimates based on a number of sources, World Bank (2000) and (2001) and IMF (2003: 20–5).
2  PCBS, Press Release of Palestinian National Accounts for 1999, Ramallah, 2000.
3  See for example, the article by Yasser Arafat, 'The Palestinian Vision of Peace', *New York Times*, 3 February 2002.

## References

Amsden, A. (1989) *Asia's Next Giant: South Korea and Late Industrialization*, Oxford: Oxford University Press.
Andvig, J. C., Fjeldstad, O-H., Amundsen, I., Sissener, T. and Søreide, T. (2000) *Research on Corruption: A Policy Oriented Survey. Report Commissioned by NORAD*, Chr. Michelsen Institute and Norwegian Institute of International Affairs.
Aoki, M., Kim, H-K. and Okuno-Fujiwara, M. (eds) (1997) *The Role of Government in East Asian Economic Development: Comparative Institutional Analysis*, Oxford: Clarendon Press.
Bardhan, P. (1997) 'Corruption and Development: A Review of Issues', *Journal of Economic Literature* 35 (3): 1320–46.
Barro, R. (1996) 'Democracy and Growth', *Journal of Economic Growth* 1(1): 1–27.
Buchanan, J. M., Tollison, R. D. and Tullock, G. (1980) *Toward a Theory of the Rent-Seeking Society*, College Station: Texas A&M University Press.
Burkhart, R. and Lewis-Beck, M. (1994) 'Comparative Democracy: The Economic Development Thesis', *American Political Science Review* 88: 903–10.
Clague, C., Keefer, P. , Knack, S. and Olson, M. (1997) 'Democracy, Autocracy and the Institutions Supportive of Economic Growth', in Clague, C. (ed.) *Institutions and Economic Development: Growth and Governance in Less-Developed and Post-Socialist Countries*, Baltimore: The Johns Hopkins University Press.
Colander, D. C. (ed.) (1984) *Neoclassical Political Economy: The Analysis of Rent-Seeking and DUP Activities*, Cambridge, MA: Ballinger Publishing Co.
DellaPergola, S. (2001) 'Demography in Israel/Palestine: Trends, Prospects, Policy Implications', paper presented at the IUSSP XXIV General Population Conference, Salvador de Bahia, Session 64, Population Change and Political Transitions.

Eisenstadt, S. (1973) *Traditional Patrimonialism and Modern Neo-Patrimonialism*, London: Sage.

Fischer, F., Said, M. and Valdivieso, R. A. (2001) 'Transaction Costs in the Palestinian Economy: A Microeconomic Perspective', in Valdivieso, R. A., von Allmen, U. E., Bannister, G. J., Davoodi, H. R., Fischer, F., Jenkner, E. and Said, M. *West Bank and Gaza: Economic Performance, Prospects, and Policies. Achieving Prosperity and Confronting Demographic Challenges*, Washington: Middle Eastern Department, International Monetary Fund.

Hall, R. and Jones, C. (1999) 'Why Do Some Countries Produce So Much More Output Per Worker Than Others?', *Quarterly Journal of Economics* 114: 83–116.

IMF (International Monetary Fund) (2003) *West Bank and Gaza: Economic Performance and Reform Under Conflict Conditions*, Washington: IMF.

Johnson, S., Kaufmann, D. and Zoido-Lobatón, P. (1998) 'Regulatory Discretion and the Unofficial Economy', *American Economic Review* 88 (2): 387–92.

Judt, T. (2003) 'Israel: The Alternative', *The New York Review of Books* 50 (16): 23 October 2003. Available online at <http://www.nybooks.com/articles/16671> (accessed November 2003).

Kauffman, D., Kraay, A. and Zoido-Lobatón, P. (1999) *Governance Matters*, World Bank Policy Working Paper No. 2196.

Khan, M. H. (1995) 'State Failure in Weak States: A Critique of New Institutionalist Explanations', in Hunter, J. Harriss, J. and Lewis, C. (eds) *The New Institutional Economics and Third World Development*, London: Routledge.

—— (1996a) 'A Typology of Corrupt Transactions in Developing Countries', *IDS Bulletin* 27 (2): 12–21.

—— (1996b) 'The Efficiency Implications of Corruption', *Journal of International Development* 8 (5): 683–96. Reprinted in Robert Williams (ed.) (2000) *Explaining Corruption*, Cheltenham: Edward Elgar.

—— (2000a) 'Rents, Efficiency and Growth', in Khan, M.H. and Jomo, K.S. (eds) *Rents, Rent-Seeking and Economic Development: Theory and Evidence in Asia*, Cambridge: Cambridge University Press.

—— (2000b) 'Rent-seeking as Process', in Khan, M. H. and Jomo, K. S. (eds) *Rents, Rent-Seeking and Economic Development: Theory and Evidence in Asia*, Cambridge: Cambridge University Press.

—— (2002a) 'Fundamental Tensions in the Democratic Compromise', *New Political Economy* 7 (2): 275–7.

—— (2002b) 'Corruption and Governance in Early Capitalism: World Bank Strategies and their Limitations', in Pincus, J. and Winters, J. (eds) *Reinventing the World Bank*, Ithaca: Cornell University Press.

—— (2004) 'State Failure in Developing Countries and Strategies of Institutional Reform', in Tungodden, B., Stern, N., and Kolstad, I. (eds) *Towards Pro-Poor Policies: Aid Institutions and Globalization* (Proceedings of the World Bank's Annual Bank Conference on Development Economics 2002), Oxford: Oxford University Press and World Bank. Available online at <http://wbln0018.worldbank.org/eurvp/web.nsf/Pages/Paper+by+Mushtaq+Khan/$File/KHAN+STATE+FAILURE.PDF> (accessed December 2002).

Knack, S. and Keefer, P. (1995) 'Institutions and Economic Performance: Cross-Country Tests Using Alternative Institutional Measures', *Economics and Politics*, 7 (3): 207–27.

—— (1997) 'Why Don't Poor Countries Catch Up? A Cross-National Test of an Institutional Explanation', *Economic Inquiry* 35: 590–602.

Krueger, A. (1974) 'The Political Economy of the Rent-Seeking Society', *American Economic Review* 64 (3): 291–303.

Lagerquist, P. (2003) 'Palestine: The Corruption of Occupation', *Middle East International*, 7 February.

Mauro, P. (1995) 'Corruption and Growth', *Quarterly Journal of Economics* 110 (3): 681–712.

Médard, J-F. (2002) 'Corruption in the Neo-Patrimonial States of Sub-Saharan Africa', in Heidenheimerm A. J. and Johnstonm M. (eds) *Political Corruption: Concepts and Contexts*, 3rd edn, New Brunswick: Transaction Publishers.

Moore, B. (1991) *Social Origins of Dictatorship and Democracy*, Harmondsworth: Penguin.

North, D. C. (1990) *Institutions, Institutional Change and Economic Performance*, Cambridge: Cambridge University Press.

Okuno-Fujiwara, M. (1997) 'Toward a Comparative Institutional Analysis of the Government-Business Relationship', in Aoki, M., Kim, H-K. and Okuno-Fujiwara, M. (eds) *The Role of Government in East Asian Economic Development: Comparative Institutional Analysis*, Oxford: Clarendon Press.

Olson, M. (1982) *The Rise and Decline of Nations*, London: Yale University Press.

—— (1997) 'The New Institutional Economics: The Collective Choice Approach to Economic Development', in Clague, C. (ed.) *Institutions and Economic Development*, Baltimore: Johns Hopkins University Press.

—— (2000) 'Dictatorship, Democracy and Development', in Olson, M. and Kähkönen, S. (eds) *A Not-so-Dismal Science: A Broader View of Economies and Societies*, Oxford: Oxford University Press.

Peres, S. (1993) *The New Middle East*, London: Shaftesbury.

Posner, R. A. (1975) 'The Social Costs of Monopoly and Regulation', *Journal of Political Economy* 83 (4): 807–27.

Roy, S. (2001) *The Gaza Strip: The Political Economy of De-development*, 2nd edn, Washington DC: Institute for Palestinian Studies.

Rueschemeyer, D., Stephens, E. H. and Stephens, J. D. (1992) *Capitalist Development and Democracy*, Oxford: Polity.

Shlaim, A. (2000) *The Iron Wall: Israel and the Arab World*, London: Penguin.

Shleifer, A. and Vishny, R. (1993) 'Corruption', *Quarterly Journal of Economics* 108 (3): 599–617.

Stiglitz, J. (1996) *Whither Socialism?* Cambridge, MA: MIT Press.

Treisman, D. (2000) 'The Causes of Corruption: A Cross National Study', *Journal of Public Economics* 76: 399–457.

US Council on Foreign Relations (1999) *Task Force Report: Strengthening Palestinian Public Institutions*, New York.

Valdivieso, R .A., von Allmen, U. E., Bannister, G. J., Davoodi, H. R., Fischer, F., Jenkner, E. and Said, M. (2001) *West Bank and Gaza: Economic Performance, Prospects, and Policies. Achieving Prosperity and Confronting Demographic Challenges*, Washington: Middle Eastern Department, International Monetary Fund.

Wade, R. (1990) *Governing the Market: Economic Theory and the Role of Government in East Asian Industrialization*, Princeton: Princeton University Press.

Woo-Cumings, M. (1999) (ed.) *The Developmental State*, Ithaca: Cornell University Press.

World Bank (1997) *World Development Report 1997: The State in a Changing World*, Washington DC: World Bank.

—— (2000) *Aid Effectiveness in the West Bank and Gaza*, Washington: World Bank.

—— (2001) *West Bank and Gaza Update, June*, Washington: World Bank.

# 2 State formation under the PNA

## Potential outcomes and their viability

*Jamil Hilal and Mushtaq Husain Khan*

The establishment of the Palestinian National Authority (PNA) in 1994 set up the institutions that it was hoped would grow into and form the core of a future Palestinian state. Its brief period of 'normal' operation over 1994–2000 provides valuable evidence about the nature of state-society relationships in Palestine, and the obstacles state formation is likely to face in the future. While the supporters and detractors of the PNA each want to focus on a partial picture of its successes and failures, the evidence suggests a more complex story of intense contestation, harsh external constraints and some unexpected strengths and weaknesses. This more complex picture provides valuable insights for identifying the governance issues most relevant for the future.

As we have seen in Chapter 1 by Khan, a number of different types of rents and rent-management capacities were in evidence in the Palestinian economy during this period. Here we want to investigate the incentives, pressures and constraints pushing the consolidation of these different rents and rent-management capacities. Some of these rents were clearly damaging for the viability of the emerging state, but others enhanced its potential viability. Some were imposed by external conditions; others were created and supported by the autonomous actions of the Palestinian Authority. Many of the rents and capacities of the PNA were consistent with those of a client state. But at the same time, we observed some rents and rent-management capacities consistent with characteristics of a predatory state, a fragmented clientelist state and a developmental state.

This chapter investigates the likelihood of some of these rents and rent-management capacities becoming more dominant over time and playing a determining role in future developments. It is difficult to measure precisely the relative magnitude of different types of rents, let alone track the development of rents, rent-management capacities and rent-seeking over time. We therefore follow a different approach. We examine the *theoretical conditions* that would favour the consolidation of each of a number of distinctive combinations of rents and rent-management capacities and we compare these theoretical conditions with observations of actual conditions in Palestine over this period. We also look at how these conditions were changing over time to assess the prospects of different state characteristics becoming stronger over time. The conditions we focus on include first *external conditions* (in particular the strategies and policies of the Israeli state), which clearly have played a significant role in determining rent-creation and rent-management in the specific context we are looking at. Second, we look at the *institutional structure and capacity* of the Palestinian quasi-state. These could directly explain the presence or absence of specific rent-management capacities. Third, we look at the distribution of power within Palestinian society, and in particular the *organization of civil society*, since this too can help explain the types of rents that were being created and the ways in which they were managed. Finally, we look at the *capacities and organization of the capitalist class* in Palestine to explain the rent-seeking strategies of emerging capitalists and state leaders.

We find that the actual conditions in Palestine *partially* supported the further consolidation of each of the incipient state characteristics that we identified in embryonic form. The eventual outcome was not a foregone conclusion, which is itself an important (and reassuring) conclusion for future policy. The rest of this chapter is organized as follows. First we identify the theoretical conjunction of factors that would be most conducive for the emergence of each of our four state types. We then look at the available evidence to see the extent to which the development of each of these state types was actually supported by conditions observed in the Palestinian territories over this period. Finally, we draw some conclusions for the future of state construction strategies in the Palestinian territories.

## Rents, rent-seeking and types of states

Table 2.1 summarizes some of the conditions that, in theory, would facilitate the development and consolidation of the characteristics associated with each of our four state types. These conditions are, in turn, broadly grouped under four headings: the external context, state capacity, the organization of civil society, and the organization and capacity of the capitalist class. Variations in each of these conditions could, in theory, promote the development of particular rents and rent-management capacities and thereby strengthen the characteristics of a specific type of state. Moreover, changes in these conditions over time could strengthen or weaken tendencies for particular state types to consolidate. These are not necessarily the only conditions that determine why some types of rents and rent-management capacities may come to dominate others, but they cover some of the most important conditions identified in the theoretical and comparative historical literature (see Khan, Chapter 1). Our main task is then to compare these theoretical conditions with the reality on the ground to examine the extent to which the actual conditions in Palestine supported specific rents, and more importantly, to identify the trends supporting the development of rents and rent-management capacities in particular directions. The conditions we discuss should not be

*Table 2.1* State types and their supporting conditions

| | Potential state types | | | |
|---|---|---|---|---|
| | *Client* | *Predatory* | *Fragmented clientelist* | *Developmental* |
| *Dominant rents defining each state* | Rents critical for state survival controlled by external power(s) and released subject to compliance | Damaging monopoly rents, direct extortions | Monopolies and transfers captured by powerful factions who can veto attempts to reallocate them | Rents for political stabilization and conditional subsidies for capitalists, both subject to performance |
| *Theoretical conditions supporting the consolidation of each state* | | | | |
| *i) The external context* | External power is militarily and economically dominant | External conditions prevent growth making predation attractive for leadership | External powers can provide significant transfer rents in the form of aid | External powers allow developmental strategies or are unable to prevent it |
| *ii) State capacity* | Weak capacity to fight external powers but strong internal policing capacity | Weak institutional capacity to push growth, but strong coercive capacities | Weak state capacity to control competing clientelist factions | State with strong capacity to allocate and manage conditional rents to accelerate investment and maintain stability |
| *iii) Organization of 'civil society'* | Social groups opposed to client-state strategy too weak to challenge it | Social groups too weak to stop predation | Clientelist factions are fragmented but well organized: can veto attempts to reallocate rents | Political factions either too weak to veto rent-reallocations or centrally organized and act in concert with state to support developmental rents |
| *iv) Organization and capacity of the capitalist class* | Some capitalists may benefit from *integration* and support it but *containment* will be resisted and requires weak capitalists | Capitalists too backward to be dynamic growth partners of the state and too weak to stop predation | Capitalists are inefficient and prefer to capture rents by allying with factions | Capitalists relatively well developed but cannot form independent social alliances to protect inefficient rents |

interpreted as *invariable*, such that the direction of state development is *pre-determined*. On the contrary, political leadership, internal political mobilization, and external assistance can make a significant difference in changing these conditions and make different outcomes possible. But for intervention to target the right issues, the critical conditions determining state viability need to be identified and understood.

In the case of the *client state*, its viable consolidation depends in the first place on external conditions. There must, of course, be an external power that has both the intention of dominating policy-making in the client state, and also the ability to do so, in terms of being able to control the allocation of significant rents necessary for the latter's survival. But the broader economic strategy of the dominant power is also critical for determining the political viability of its client-state strategy. An *integrationist* strategy that allows economic growth to improve in the client state is obviously more viable from the perspective of the client compared to a strategy of *asymmetric containment* that seeks to achieve leverage by maintaining the economic vulnerability of the client and uncertainty about further penalties in case of non-compliance. The containment strategy is politically less viable, and requires a high degree of internal repression in the client-state for its implementation (Chapter 1 by Khan). Second, in terms of the state's institutional capacity, the client state by definition cannot have the military capacity to stand up to external efforts to dominate it, but it must have sufficient policing capacity to deal with internal opposition. These two conditions are to some extent inter-dependent. An integrationist strategy can survive with less policing capacity, but an asymmetric containment strategy is likely to require significant internal policing. Ultimately, if the economic vulnerability inflicted by asymmetric containment is very severe, no amount of internal policing is likely to be sufficient for maintaining the viability of the client state.

Third, social groups and classes opposed to the client strategy must be sufficiently weak and disorganized for the state leadership to be able to pursue any variant of a client-state strategy. Finally, as for internal capitalists, with *asymmetric containment*, the client state would be unlikely to get support from any of its own capitalists and would require either an absent or very weak capitalist class. However, an *integrationist* client state *could* get support from sections of capitalists who did not produce goods that were directly competing with the products of the dominant economy. These capitalists, typically at the lower end of the technology ladder, may benefit from greater access to markets in the more advanced economy and possibly from cheaper inputs as well. More advanced capitalists producing products similar to the ones produced in the dominant economy are likely to seek state assistance to improve their technological capacity, and are therefore likely to oppose even an integrationist strategy since in many cases this is likely to destroy them or prevent their growth.

Many of the conditions that supported the consolidation of a client state could be observed in Palestine over the period we are looking at. Israel would clearly only proceed with even its limited steps towards Palestinian state formation on the basis of maintaining significant leverage over the Palestinian quasi-state. Not surprisingly, the PNA's institutional capacity was biased towards policing, as one would expect. The internal social fragmentation of Palestinian civil society supported client-state strategies by preventing the development of broad-based or concerted opposition to the territorial boundaries, state powers and degree of sovereignty accepted by the PNA. The role of the capitalist class was more complex and reflected the ambiguous Israeli economic strategies towards the Palestinian territories. To the extent that integration was on the agenda, some Palestinian capitalists were happy to support a client state, hoping to gain from trading and investment opportunities. Others, particularly the expatriate capitalists, were less keen as they saw potential obstacles in the path of more advanced Palestinian capitalists like themselves. But in fact the emerging Israeli policy towards the Palestinian state veered towards asymmetric containment rather than integration. This fact alone made the client state politically and economically unviable in Palestine. As a result, relationships between the PNA and Israel remained fraught and indeed became worse over time. By the time of the Second *Intifada*, far from remaining a client, the PNA came out against Israel with its limited military forces.

*Predatory state* characteristics begin to emerge when public officials seize or extract resources by creating predominantly *damaging* rents that impoverish society. The conditions that might create a predatory state are interesting because creating damaging rents is not rational for state leaders who face no constraints. Rational leaders usually do better by creating and maintaining growth-enhancing rents and rights, since these allow them to extract an even greater amount from society over time. Resource extraction in the form of rent-sharing by state leaders in a context of rapid economic growth would by definition not be predatory and could even be consistent with a developmental state (see Khan, Chapter 1). Special conditions are required to induce strictly predatory strategies, as summarized in Table 2.1. First, external conditions might be so adverse that the state had no hope of implementing growth-promoting strategies. If this happened, the best strategy for state leaders would be to extract as much and as fast as possible, since their hold on power would be unlikely to last very long. The creation of damaging predatory rents may then allow rapid resource extraction at the price of accelerating the decline of the economy. Second, the absence of institutional capacity to create growth-enhancing rents would also enhance predatory tendencies. The complete absence of a competent economic bureaucracy that can manage growth-enhancing rents for investors may induce state leaders to create damaging rents to extract resources since in any case they are not capable of creating growth-enhancing rents. Third, predation can only take place if the internal organization of society *allows* predatory strategies on the part of the state. Social factions, typically led by members of the 'middle classes' in developing countries, have to be weak enough to be unable to resist predatory state strategies. And finally, the capitalist class has to be under-developed and lack significant developmental capacity. The absence of a skilled entrepreneurial class would make predation more likely. The absence of potential capitalist capacity means that predation does not result in any lost opportunities for the state, since growth is unlikely anyway.

Some of these conditions held in Palestine over our period. External constraints in particular were severe, and growth possibilities were limited by the asymmetric containment that Israel sought to impose. The developmental capacities of the state were also limited, though as we shall see, key decision-makers *were* able to direct rents to promote growth. Civil society was weak and fragmented, again supporting predatory behaviour, aided by institutional constraints on democracy. But on the other hand, a relatively developed capitalist class existed, particularly in the form of expatriate capital, creating incentives for the leadership to play a longer term developmental game. The relative autonomy of the state paradoxically also aided these developmental attempts, as we shall see later. Thus the conditions supporting predatory tendencies within the PNA were at best contradictory.

*Fragmented clientelist state* characteristics develop when the central state loses the ability to police the allocation of rents. The predominant rents are now redistributive transfers to powerful factions who can *dictate* the allocation of rents and *veto* their re-allocation (Khan 2000 and Chapter 1 in this volume). As a result, even if the state leadership wants to remove unproductive rents, or to redirect rents to more productive groups, it finds that it cannot do so. After a while, most rent allocations in fragmented clientelist states turn out to be damaging rents that benefit unproductive groups. Here, external factors are less important, but the availability of foreign aid can make things worse by providing a large pool of resources for redistribution which competing factions can fight over. Like the predatory state, a fragmented clientelist state also lacks the institutional capacity to implement growth-enhancing strategies. But the most significant condition promoting a fragmented clientelist state is a strong but fragmented civil society in the form of parties or factions often led by political entrepreneurs from the 'intermediate' or middle classes. In the extreme case, these groups and factions can effectively protect their rents despite the wishes of the executive. In the Palestinian context, external conditions and weak state capacity could have supported moves towards a fragmented clientelist state, but civil society was paradoxically *too* fragmented, and *powerful* factions of the type observed in fragmented clientelist states did not emerge. We find virtually no examples of cases where powerful factions overturned or vetoed executive decisions about rent-creation, allocation or rent-management.

Finally, *developmental state* characteristics are strengthened in proportion to the state's ability to allocate and manage rents to maintain political stability while enabling a capitalist class to develop and acquire technological capacity. For this to happen, external conditions have to be such that developmental interventions are either encouraged, or at least, not thwarted. Ultimately, this requires not only full sovereignty but also conducive international economic conditions and accommodating trading partners. Second, developmental strategies also require a minimal institutional capacity on the part of the state to identify and support growth-enhancing sectors and activities, and manage rent-allocation so that inefficient groups are not able to capture rents. Third, and most important, internal political conditions have to allow the state to manage rents to promote growth. In particular, the state has to have the capacity to *withdraw* rents if the recipient proves to be incompetent or the firm or sector proves to have been badly chosen in the first place. Subsidy withdrawal requires that recipients of rents are not able to buy or construct coalitions that can resist the state if rent-withdrawal becomes necessary. This in turn requires either very weak social factions so that clientelism cannot be used to protect inefficient rents, or a strong but centralized or 'corporatist' organization of social interests such that agreement can be reached centrally on the optimal allocation of rents. The worst outcome is an intermediate degree of fragmentation that allows fragmented clientelist coalitions to veto rent re-allocations (Khan 2000 and Chapter 1 in this volume). Finally, the developmental state requires as its partner an emerging capitalist class that has the capacity and experience to respond to incentives to attract investment and generate growth. Our conditions deliberately give less importance to the intentions and quality of the state's leadership even though this is clearly also important. Nevertheless, if the conditions identified above are fulfilled, it is very likely that the state leadership will over time behave in a developmental way out of self-interest, as developmental strategies will then deliver the greatest benefits for the leadership.

In terms of our conditions, external conditions were clearly adverse for constructing a developmental state in Palestine. Israeli control over the Palestinian economy and public finances was severely detrimental to any autonomous Palestinian economic development. On the other hand, the ensuing asymmetric containment created a growing perception within the PNA leadership that economic development was essential for its own survival. Paradoxically, the centralization of power meant that the PNA had *some* state capacity to allocate rents in ways that could promote a capitalist transformation. At the same time, the extreme fragmentation of Palestinian civil society, whilst damaging for democracy, meant that fragmented clientelist pressures from powerful factions for rent allocation were minimal. The construction of centralized and corporatist political organizations to resolve conflicts between factions did not therefore prove to be necessary. Finally, and most importantly, the existence of an advanced capitalist group in the form of expatriate capitalists provided the PNA with credible developmental partners. In the next four sections we discuss in turn, external conditions, state capacities, the organization of civil society and the organization and development of the capitalist sector in Palestine. This is then used to evaluate the likelihood of critical characteristics of each of our state types consolidating and eventually dominating in the Palestinian context.

## The external context

The external context has been more important in the Palestinian context than in virtually any other emerging state in the developing world. To appreciate this we have to remind ourselves that many of the critical features of the impact of Israel on the Palestinian economy and society began long before Oslo. The 1967 occupation, and before that the setting up of the state of Israel in 1948 in historic Palestine had an enormous impact on what at each stage was left of Palestinian economy and society. From the outset, the Israeli state was not just a normal colonial state but also one that justified its colonialism and expansion by divine right and the historical injustices suffered by Jews in Europe. This made the dispossessions, the seizures of land and the building of settlements much more difficult to fight on the Palestinian side and explains some of the desperation and fragmentation observed in Palestinian society. In this section we will look at the factors that most directly impacted on the operation of the PNA, and are likely to affect the future prospects of a Palestinian state.

### Colonial impediments to Palestinian development

The history of Israeli occupation and the impact this had on the class and social organization of Palestinian society is well known. The establishment of the state of Israel in 1948 in historic Palestine resulted in the expulsion of more than 700,000 Palestinians from what became Israel and many of them settled in refugee camps in the West Bank and Gaza Strip. The economy of these territories was thus dominated by the refugee economy from 1948 onwards. The occupation of the West Bank and Gaza Strip in 1967 further undermined the power base of the traditional landed and commercial capitalist classes (Kimmeling and Migdal 1994), and at the same time, it erected insurmountable obstacles for further indigenous economic development and the emergence of an industrial capitalist class. As an occupational force, Israel imposed political, economic and administrative restrictions, including the use of military orders that adversely affected Palestinian economic activity in WBG. These included the confiscation of prime Palestinian land for settlement building that aimed to change the ethnic character of the WBG using Jewish immigration to populate these areas. Colonial settlements were built on the best agricultural areas with easy access to water and wells. For Palestinians, on the other hand, there was strict rationing of water use and restrictions on construction activities. Israel introduced total control over financial institutions and the import and export trade. New taxation was imposed on the Palestinians that, in the fashion of other colonial occupations, was ostensibly imposed to pay for the costs of administration.

These interventions added up to a set of restrictions, seizures and extractions which limited autonomous Palestinian economic activity and made it practically impossible for a 'national' bourgeoisie to emerge in the WBG (Abed 1988; Aruri 1989).

### The fragmentation of Palestinian society

Apart from preventing the development of a Palestinian capitalist class, Israeli rule seriously fragmented Palestinian society, and the middle classes in particular (Heiberg and Øvensen 1993; Kimmerling and Migdal 1994). Unlike the British colonial power in Asia and Africa which ruled through the incorporation of large parts of the indigenous middle classes as administrators and allies, the Israeli colonial occupation was much more like the Japanese one in East Asia, where all key administrative positions were controlled by the occupying military power and the indigenous population was controlled largely by military means.[1] Israel could follow such a strategy because of overwhelming military might and because it was primarily interested in the occupation and acquisition of land without a clear policy for the administration or otherwise of the Palestinian people. This has been frankly acknowledged by historians on the Israeli side such as Shlaim (2000) and Pappé (1999).

The Palestinian territories prior to the Oslo Accords were directly administered by Israel with a limited and low-level role for Palestinians in the 'Civil Administration'. The latter was a deliberately misleading term for the pre-Oslo administration that was headed by an Israeli colonel, subject to the Israeli Ministry of Defence, and under the direct command of an Israeli general (Halper 2001). At its height the Israeli Civil Administration employed around 20,000 Palestinians, mostly at the delivery end of the health and education sectors. There was no need to involve middle-class Palestinians at higher levels of the administration. Nor did the Palestinian middle class have the political power to demand incorporation as was typical in many British colonies before independence. Israel had the military power and international support from major powers to clamp down on any organized expression of Palestinian nationalism, for instance by outlawing the PLO and all its factions. It activated British mandate emergency laws on a protracted basis to 'administratively detain' (imprison without trial) several tens of thousands of Palestinians, expel many thousands of activists from the WBG, and demolish hundreds of Palestinian houses to punish the families of those actively opposed to the occupation. Under such a military and coercive administration, the political and organizational development of a Palestinian middle class was necessarily very limited. The Palestinian middle class was also effectively excluded from employment in Israel. Instead, until the first Iraq War, the oil economies of the region were the main employers of Palestinian professionals from the WBG.

### Selective and detrimental integration into the Israeli economy

As a colonial power and the dominant economic power of the region, Israel's economic strategy towards the occupied territories critically affected the latter's pattern of development. Since 1967, Israel was primarily interested in appropriating resources through land confiscation, appropriation of water resources, and settlement building. It was also to a lesser extent interested in the exploitation of cheap unskilled labour (people who commuted to Israel on a daily basis to minimize social security claims), and the creation of a captive market for Israeli goods. All of these Israeli objectives were potentially detrimental for long-term Palestinian development. Nevertheless, the pre-Oslo colonial policies of the Israeli state did have some limited *integrationist* elements. In particular, employment in the Israeli labour market, even though restricted to unskilled workers, did yield short-term relief to the Palestinian economy. At a time when Israeli agriculture and industry were protected from competitive Palestinian products, Israel opened its market to Palestinian unskilled and semi-skilled labour. As a result, some 40 per cent of the WBG labour force was employed in Israel (comprising some 10 per cent of the Israeli labour force) till the early 1990s.[2] Labour was the major WBG export (to Israel and to other countries) till the first Iraq war. At the same time, the WBG became the second biggest export market for Israeli goods, second only to the USA. Even though the Palestinians were selling cheap labour to buy Israeli products that were relatively expensive at world market prices, Palestinians working in Israel were better off than those employed in the WBG where wages were even lower. The higher wages received by Palestinian workers in Israel, relative to wages paid in the WBG, and even relative to many middle-class occupations, had a levelling effect on differentials between middle- and working-class incomes in these areas. This reflected itself in patterns of consumption, particularly the ownership of durable goods. But even to enjoy this unequal exchange, the occupied territories were administered entirely through taxation raised from the Palestinian population, and moreover, they were prevented from following autonomous developmental strategies.[3]

While Israel was clearly interested in political domination and occupation, even this pattern of occupation could, in theory, have resulted in sustained improvements in Palestinian living standards *if* over time the pattern of economic exchanges had become less restrictive against the Palestinians. If Israel had allowed integration to deepen, we would have expected to see a sustained increase in the percentage of the Palestinian labour force employed in Israel. In particular, there should have been a loosening of the implicit ban on the employment of professional and middle-class Palestinians in Israel. In addition, there would have been a reduction of protection such that industries located in the occupied territories could grow by enjoying access to Israeli markets and capital. If all this had happened, the Palestinian economy *might* have developed more rapidly even if the development was unequal and led by Israeli rather than Palestinian capitalists. However, before Oslo, the employment of unskilled workers remained the dominant aspect of Palestinian 'integration' with the Israeli economy. There is little evidence that integration was moving in the direction of greater employment of skilled Palestinians in Israel or of faster industrialization in the occupied territories.

### Post-Oslo tightening of Palestinian labour mobility

In principle, the signing of the Oslo Agreements could have allowed Israel to move forward on economic integration now that the question of the political status of the occupied territories was on the way to being resolved. Instead, one of the most damaging aspects of Israel's response to the signing of the Oslo Accords was that it saw an opportunity to formalize aspects of asymmetric containment that had already been built up since the early 1990s and indeed to extend these controls. Its implicit strategy towards the Palestinian economy thus changed from one of reluctant and partial *integration* to one that developed rapidly into *asymmetric containment* (see Chapter 1 by Khan, and Chapter 3 by Zagha and Zomlot). While the PNA gained *limited* control over *some* territories within the WBG, Israel made permanent and formal its newly developed capacities to control the movements of Palestinian goods and people through a complex network of checkpoints and began to extend these systems. These could be used to stop not only movements between the Palestinian territories and Israel, but also movements between the Palestinian enclaves themselves. The extension of 'border controls' was a dramatic break with the pre-Oslo period and imposed *new* restrictions and hardships. It also increased the uncertainty of Palestinian employment within Israel and in the occupied territories because these 'borders' could be sealed on a day-to-day basis (Zagha and Zomlot, Chapter 3).

WBG employment in Israel declined from its peak of around 40 per cent of total WBG employment in the pre-Oslo period to a low of around 14 per cent in 1996. Given that Israel also wanted to ensure security compliance on the Palestinian side over this period, developing its ability to block movements of labour and goods selectively and at short notice was consistent with a strategy of ensuring compliance through the threat of sanctions. The new controls over labour movements were one of the pillars of *asymmetric containment*. The labour front caused particular hardships on the Palestinian side because the Israeli restrictions coincided with the imposition of restrictions on the entry of Palestinian labour to the oil-producing Gulf states in the aftermath of the first Iraq war of 1991. An immediate impact was that Palestinian employment in Israel fell at a time when labour shortages in Israel were met by importing non-Jewish labour from Eastern Europe and the Far East. Thus the asymmetric containment strategy had costs for Israel too, but the cost to the two economies was itself asymmetric.

Once the physical apparatus for controlling labour movements had been fully established, restrictions on Palestinian employment in Israel began to be relaxed from 1998 up to September 2000. At the end of 1999, the number of Palestinians working in Israel or its settlements had crept back up to 139.1 thousand or 22.4 per cent of total WBG employment (MAS 2000: xii). In the second quarter of 2000 the number grew further to 143.4 thousand but as a percentage of total WBG employment, the figure was unchanged at 22.3 per cent (PCBS 2000a).

Thus, far from the post-Oslo economy offering Palestinians any improvement on the employment front, Israel's new ability to impose border controls on a territory that was effectively occupied, encircled and heavily dependent on Israeli labour markets increased Israel's economic control over the WBG without any greater economic integration. The main effect of *asymmetric containment* was a much greater economic *vulnerability* of Palestinian employment and trade. The growth of Palestinian employment in Israel in the late 1990s back towards its earlier levels did not reduce Palestinian vulnerability because by now labour was streaming in and out of heavily armed checkpoints on a daily basis to go to work. This explains the paradox that Palestinian frustration was growing before the Second *Intifada* while employment in Israel was returning to earlier levels. The essential aspect of asymmetric containment was that the new security and checkpoint apparatus could stop the movement of labour and goods within the WBG on a daily basis and without advance notice (for its impact on the Palestinian economy see UNSCO 2000). The efficacy of the containment system was proved when the Second *Intifada* began. Palestinian employment in Israel was immediately and drastically curtailed. The movement of Palestinians *within* the WBG also came to an almost total stop.

### Israeli controls over Palestinian land and resources

Since Israel initially saw the Occupied Territories as an integral part of its territories, control over land and resources was one of the main aims of the Israeli occupation of 1967. As a result, there were a plethora of controls over Palestinian access to the natural resources of the WBG. Palestinian claims on natural resources were controlled and restricted, with a wide range of restrictions covering everything from digging wells to fishing. One of the problems with Israel's strategy of phased withdrawal from areas in the WBG was that it intended to retain control over almost all the strategic resources of these areas for an indefinite period *after* it had theoretically withdrawn. In particular, Israeli settlements sat atop all the critical aquifers of the West Bank. This prevented any substantial expansion of Palestinian agriculture or of water-dependent industry during the Oslo period or beyond, until the status of water and of the settlements had been decided. Even the mineral resources of the Dead Sea remained under Israeli control. Thus, the PNA as a quasi-state had no access to its 'own' natural resources. Indeed, even under the 'final' offer that was available to Arafat at Camp David, Israel would retain control over critical areas such as the Jewish settlement city of Ariel and its surrounding areas that sits on top of the major aquifer in the West Bank (Halper 2001). The implication was that the future Palestinian 'state' would remain dependent on enclaves belonging to a foreign country for access to water under its own territory.

### Israeli controls over PNA revenues and trade

The Oslo Accords and the Paris Economic Protocol gave Israel a significant degree of control over the fiscal revenues available to the Palestinian quasi-state. In addition, since for 'security reasons' Israel remained in control of all borders with the outside world, the foreign trade of the Palestinian territories remained entirely with or through Israel, giving Israel control over the movement of all goods into and out of the Palestinian territories. More critically, as the Palestinian territories remained in a customs union with Israel, the latter collected the duties on Palestinian imports from the outside world, with an agreement in the Paris Economic Protocol to pass these on to the PNA. Following the setting up of the PNA, the WBG continued to import 90 per cent of its total imports from Israel or through its ports, and it exported 95 per cent of its total exports to or through Israel. Even the small amount of trade that the Palestinian economy could conduct directly with third countries such as Jordan could be stopped at short notice as Israel controlled those borders as well. The Palestinian economy remained totally dependent on Israel for its electricity, international communications, fuel, almost all its cement and more than 40 per cent of its water, which had to be purchased from Israeli companies even though they were appropriating the water from the underground aquifers of the WB (PCBS 2000c: 18).[4]

For all these reasons, the PNA had a low internal income-tax base. It was dependent, to a large extent, on aid from the donor community, on agreed transfers from Israel of customs duties collected on goods imported from abroad by Palestinian companies, on remittances by Israel of taxes collected from Palestinians working in Israel with work permits, and remittances by Israel of VAT collected on goods exported to Palestinian areas. Direct income tax formed a meagre 7.6 per cent of total PNA revenue in 1999, compared to tax clearance from Israel, which contributed 63 per cent in the same year (PA 2000; in Chapter 3 of this volume Zagha and Zomlot provide more details on taxation). Apart from delays and disputes in the calculation of these tax remittances, the ability to delay or even stop these transfers gave Israel significant leverage over the PNA. This capacity too was fully demonstrated when the Second *Intifada* erupted in 2000: Israel immediately held back all funds due to the PNA as a way of exerting political pressure. In the same way, but with somewhat different objectives, international donors have used aid as a tool to encourage the PNA to stick to the 'peace process', and to keep the PNA operational for this purpose.

### Effects of external controls: Petty corruption, monopolies and special accounts

The external control that Israel insisted on under Oslo defined the higher-level governance architecture that in turn defined lower-level options available to the PNA. Clearly, our evaluation of rent-management and governance practices has to take into account the alternatives allowed under these arrangements.

#### Petty corruption

It is widely recognized that many types of petty corruption and monopoly rents followed directly from the system of control established by the external power. The most obvious and immediate effect of the mechanisms of controlling movements of goods and labour was to create a complex mosaic of territories and 'gates' within the Palestinian territories. With the signing of the Oslo Agreements, some areas in the WBG came under the jurisdiction of the PNA, some under joint Israeli and Palestinian jurisdiction but many remained entirely under Israeli control. Moving from place to place even *within* the WBG now became much more tortuous, time-consuming and often dangerous for Palestinians than it had been before Oslo. The system of gates and gatekeepers inevitably created its own associated system of petty corruption by gatekeepers. There were reports of small-scale extortion by Palestinian security officials, the victims often being small traders, shop-keepers and others. These opportunities for petty extortion thus followed directly from this system of control.

#### Trading monopolies

The Palestinian trading monopolies had significant economic effects, but here too, their economic and political implications cannot be understood without taking into account the context of external controls dictated by security-first considerations. Israeli control over Palestinian borders meant that the PNA lacked any fiscal ability to determine border prices and its trade and tax revenues were almost entirely controlled by Israel as part of the design of the Oslo architecture. Almost the only power of the Palestinian 'state' was its ability to restrict the movements of goods *within* the territories exclusively under its control. This power turned out to be quite useful because Israel itself was far from a free market, and many key commodities like fuel and cement were sold in Israel at prices well above world market prices by cartels or monopolies. The Palestinian ability to obstruct sales by Israeli monopolies or cartels in Palestine eventually led to agreements that effectively shared these monopoly rents. The 'solution' was the creation of Palestinian trading monopolies that imported fuel and cement from Israeli monopolies at lower than Israeli retail prices and sold them on at Israeli retail prices or even higher. These arrangements allowed the Palestinian monopolies to make easy margins in these trades, and it allowed Israeli monopolies to maintain high prices within the custom union as a whole (see also Chapter 5 by Nasr). Israeli acquiescence was undoubtedly assisted by the calculation that this was a way of maintaining Israeli monopolies since even limited direct Palestinian imports may have made Israeli monopoly prices unsustainable within the customs union. But perhaps more important for the Israelis was the consideration that this arrangement created yet another PNA rent that Israel could turn on and off as a way of retaining influence and leverage over its leadership. From the Palestinian perspective, the monopoly arrangement offered lucrative rents for the PNA and associated individuals. Moreover, while the Paris Protocol did allow limited imports of commodities like cement and fuel from non-Israeli sources, as long as Israel policed the external borders of Palestine, it could delay and obstruct imports of vital commodities by Palestinians even for the limited quantities allowed under the terms of the Protocol. In this context, the absence of Palestinian trading monopolies would very likely not have meant lower prices for Palestinian consumers, but it would have meant that the Palestinian quasi-state would have lost substantial revenues.

These arrangements collapsed following the Israeli re-occupation of Palestinian administered areas post-2000 and the collapse of almost all Palestinian institutions. From a 'good governance' perspective, the reforms accepted by the PNA between 2000 and 2003, at a time when it was under an Israeli blockade and its institutions were collapsing could still be construed as progress. Indeed the International Monetary Fund (IMF) was very positive about the reforms under which the Palestinian leadership agreed to reduce the monopoly rents of their trading companies and to prepare them for privatization (IMF 2003: 102). The measures adopted included imposing price controls on cement sales in the Gaza, allowing Jordanian companies to sell cement directly to Palestinian importers, and giving a commitment to prepare these companies for privatization. The IMF recognized that this would *considerably reduce* the revenues of the Authority, but was pleased that privatization was now on the agenda. Our analysis makes us less sanguine. Palestinian trading monopolies were clearly responsible for higher prices for Palestinian consumers compared to world prices and were responsible for a number of irregularities. In the normal course of events, this would be highly undesirable. The question remains though, whether, after the dust settles, Israel will be willing to withdraw from its control over Palestinian borders with the outside world that allows it to block imports of vital commodities at short notice on grounds of security. Imports of cheaper fuel and cement also threaten Israeli monopolies because some leakage of these commodities to Israel is inevitable. This too might induce Israel to use its powers to preserve the commercial interests of Israeli companies. Over time, it is very likely that Israel will use its border controls to persuade Palestinian companies to import from Israelis rather than risk seizures of their imports at the border. As a result, prices for Palestinian consumers might not come down significantly. The only achievement may eventually be a loss of monopoly rents to Israel and a future Authority that is even less financially viable. In other words, unless the client-state architecture is dismantled, these governance reforms may *reduce* the viability of the state apparatus that replaces the PNA and increase the rent-extraction by Israeli companies from Palestinian territories. There is no indication that Israel is willing to dismantle this control apparatus. As for the privatization of Palestinian assets, preparing for this now is almost surreal before violence and uncertainty can be ended by *first* creating a viable Palestinian state. We will return to this issue a little later.

*Special accounts*

At least as widely discussed have been the so-called special or secret accounts of the leadership that enabled some public funds to be allocated by the executive outside the budget. These accounts clearly violate good governance criteria of transparency and accountability, and are clearly not desirable in the long term in any state. What is perhaps less widely recognized is that these accounts were not secret at all and Israel and the external powers colluded in allowing the Palestinian leadership to exercise non-transparent control over part of its tax revenues. Israel even paid some Palestinian tax revenues into these 'secret' accounts. For instance, petroleum excise duties collected by Israel and due to the PNA were paid into an Israeli bank account controlled by Arafat and his financial advisor Muhammad Rashid (IMF 2003: 88). Some revenues from government trading monopolies that operated with the collusion of Israeli monopolies in fuel and cement also went into these unaudited accounts. Finally, some of the money in these accounts was possibly from sources such as kickbacks that could not be audited.

Israeli denunciations of the Palestinian leadership's secret accounts only began when it was clear that the PNA executive was not sufficiently dependent on Israel to use these secret funds only in ways approved by Israel. Its earlier collusion in these arrangements and its later criticism of Palestinian 'governance' can be explained if we remember the big picture of what the Oslo arrangements were all about. Both sides took a gamble from their own perspective (see Chapter 1 by Khan for a discussion of the client-state strategy). The Israeli gamble was that the PNA would emerge not just as a client state but also one that accepted asymmetric containment. The PNA leadership was willing to accept aspects of a client state but gambled that it could then further Palestinian economic and political aspirations and achieve a viable and dynamic state. Given the aspirations of both sides and the overall structure of external control, handing over part of Palestinian tax revenues directly to the PNA leadership was a rational component of Israel's 'client-state' strategy. It increased the ability of the PNA to carry out the necessary political stabilization, and to prioritize security expenditures in ways that might be difficult if revenues went through the Ministry of Finance and were subject to public scrutiny (see also Chapter 1 by Khan). From the perspective of the PNA, these resources enhanced its room for manoeuvre in emergencies. It was only when it turned out that the Palestinian leadership was not willing to accept a client state on the terms offered, and may indeed have been using these resources to attempt to break out of asymmetric containment, that Israel and its allies pointed out the 'governance failure' associated with unaudited accounts. Since Arafat's objections to the state being offered were well-known by then, it was convenient from a number of perspectives to attribute all failures to the venality of the PNA leadership.

### Effects of asymmetric containment

We have argued that asymmetric containment was not a necessary outcome of Oslo but reflected additional strategic decisions within Israel (see also the discussion in Chapter 1 by Khan). The asymmetric containment strategy had critical implications for governance and rent-creation in the PNA. On the one hand, it created strong Palestinian incentives for pushing development since a viable client state was not on offer. In this context, the hidden accounts and the profits of PNA enterprises assisted the PNA *to hold out against Israeli pressure exerted through asymmetric containment*. On the other hand, in the longer run, containment also meant that even the PNA's second-best developmental options faced serious constraints, and this created growing antagonisms between Israel and its putative client state. In fact, the PNA eventually became the target of Israeli attacks during the Second *Intifada* that began in 2000. We will examine the developmental interventions of the PNA in a later section. Here we examine the implications of asymmetric containment for executive discretion and the special accounts.

We have seen that the unaudited special accounts under the control of the PNA president were to some extent necessitated by the inconsistent aspirations of Israelis and Palestinians that the Oslo architecture attempted to resolve. But the Palestinian executive also had incentives to expand the scope of these funds given its perception that it needed financial flexibility in a context of growing containment. The fiscal dependence of the PNA on Israel created strong *incentives* to extend its 'unofficial' sources of income given the highly vulnerable sources of 'official' income. Of course, a predatory executive could also use these arguments to justify its refusal to open accounts to public scrutiny. The existence of unaudited contingency funds inevitably led to some misallocation and misappropriation.[5] Even if secret accounts did not lead to misappropriation on a scale that would lead us to describe the state as predominantly predatory, this does not mean that resources were always allocated efficiently from the perspective of

Palestinian development. Nevertheless, the Palestinian Authority facing asymmetric containment had strong incentives to manage these funds efficiently to sustain its freedom of manoeuvre.

The PNA leadership consistently argued that it needed to have these contingency funds if aid from the donor community, or customs and VAT clearance from Israel were withheld or cut. Contingency funds would be necessary to maintain, at least for a time, the PNA bureaucracy and the patron-client networks necessary for the stability of the regime. Reserve funds would also be needed to reactivate the PLO should the peace process or the PNA completely collapse. Events following the collapse of the Camp David talks suggest that these contingencies were not necessarily far-fetched. The combination of political vulnerability and the centralization of power can explain why attempts to bring unaudited reserve funds under the scrutiny of the legislative (in the form of the Palestinian Legislative Council (PLC)) had limited success before the collapse of 2000.[6] Reformers often did not understand that if they were unable to change fundamentally the external constraints, reforms that implicitly reduced the flexibility of the leadership could worsen its already vulnerable position.

After the collapse of PNA institutions under the Israeli re-occupation that began in 2000, there were gradual moves towards greater transparency in the PNA's budget. These moves accelerated during 2002–03, when the economic and political situation in Palestine began to deteriorate rapidly. By 2003, when the Palestinian population was encircled in hundreds of pockets by the Israeli army, external pressure was able to achieve a degree of openness and transparency in the PNA's budget that was so impressive that the IMF described it as 'quite exceptional in the Southern Mediterranean region' (IMF 2003: 99). While the reforms look good on paper, they can be interpreted in two different ways. Either the economic and political crisis made the leadership recognize that it had to concede to reforms that would actually improve its own political viability and the economic prospects of the Palestinians, or the situation had become so hopeless that the leadership conceded to reforms that would make future progress along a security-first route even more difficult to achieve. Since budgetary transparency has implications for a wide range of activities, both possibilities are likely to be true depending on which activities we look at, but the second possibility has serious consequences for any effective re-starting of Palestinian state formation with the security-first conditions that Israel is bound to insist on. This leads us to ask why Israel has been keen to support governance improvements in the PNA post-2000. It may be hoping that with greater transparency, the fiscal flexibility of the Palestinian Authority will be significantly reduced. If *at the same time*, revenue remains dependent on Israeli transfers, *and* budgetary priorities continue to be set by security-first concerns, this would further increase the bargaining power of Israel vis-à-vis the Palestinian Authority. A future Authority may eventually accept that it had no option but to accept asymmetric containment and opt to survive by keeping its vulnerable fiscal revenues coming through by spending these in transparent and pre-determined ways. Unfortunately, this calculation ignores the expectations and mobilization of Palestinian society, which is not likely to accept the spending priorities (and even more so the actions) required to achieve security for Israel while the Palestinians live in asymmetric containment, regardless of the options available to its leaders. A more likely outcome is that even limited progress towards a two-state outcome under the security-first (or client state) route will be ruled out since no Palestinian leadership is likely to survive under these pressures.

### A summary of the implications of the external context

Clearly, of all our state types, external conditions were most conducive for the consolidation of a client state. In fact, the higher level architecture of Israel–PNA relationships under Oslo had been deliberately constructed to enable the consolidation of a client state. But Israel's insistence on having both a Palestinian client state *and* an asymmetric containment strategy must be judged to have been unsustainable given Palestinian aspirations and the degree of mobilization of Palestinian society. Such a client state could only survive using excessive internal repression, and it only remained minimally viable because the executive used unconventional methods like monopolies, special accounts and (as we shall see later) centralized executive powers to sustain its viability. Even these could not prevent frequent outbreaks of violence given slow progress towards credible statehood. It would clearly be misleading to attribute violence and poor economic performance in the Palestinian territories to executive centralization or the corruption associated with unaudited accounts and trading monopolies if the latter were to some extent *responses* to the externally imposed governance architecture. The experience of the first phase of state formation suggests that only an *integrationist* client state *may* have been viable in Palestine. If economic integration was not acceptable, for whatever reason, it follows that a client-state strategy of any type is likely to be unviable in the future.

External conditions also had implications for a number of our other state types. The historical impact of the arrival of Zionism in Palestine weakened indigenous capitalist development, and to that extent made a developmental state less likely. Asymmetric containment was also directly contrary to any developmental strategies on the part of the Palestinian Authority. But paradoxically, the pressure of asymmetric containment on the executive could only increase its commitment to autonomous developmental strategies. The migration of many Palestinians to other countries had created an expatriate Palestinian capitalist class that enhanced the possibility of developmental strategies, and we will return to this later. On the other hand, the imposition of asymmetric containment could also have strengthened tendencies towards predation since it made developmental outcomes vulnerable, and ultimately dependent on an eventual dismantling of the client-state apparatus.

## State capacity under the PNA

State capacity in our framework refers to the institutional capacity of a state to create and maintain different types of rents. Since each of our state types is defined by the predominance of particular rents, each requires specific state capacities to create and manage these rents. A *client* state has to be able to effectively police the domestic population and maintain social order, as well as to distribute the rents controlled by the external power to stabilize vital domestic constituencies. With *asymmetric containment*, its policing capacity would have to be much greater to deal with much more serious internal opposition. However, even with moderately well-organized internal opposition, no amount of policing capacity may be sufficient to make a client state based on asymmetric containment politically viable for too long. *Predatory state* characteristics are likely to develop if the state has a repressive apparatus that can deal with social opposition while enabling the extraction of resources from society. How extensive these policing capacities have to be, once again, depend on the strength of internal opposition to predation. *Fragmented clientelist state* characteristics are likely to develop when the state lacks the capacity to police internal factions and instead maintains a precarious political stability *primarily* by allocating rents to shifting coalitions of factions. Both fragmented-clientelist and predatory states are likely to be characterized by poor quality bureaucrats and/or bureaucratic structures that are unable to allocate or manage rents for development.

The institutional capacities required for strengthening *developmental state* characteristics are more demanding. The political-administrative structure has to be able to create and manage developmental rents and to withdraw or destroy value-reducing rents. This requires a state leadership, and eventually a bureaucracy with the appropriate skills, incentives and powers to monitor rent-allocation and performance. The more backward the economy, paradoxically the easier it is to identify the investments that need to be attracted and the technologies that have to be learned. A developmental state also requires a political leadership with the incentive to push development and the capacity to enforce these decisions. The political and institutional structures that have proved adequate for these tasks have, however, differed greatly from case to case, as an examination of the high growth economies in Asia shows. Developmental states have sometimes been authoritarian, as in the case of South Korea or Taiwan in the 1960s and 1970s, and sometimes moderately democratic, as in the case of Malaysia in the 1980s and 1990s. Predatory or fragmented clientelist states have also sometimes been democratic and sometimes authoritarian. In other words, neither democracy nor authoritarianism is necessary or sufficient as an institutional guarantee for a developmental state (see Chapter 1 by Khan). But all successful developmental states have had the institutional and political capacity to allocate rents to enhance growth and maintain political stability. In the remainder of this section we discuss the ways in which the *institutional structure* of the

PNA may have helped or hindered the creation and management of the rents appropriate for each of our four state-types.

### The primacy of policing and the centralization of authority

At first sight, many of the institutional capacities of the PNA appear to be most appropriate for a client or a predatory state. This is not surprising since the initial focus of externally assisted institutional capacity-building in the PNA was in the areas of policing, surveillance, and the maintenance of internal order. The PNA had to prove its 'capacity' in these areas in order to make progress towards statehood. This meant essentially proving that it was able and willing to use repression on a sufficient scale to satisfy Israel that it could transfer to it the job of policing the Palestinians in the occupied territories. A number of competing security forces were set up within the PNA structure, each answerable directly to the President. A multiplicity of security forces would not make sense in a normal state but in the limbo status in which the PNA found itself, this institutional structure was not accidental.

Arafat's administration had to prove its ability to carry out a highly unpopular repression of its own people at a time when almost no progress towards Palestinian statehood could be demonstrated. The President therefore needed an enormously powerful security apparatus, and yet to ensure that the security chief did not become the most powerful person, particularly given that every other aspect of the state was extremely under-developed or absent. The mechanism through which the executive retained its power in such a context was through the device of setting up a number of competing security agencies, each of whose chiefs was dependent on the president for their position. The Palestinian Police Force alone employed more than 30,000 persons, giving a police-to-population ratio of 1 to 75, one of the highest in the world (Pederson and Hooper 1998: 5). The fact that there were a number of other parallel security forces effectively doubled this number. According to a reliable source, personnel employed across these security forces amounted to 50 to 60 thousand, with an annual salary budget of $200 to 250 million.[7]

A consequence of this extensive policing apparatus was that it further strengthened the executive in the form of Arafat. But under the Oslo architecture the Palestinians had to prove their ability to police opposition to the Israeli occupation *before* the occupation ended. It is unlikely that greater democratic control over the security apparatus would have delivered better results, given that most Palestinians were against the security-first route to statehood. In any case, it is important to remind ourselves that Arafat was the democratically elected president of the PNA and enjoyed enormous legitimacy. The general election of January 1996 was largely free and democratic (Rubin 1999: 49–51). Although the Islamists and some small left-wing secular PLO factions boycotted these elections, over 80 per cent of the electorate participated in the general and presidential elections that gave Arafat an overwhelming majority, and permitted his faction (Fateh) to dominate the legislative council (Hilal 1998a).

The popular support for Arafat was based on a gamble by the leadership, the precariousness of which was not always appreciated outside Palestinian society. It was premised on Arafat's system being able to deliver both independence and economic prosperity to a large enough number of Palestinians rapidly enough to undermine support for the Islamist opposition. Israeli economic policies towards Palestine that we described earlier, in particular the random closures, the continuation of settlement activity, the delays in implementation and finally the insistence at Camp David on further territorial concessions, however small, seriously upset this calculation. A poll conducted five months after the Second *Intifada* began showed a dramatic rise in popular support for Hamas in the Gaza Strip, equalling for the first time the support enjoyed by Fateh.[8] The hardening of popular opinion against the security-first Oslo route means that it may be even more difficult to combine democratic control over the executive with a security-first route to statehood in the future.

The president of the PNA was not only directly in control of all the security services but also of all ministries and public bodies. As the elected president of the PNA, Arafat combined this position with that of chairman of the Executive Committee of the PLO to construct a loosely defined institution called the 'Palestinian leadership'. This institution included all strategic posts: ministers, Executive Committee members, the speaker of the Palestine National Council, the speaker of the Palestinian Legislative Council, the heads of the main security agencies, and Arafat's main advisors (including his economic adviser who managed much of the PNA's investments). Directly or indirectly, most of these individuals owed their positions to Arafat personally.[9] This 'leadership' did not include representatives of the business community, the opposition, or popular organizations. The private sector was very weak, as were popular organizations, while the Islamic opposition opted to keep itself out of all PNA and PLO institutions.

A large number of security forces could potentially have resulted in the development of forms of localized warlordism that would have been consistent with fragmented clientelism. But the conditions at this time were such that no second-tier security chief could survive without Arafat's support, and as a result, localized warlordism did not emerge. Rather, the multiplicity of security agencies was a manifestation of, and indeed further reinforced, the centralization of authority. The central control over the coercive apparatus in turn meant that other aspects of institutional power were also effectively centralized. The effects of this centralization were not necessarily negative. Under some conditions, the centralization of power *can* support developmental states. If centralization allows the executive to resolve factional conflicts and override interests opposed to necessary restructurings of economy and society, it can accelerate social transformations (Amsden 1989; Wade 1990; Okuno-Fujiwara 1997 show how this happened in East

Asia). However, for centralization to have developmental effects, the state must have both the incentive to push development as well as the capacity to overcome the opposition of powerful coalitions which may oppose specific developmental strategies. We examine these later, but first we look at a number of other factors that contributed to the centralization of power.

### Multiple legal systems and weak separation of powers

A number of additional features of the Palestinian situation helped the PNA leadership to further centralize its power. One was the operation within the Palestinian territories of multiple legal systems. The West Bank operated under laws inherited from the period of Jordanian rule and the Gaza Strip under laws inherited from the Egyptian Administration. There were also Emergency Laws from the British Mandate period that continued under the Israeli occupation. The plurality of legal systems and the potential for conflicts and confusion made it necessary for the President of the PNA to adopt prerogatives to make and interpret the day-to-day rules of governance. This in turn made it almost impossible to separate powers within the quasi-state. Arafat was able to use security courts to rule not only on matters of security but also on criminal and civil cases, and indeed on matters related to taxation. In addition, Arafat remained the chair of the Executive Committee of the PLO, which maintained its own revolutionary courts. Thus while the executive undoubtedly used this situation to strengthen its own position, it is also true that given the confused system of property rights and legal systems, not to speak of the limited jurisdiction of the Palestinian legislature to rule on these issues under the Oslo Agreements, a centralized executive was functionally necessary.

The separation of powers was also complicated by the fact that the president of the PNA had also been the leader of the largest political organization (Fateh) that in turn had dominated the PLO since the late 1960s. By virtue of this, and of being the main force behind the Oslo Accords, Fateh came to command the executive and legislative branches of the quasi-state, and to control its mass media. Hence, the president could rely on both PNA structures (particularly the security services) and on Fateh, as alternative power bases. This enabled him not only to undermine the PLC as an elected legislative body, but also to undermine the PNA's leading executive institutions (such as the ministerial council) as well as bodies of the PLO (its Executive Committee, the PLO Central Council, and the Palestine National Council). The uncertainties in the situation and the confused legal framework under which the PNA was set up allowed Arafat to activate PLO institutions only on those occasions where they served a specific political purpose.

This highly centralized power structure permitted the apex to marginalize the PLC (helped by its large Fateh majority), and to foil attempts to institute a political system with a clear separation of powers that would limit and check the President's authority. Thus, the President could easily delay the promulgation of the Basic Law passed by the PLC that aimed to institution-alize the separation of powers and limit the powers of the executive. While some centralization of power was functionally necessary for the reasons described earlier, it is also clear that Arafat's personal political pre-eminence and strong Palestinian support for national unity against the occupying power helped to further this centralization. But equally, to attribute the centralization entirely to Arafat's political machinations would be wrong. Any effective leader under a security-first route to statehood and with the economic and political restrictions enshrined in the Oslo architecture would have to achieve significant executive centralization to operate at all.

### Developmental rent-management capacities

Not surprisingly, while some aspects of the PNA's political and institutional structure were potentially damaging for economic activity and for the general investment climate, others were unexpectedly conducive for development given the otherwise adverse political conditions. On the one hand, the multiplicity of legal systems, the absence of a clear rule of law based on judicial indepen-dence, and the ability of the executive to over-ride bureaucratic decisions were institutional conditions at variance with what investors in more advanced economies are used to. In particular, the concentration of power in the hands of the executive could potentially have been used in a predatory way to extract resources from investors and others. Undoubtedly some investors stayed away because of these dangers. In addition, some economic activity was no doubt adversely affected by the arbitrary actions of the executive.

The developmental capacity of the state was also limited by the very constrained powers of the quasi-state to which we have already referred. But despite the fact that the quasi-state lacked many of the normal powers of a state, it did have powers to allocate and rescind licences and contracts, and the power to enhance returns for investors in particular sectors. It could do so by allowing the creation of monopolies, or by allowing some investors to set prices through the exercise of state sanctioned market power in the internal market. Each of these state capacities potentially gave the state the ability to create rents that could make investment in particular sectors attractive. The quasi-state could also use its discretionary power to make sure that utility bills and taxation demands could be informally rene-gotiated to ensure that profitability in key enterprises or sectors was maintained. Last but not least, the PNA did enjoy a sufficient centraliza-tion power to be able to protect major enterprises from possible decentralized extortion demands of local 'mafias'. There is evidence that the PNA leadership used all these rent-creation and rent-protection possi-bilities to attract investments and to ensure that investment was directed towards sectors such as tourism and communications infrastructure that it believed would most contribute to future prosperity.

This invites us to probe deeper into the incentives of the leadership. A number of factors specific to the Palestinian context may have helped to create incentives for developmental interventions by the quasi-state. First, the conflict with Israel provided strong incentives for the executive to strengthen the national economy, in the same way that conflicts with neighbours provided incentives in South Korea, Taiwan, and other emerging Asian economies. In Palestine these incentives soon became much stronger when it became clear that there would be a long interim period with no clear end point during which Israel would continue to have control over critical aspects of Palestinian fiscal capacity, trade and borders as part of its containment policy.

A second factor that helped was the centralization of power within the PNA that enabled the executive to intervene in the allocation of resources and contracts in ways that ensured that economic performance was maintained. It allowed the executive to exercise control over lower-level bureaucrats and functionaries such that state decisions could actually be implemented. This in itself was an achievement given the problems of implementation faced by most developing countries with fully fledged states. In Palestine, appointments to all leading positions in the bureaucracy as well as the political structure (directors, general directors, deputy ministers and ministers) required the written approval of Arafat, as the head of the PNA. He could equally remove them with a single letter. As a result, the Palestinian quasi-state apparatus could rapidly implement decisions of the executive. The executive could also, as a result, rapidly correct mistakes once discovered.

Third, the blurred boundaries between the state and the political leadership paradoxically created incentives for the political leadership to take an interest in the profitability and viability of key enterprises. The grey boundary between the political leadership and the state meant that the political leadership effectively controlled state assets and benefited from their income that often remained outside the budget and directly enhanced the financial flexibility of the leadership. As part of its attempt to maintain and enhance its own economic viability, the political leadership began to acquire and own shares in new enterprises, and even to invest in shares of foreign companies. While these attempts by the executive could be characterized as predatory, they are also reminiscent of the Kuomintang's acquisition of shares in key Taiwanese public sector industries in the early years of Taiwan's development, which created strong incentives for the political leadership to make sure that economic growth was not impeded by an inefficient and loss-making public sector (Wade 1990). If the profits of the ruling group come from share ownership in key 'public sector' enterprises, it is unlikely that these enterprises will remain inefficient for long if the executive has the power to enforce its decisions and is reliant on a long-term flow of income from these assets. In Taiwan, the presence of external threats and the absence of powerful internal coalitions that could potentially block the leadership created a combination of incentives and capacities that ensured that leadership stakes in public sector enterprises did not lead to short-term asset stripping but to a longer-term concern with enhancing economic viability. Although economic and political circumstances in Taiwan in the 1950s were very different, a similar combination of external threats and an absence of powerful internal coalitions that could contest the decisions of the executive also obtained in Palestine. It is not entirely surprising that Palestinian public sector enterprises were relatively profitable. In 1999, for instance, the rate of return achieved in the PNA's public sector holdings was 22.4 per cent of their asset value (IMF 2003: 89).

The PNA's shares in enterprises were managed through the Palestinian Commercial Services Company (PCSC), a holding company chaired by President Arafat's chief financial adviser (Khalid Salam, also known as Mohammad Rashid). The PNA's Ministry of Finance was not sure whether it should treat the PCSC as a private or as a public company since its registration did not specify its legal status. This confusion continued until in June 2000 the PNA formally acknowledged that the PCSC investments were public investments, and it also signalled its intention to eventually privatize all public enterprises. At that time, the PCSC had shares in 33 private firms or subsidiaries. These companies ranged from the Jericho Casino to the Palestine Telecommunication Company or Paltel. The percentage of shares owned ranged from 100 per cent (for two companies including the Cement Company), which were therefore by definition totally public sector, to 5 per cent in a number of companies that were effectively public–private partnerships. The PNA put the total market value of its shares at $292 million at the end of 1999. In addition, the PNA declared ownership of land and other property valued at another $10 million, and other funds (not specified in the report) valued at $42 million (PA 2000: end table).

By May 2000, the IMF and the World Bank succeeded in putting pressure on the PNA to agree to restructure these public investments through privatization (PA 2000). The President agreed to set up a Palestinian Investment Fund (the PIF) to which all holdings of the PNA were to be transferred. All income from these assets would henceforth be paid into the central fiscal budget through a treasury account, and these assets were to be privatized as soon as practicable. But there was little progress in implementing these changes until well after Israeli attacks decimated the institutions of the PNA during the Second *Intifada* and made the prospect of statehood at best a very distant aspiration. It was under these conditions that the PIF was finally set up in October 2002 under the Ministry of Finance and managed by Arafat's financial advisor, Mohammad Rashid. In January 2003, PNA assets were estimated at $633 million, and included 67 enterprises and some liquid assets. This was almost double the $345 million valuation of PCSC assets in 1999, suggesting that the earlier coverage had been incomplete (IMF 2003: 101).

While these changes met with the approval of the World Bank and the IMF, the expected results of these reforms are likely to prove more complex than the good governance approach suggests. The PNA conceded to the implementation of these changes at a time when the limited state-like characteristics of the PNA had disappeared, its institutions had been destroyed, the President was besieged in his compound and the Palestinian territories were effectively under Israeli occupation once again. In contrast, when the PNA *was* operating as a quasi-state, its holdings of 'public' assets through the PCSC created incentives for effective management in a context of considerable uncertainty, and generated incomes that helped sustain the quasi-state's viability. The leadership relied on the income from these key assets, *and* it was politically secure enough within its own constituency to be able to take a long-term view. These two factors ensured that the leadership had strong incentives to manage these assets effectively and moderated any potentially predatory tendencies within the state as far as the assets of these critical firms was concerned. This might explain why Palestinian public sector investments, unlike those in many other developing countries, achieved very high rates of return. These arrangements were far from ideal. A transparent and accountable use of revenues would normally be highly desirable. But in the specific context of Palestinian state formation, our earlier discussion of the contrary implications of budgetary transparency is again relevant.

Moreover, if the external conditions remained, and income from public assets was paid into a budget whose security priorities were set by a foreign power, the managers of these assets may have significantly diluted incentives for their effective management. While the necessity of constructing a viable economy in Palestine is widely recognized, the conventional wisdom about how capitalism is to be constructed in contexts like Palestine is very unrealistic. The reason why the IMF and the World Bank were excited about the creation of the PIF is that they saw it as the first step towards privatization, which they assume will help to create a viable capitalism. But privatization is an almost surreal expectation in contemporary Palestine given the realities on the ground, the absence of potential investors inside the territories, and the absence of any state structures that might assure overseas Palestinian investors to invest in territories encircled, occupied and disputed by a hostile power. In most developing countries, the problem is that a ready-made capitalist class that has the capacity to run enterprises does not already exist, nor do ready-made state structures that can regulate a capitalist economy. In Palestine, the state itself does not exist. In such contexts, developmental states have to be constructed with the requisite rent-creation and rent-management capacities before it makes sense even to start planning for privatization (see Chapter 1 by Khan).

*A summary of the implications of institutional capacities*

The institutional structure of the PNA thus had a number of features relevant for our discussion. The centralization of power was the key characteristic of the PNA, and this could potentially support all of our state types except for *fragmented clientelism*, which requires a central state apparatus that is too weak to overcome the demands of powerful redistributive coalitions. Institutional capacity was particularly appropriate for the consolidation of a *client state*, and indeed many aspects of centralization were design features of the state apparatus that was set up as part of the Oslo Agreements. However, while the PNA may have been sufficiently centralized to maintain order under an integrationist Israeli strategy, it probably lacked sufficient repressive capacities, and certainly the will to exercise the capacities it did have, to support an Israeli strategy of asymmetric containment. Given the latter strategy, the centralization of power within the PNA could have had two quite different outcomes. It could have led in the direction of supporting *predatory state* characteristics if the executive gave up all hope of a long-term future and decided to make as much as it could in the short-run. Or it could have led in the direction of enhancing *developmental state* characteristics if the executive tried to break out of the impasse by creating more economic space for itself. While we will look at some instances of predation later, we also find a number of instances of developmental interventions by the PNA, which in turn are explicable in terms of the incentives, constraints and capacities discussed in this section.

## Civil society organizations

States do not intervene or create rents in a vacuum but often do so in response to either demands coming from society, or in the face of social opposition. To explain the types of rent-creation and rent-management a state is engaged in we need to look at the social history of a society, and in particular, the distribution of organizational and bargaining power between different classes and groups. Looking at civil society organizations is one way of examining this distribution of power. The development of *client-state* or *predatory state* characteristics would require weak and highly fragmented social organizations that could not resist the rent-creation or extortion imposed by the state. On the other hand, *fragmented clientelist* state characteristics can only emerge if there are a large number of well-organized social factions that are strong relative to the state. The strengthening of *developmental state* characteristics is more complex. A developmental state can operate with very fragmented social organizations, as in the North East Asian countries. Social fragmentation can allow a strong state to push through painful structural changes rapidly. But developmental states can also operate with centrally organized 'corporatist' social organizations. These allow the state to rapidly reach agreements about rent-allocation to maximize growth, and subsequently to enforce these decisions. Variants of corporatist developmental states existed in Malaysia in the 1980s and in post-war Scandinavian countries.

### Fragmented middle classes

We have already seen how Israeli colonial rule resulted in a weak and fragmented Palestinian middle class. In developing countries, the 'middle class' consists of intermediate classes who are neither working class/poor peasant on the one hand, nor owners of significant land, capital or other productive assets on the other. Unlike advanced countries, where the middle class consists largely of professionals, in developing countries they consist predominantly of petty traders, the petty bourgeoisie, the educated unemployed, rich peasants, as well as some professional white-collar workers. The organization of these intermediate classes is critical for understanding civil society in developing countries since they play a disproportionately important political role in these societies. Their organizational power and their degree of fragmentation can determine and set limits on the types of rents and interventions developing country states can create. Palestine was historically one of the more advanced regions in the Arab world in terms of education and therefore in the strength of its intermediate classes. In addition, the 1970s and 1980s saw the establishment of a number of new universities in the WBG. However, since the 1950s there has also been a strong trend of emigration out of the WBG, particularly among the professional middle class.

Following the establishment of the PNA in 1994, a huge increase in university education took place. The number of university students increased from 29,380 (16,042 males, and 13,338 females) in 1994/95, to 66,050 (35,696 males, and 30,354 females) in 1999/2000. In community colleges, student numbers showed a smaller increase over the same period from 4,110 to 5,157 (MAS 2001: Table 4.15). According to the Palestinian population census of 1997, some 5.4 per cent of the population of the WBG aged over 15 had a university education (MAS 2001: Table 1.4). A further factor that accelerated the growth of the Palestinian middle class in the post-Oslo period was the return of the cadres of most PLO political parties after the 1994 Accords were signed. The 1997 population census shows that by then some 10.5 per cent of the population of the WBG (267,355 persons) were returnees, or persons whose usual place of residence had been outside Palestine. Around 24.1 per cent of the returnees returned between the first Iraq war of 1991 and 1994 and another 48.5 per cent returned after the establishment of the PNA in 1994. Since Israel had always employed only unskilled and semi-skilled Palestinians, middle-class Palestinians had had to find employment elsewhere, primarily in the Gulf states. But following the war of 1991, Palestinians in Kuwait were forced to leave, returning to Jordan or the WBG. Data shows that returnees in general had higher levels of education than non-returnees. Of those aged 10 or over, 14 per cent of returnees had a university education, compared to 4.5 per cent of non-returnees. Returnees were also predominantly of working age with 68.8 per cent between the ages of 15 and 65, compared to 49.4 per cent in the case of non-returnees (Maliki 2000: 53–62).

But the steady growth in numbers of the Palestinian middle class in the 1990s did not result in a proportionate growth in their political power and influence. Despite many obvious differences in the historical context, the arrival of the PLO in the occupied WBG in 1994 can *in some respects* be compared to the arrival of the Kuomintang administrative and military apparatus in Taiwan from mainland China in 1949. In both cases, the incoming state apparatus was much better organized than the domestic population and consequently enjoyed a high degree of relative autonomy in policy-making and resource allocation. In both, the new state had powerful incentives to develop the domestic economy. In both, the boundaries between state and party, and between party and leader were blurred, arguably creating incentives for the top leadership to manage critical assets effectively. In both, there was access to foreign technology and a willingness to use it. But there were differences too, particularly in the international context, and in the degree of internal turmoil. The PNA was not a proper state, and large parts of its territories continued under foreign occupation, with the additional imposition of a containment strategy. Moreover, its development came to a (temporary?) end in 2000, leaving very few years of experience on which to base international comparisons. In addition, in the Palestinian case, while the middle class was relatively disorganized, it was nevertheless more politicized than in the typical East Asian country. As a result, the leadership faced greater criticisms for actions that appeared to be driven by the executive compared to East Asian states doing similar things at an equivalent stage of their development. Nevertheless, the comparison with East Asia is useful for suggesting that despite its size and politicization, the fragmentation of the Palestinian middle class allowed the executive to act for a time in ways that were closer to the experience of East Asian countries than the typical developing country with well-organized client factions.

Two features characterized the Palestinian middle classes in the WBG in the period under study: fragmentation, and a very low level of organization, despite a high degree of politicization in terms of ideology and aspirations. If fragmentation had been combined with a high degree of independent organizational and political power, this could have led to fragmented clientelism. But fragmentation combined with very weak organizational power of factions allowed a strong executive-led state to consolidate. The Palestinian intermediate classes were fragmented by geography (the territorial division of the occupied territories into the West Bank, the Gaza Strip and East Jerusalem, and beyond that into a large number of 'cantons' separated by Israeli controlled territories and gatekeepers). They were also fragmented by sector of activity (PNA, NGOs, private sector or political parties), by ideology (PNA, the secular opposition, the Islamist opposition, or independent) and by membership of different types of organizations (bureaucratic, traditional and modern). It had remained organizationally weak because of the occupation and repression by Israel that resulted in the exclusion of the middle classes from politics and administration. After 1994, it found in addition that it faced a relatively well-organized and to some extent imported state apparatus in the form of the PNA. Individuals and factions within the middle classes did achieve privileged access to resources based on *wasta* (mediation) and *mehsubia* (patronage); that is, through the use of political, personal, family or regional connections and relationships.[10] But because of their organizational weakness, these mechanisms allowed the middle class to be easily incorporated into the state formation strategies of the executive.

### Middle class growth under the PNA

The establishment of the PNA resulted in a rapid growth in the relative share of middle class employment in the WBG. In 1999, some 22.5 per cent of all employed persons in the WBG were classified as legislators, senior officials and managers, professionals, technocrats, and clerks, and a similar percentage (22.7 per cent) were in crafts and related occupations (PCBS 2000b: Table 26). Almost all of those in the first category were middle class. A smaller percentage of the second category (consisting of skilled artisans and craftsmen) could also be classified as middle class. Compared to these figures, in 1992, Israeli data for the same job classification in the WBG (but excluding East Jerusalem) indicated only 11 per cent of all employed persons were in occupations of the first category (administrators, professionals, technocrats, and clerks). Thus, the share of this category in total employment virtually doubled soon after the PNA's creation. In absolute numbers, the number of employees in this category increased more than threefold between 1992 and 1999, excluding East Jerusalem.[11] In contrast, the percentage reported in the second category (skilled artisans and craftsmen) declined in 1999 compared to the 1992 figure of 29.4 per cent (ICBS 1993: Table 27.20).

Some individuals in other categories should also be classified as middle class. In 1999 employers formed 5.5 per cent of all economically active persons, and the self-employed another 18.7 per cent (PCBS 2000b: Table 25). A large percentage of 'employers' ran very small enterprises (employing less than five persons with very little capital and simple technology). These petty-bourgeois employers should be classified as middle class. Similarly, many of the self-employed were craftsmen working, like most employers, in the small-scale informal sector of the economy and they too would be middle class in a developing country context. A small percentage of the self-employed were also professionals (architects, engineers, doctors, etc.), who were clearly middle class. The share of middle-class employment when all these individuals are added to the first category (administrators, professionals, technocrats, and clerks) would thus very likely be between 30 to 40 per cent of total employment.

Two main motors drove the rapid growth of middle-class jobs after the setting up of the PNA. The first was the political imperative of the emerging state to increase public employment as a way of distributing rents to maintain political stability. The second, which we will discuss later, was a related process of NGO growth, driven largely by external funding and externally distributed rents, and this too was partly motivated by a donor commitment to maintain political stability. The political imperative within the PNA was responsible for government employment reaching 17.9 per cent of total employment by the last quarter of 1999 (the rate in the Gaza Strip being double that of the West Bank). In comparison, 59.4 per cent of employment was in the private and NGO sectors, and 22.7 per cent in Israel and Israeli settlements (MAS 2000: Table 3.2).[12] The PNA had to absorb PLO cadres into the state apparatus, absorb Palestinians previously employed by the Israeli Civil Administration, and reward cadres of the ruling party. The regime, as we explained earlier, required a large security force and it needed to co-opt the more influential traditional families. In other words, public employment creation was not driven solely or even largely by the needs of administrative efficiency or economic rationality. It was also and perhaps largely driven by the rationality of state-building and regime maintenance. Hence factors such as the containment of opposition and discontent, and the need to enlarge the regime's political base across regional, kinship, and other parochial or traditional solidarities were critically important.[13]

The Israeli imposed Civil Administration of the WBG had employed some 20,000 Palestinians at the time it was taken over by the PNA. Six years later the number on the payroll of the PNA in its various institutions and agencies (including education, health, and security forces) had reached 120 thousand. Public employment in high positions (minister, deputy minister, director or head of one of the state agencies) carried valuable privileges (including, in most cases, a VIP card, the free use of a car and telephone, and rent-free housing). It also provided a level of income that would not, in most cases, be otherwise attainable by persons of similar qualifications elsewhere in the local economy. Thus public office was turned into a reward for political and/or personal loyalty, and thus a powerful mechanism through which the regime distributed rents to maintain political stability.

The number of ministers or officials with ministerial rank grew from 14 in May 1994 (when the PNA was established) to 23 in 1996 (after the general and presidential elections), to 33 (some without portfolios) by August 1998. In addition to the ministries, there were also some 75 public bodies linked directly to Arafat or his office, including a public monitoring unit set up and accountable only to the president.[14] The increase in the number of ministries and security agencies seemed to be aimed at the enlargement of the circle of the PNA's clientele, to include, among others, critics from the PLC and representatives of political parties who wished to be in the government. On the other hand, loud critics holding sensitive positions (such as chairs of PLC committees), were pressurized, out-manoeuvred or replaced by more amenable members. Positions of deputy ministers, general directors, and heads of agencies (civilian and military) and public institutions were predominantly awarded to Fateh cadres (Hilal 2002). Other political parties were offered a quota of positions as political favours, not as entitlements.

The interesting question for the state formation process is whether the allocation of rents to different middle-class individuals and groups was determined from below by the relative power of competing organizations, or decided from above in ways which furthered the objectives of the executive. This judgement is important to distinguish between what we have called a *fragmented clientelist* state captured by factions who can dictate the creation of jobs and rents, and a *developmental* or a *client* state where the allocation of rents is centrally determined by the economic and political objectives of the state leadership. In the Palestinian case, the evidence suggests that political rent allocation was a mechanism through which the president of the PNA consolidated the centralization of power by accommodating middle-class individuals and groups on terms determined by the state and on condition that they supported state policies. This would be consistent with characteristics of a client or developmental state rather than a fragmented clientelist one.

This helps to explain the paradox that despite the growth in the size and employment share of the middle class, its political influence *declined* with the establishment of the PNA. The middle class was aware of this, and indeed there was a broad-based middle-class disenchantment with the PNA. A much higher percentage of those with university education were found in opinion surveys to be critical of the PNA than those with little or no education. A higher percentage of the educated young also expressed a readiness to emigrate permanently.[15] This is particularly significant since substantial economic opportunities were emerging for the middle classes. The main beneficiaries of the PNA rent-allocation strategy through public sector job creation was the strategic strata of the middle class who secured managerial positions in the middle and upper echelons of the public administration in return for their support for the state formation process. But wider sections of the middle class also benefited in a number of ways. The subsidized expansion of higher education mainly benefited the middle class. Significant autonomy was also granted to NGOs (see p. 98), allowing job creation for new sections of the middle class based on foreign inflows. Popular organizations and professional associations also offered positions of privilege, contests for which took place on the basis of political affiliation. Political parties too provided positions of privilege, as well as getting direct rent-redistributions from the executive.

All this was in addition to the educated middle class being the main beneficiary, apart from the capitalists, of the expansion of the private sector. The growth of the financial sector provided the most striking area of middle-class employment growth in the private sector. By 1999, there were some 22 banks, Palestinian, Arab and international, with some 115 branches, nearly all of which opened after the establishment of the PNA in 1994.[16] A stock exchange was established in 1997, and by the summer of 2000 some 25 companies were listed. The number of insurance companies increased from

1 in 1994 to 8 in 2000. There was an even more significant increase in the number of hotels, restaurants, and travel agencies. The apparent paradox of the political disenchantment of the middle class in a context of growing economic opportunities suggests that the PNA leadership had effectively limited the autonomous powers of the middle class and made their economic opportunities conditional on their political quiescence.

### The struggle for liberation and political centralization

As with other national liberation struggles, the Palestinian struggle had from the beginning recognized the importance of maintaining political discipline. As part of a system of political consolidation, the PLO had since the early 1970s operated a system of distributing funds to its affiliated parties in a centralized way. The political rents available to the PLO decreased sharply following the first Iraq War early in 1991 that in turn led to a sharp reduction in the regular transfers of rent to PLO factions. Later in that year, Fateh, the leading faction of the PLO, supported by some smaller factions, agreed to join the Madrid peace conference and two years later the Oslo Accords were signed. The result was dissension within the PLO, with a number of political factions rejecting the Oslo Accords and freezing their membership in the PLO Executive Committee. This led Arafat, as the chairman of the Executive Committee and later head of the PNA, to be more selective in his use of rent-allocation as a political tool. As the flow of funds to the PNA increased after Oslo, the allocation of funds to political groups became a tool of incorporation, not within the PLO framework, as was the case previously, but now within the framework of the PNA. The president of the PNA effectively became the authority determining who would get these allocations, and their size and frequency. Although most of the PLO political parties had their own financial resources, the political rent-allocation allowed the president of the PNA to exercise considerable leverage in maintaining political stability.

Rent allocation to political parties was not confined to cash handouts. It included other forms of rent (offices, cars, VIP cards, appointments of party cadres to the public administration, and so on). All this operated as an integration mechanism for the stabilization of the PNA regime. Opposition political parties recognized the new power centred in the PNA, and accepted, more or less, that they had to work within the ceilings set by the regime. Islamist factions, never having been part of the PLO, were never part of the PLO rent-distribution system. They emerged outside it, maintained their organizational, political and financial autonomy from the PLO, and relied on other sources of funding (both local and external) for their organizations and activities. This does not mean that attempts were not made to incorporate them. But when they failed, the President of the PNA relied on repressive measures, such as the imprisonment of their leaders and cadres and the closure of Islamic charitable institutions.[17]

Other civil society formations, such as mass organizations, professional associations and trade unions posed even less of a problem for the regime. They had lost much of their social base and mobilizing capabilities earlier in the 1990s after the erosion of the popular character of the First *Intifada* (1987–92). PLO factions had created the main body of these civil society formations as civic associations with the aim of organizing opposition to the Israeli occupation, while providing services to needy sectors of the population. Following the Oslo Accords, and the removal of restrictions on political parties in Palestinian-controlled areas, these associations lost their original function as arms of political parties. Many transformed themselves into professional NGOs, while others (such as trade union federations, women's federations, youth associations and so on) lost much of their constituency, and with that, their political credibility (Hilal 1998b). The main factor behind their demise was their inability to create a new organizational and programmatic role in the emerging political field. Most retained their headquarters and branch offices but depended on external financial resources. In the absence of an organized constituency, many popular organizations became *de facto* NGOs and collapsed into venues for personal rent-seeking based on access to external institutional and political donors. Most professional associations (lawyers, doctors, engineers, teachers, and others) were better organized than popular organizations, and unlike NGOs, had a well-defined and stable constituency. However, the ruling party, Fateh, dominated most of these associations, though it often had to engage in vigorous competition with the Islamists. Hence, most professional associations tended to avoid voicing open criticisms of the PNA.

### The anomalous role of NGOs

Apart from the PNA's job creation, the second major process that contributed to the enlargement of middle-class employment was the proliferation of non-governmental organizations or NGOs throughout the late 1980s and 1990s. In Palestine, NGOs in the form of human rights advocacy groups, 'developmental' and service-oriented organizations and so on, were often the descendants of organizations formed by left-wing political factions that later succeeded in detaching themselves from their mother organizations. But they did so at a cost. Their 'professionalization' and the attendant transformation of organizational structures and agendas were necessitated by the requirements of international donors. This meant two things: dependency on short-term foreign funding, and delinking from political parties that lost them their organized constituencies. In addition they had to face occasional PNA attempts to limit their operational autonomy.[18]

The PNA did in the end change the very restrictive legislation originally proposed to govern NGOs, and approved legislation that left the NGOs with a tangible degree of autonomy. It even erected a ministry to deal with NGOs, aiming no doubt, to integrate them into the state framework. But the success of NGOs in keeping their autonomous space should not be entirely attributed to their own strength. They worked closely as a lobby with the PLC, many of whose members were sympathetic to the cause of NGOs, and a few PLC members were directly involved in these organizations. They also received direct and indirect support from the World Bank and international donors, who assured the PNA that the funds going to the NGOs were not coming from resources earmarked for the PNA.[19] The fact that the NGOs acted as providers of jobs and services to the poor in a situation character-ized by high rates of unemployment and poverty was also relevant for persuading the PNA leadership not to encroach too much on their space.

However the NGOs' autonomy remained precarious. Most NGOs ran small-scale organizations, with short-term budgets and a small and unstable number of beneficiaries. At the same time, they provided their middle-class leaders with status, income and privileges unattainable in alternative oppor-tunities, in other words, access to a range of rents.[20] Access to these rents kept them independent of the PNA, but highly dependent on fickle foreign donors.[21] Most NGOs were not interested in confronting the PNA, as it was rarely in their interest to antagonize the executive. In sum, NGOs in Palestine, as elsewhere in much of the developing world, did not necessarily provide an alternative *organizational* structure through which the middle and other classes could effectively constrain executive authority. Given the fact that the Palestinian middle class was fragmented and organizationally weak, the NGOs, if anything, contributed to the continuation of these features. By enabling many entrepreneurial and organizationally skilful middle-class individuals to acquire leadership roles in small well-funded organizations, the NGO structure contributed to the quiescence and incorporation of the middle class, while contributing to some service delivery functions. In the context of considerable social tensions and uncertainty in the Palestinian territories, the NGO sector may have positively contributed to social stability by providing rents to socially conscious middle-class individuals and opportunities to deliver socially desirable services.

The working class benefited the least from the regime emerging under the PNA. On the one hand, the PNA was committed to basic education and health for all. The ministry of social affairs provided assistance to very poor families, the United Nations Relief and Works Agency (UNRWA) continued to assist the extremely poor in refugee camps, and local NGOs, such as *Zakat* committees, together with international NGOs attended to marginal groups. Nevertheless, such services did not compensate for the highly precar-ious labour market that the working class and other marginal social groups faced since the Oslo Accords. The fragmentation of the working class, geographically and into different labour markets, did not help its bargaining power. This was compounded by weak labour organizations and the fragile and dependent Palestinian economy. Moreover, it was the working class that was the hardest hit in terms of unemployment and poverty rates by Israel's asymmetric containment strategy, and this capacity to debilitate became fully visible in the aftermath of the Second *Intifada*.

*A summary of the implications of social organization*

Our review of different aspects of middle-class organization shows how the fragmentation and disorganization of the middle class allowed the PNA to organize their incorporation on terms determined by the executive. Even in the NGO sector, the apparently autonomous activities of these organizations arguably contributed to the PNA being able to maintain its centralized hold on power. While such a distribution of power between the executive and those who could potentially constrain it could support *predatory* or *client-state* characteristics, in the context of the Oslo interim period, it also allowed the executive to allocate and manage some rents in a *developmental* way. The quasi-state could allocate rents and resources without powerful factions being able to determine the terms of these allocations. The least likely outcome given the organization of Palestinian civil society organizations was the development of *fragmented-clientelist* state characteristics, which require the presence of a number of competing parties and factions with significant bargaining power relative to the executive powers of the state.

## The indigenous and expatriate Palestinian capitalists

The degree of development of the capitalist class clearly has important implications for the rent and intervention strategies of any state. The more developed the capitalist class, the more likely it is that the state will follow *developmental* strategies of the East Asian type. If the capitalist class has the capacity to acquire and use technology, conditional rent allocation to this class to accelerate growth can provide high economic and political returns for the state leadership. The Palestinian paradox was that its capitalist class was dualistic, with an indigenous capitalist class that was under-developed because of decades of Israeli occupation. On the other hand, expatriate Palestinian capitalists were more developed than capitalists in many other developing countries with equivalent per capita incomes. This dualism resulted in an implicit PNA strategy of trying to accelerate economic development by prioritizing the needs of the expatriate bourgeoisie while ignoring for the time being the demands of smaller and less advanced indigenous capitalists. This resulted in a bias in state support for capital-intensive investments in the tourism and communications sectors and a relative neglect of artisan manufacturing, agriculture, and petty businesses. While this strategy had costs, particularly in terms of the distribution of benefits, it was not necessarily entirely flawed if the priority was to accelerate economic growth. If rapid progress towards statehood had been achieved, the PNA's economic priorities in developing the tourism sector may well have provided significant returns for the Palestinian economy.

Indigenous Palestinian capitalists in the WBG were historically weak and under-developed because they had to operate under an external rule that imposed multiple restrictions on their development (Diwan and Shaban 1999). It lacked serious capital and it lacked political legitimacy since it had played a marginal role in the national liberation movement. On the other hand, the expatriate Palestinian capitalists, located in the oil-rich Gulf states, North America and Europe had significant blocks of capital. They were also eager to invest in Palestine for a combination of national-istic and profit-seeking motives. But they too had tenuous relations with the national movement, and when they appeared in the WBG after the estab-lishment of the PNA, they were clearly junior partners of the state leadership. The PNA granted expatriate capital privileged access to Palestinian markets and to major projects, and set contracts and conditions to ensure that these critical investors earned sufficient rents to compensate them for the precariousness of their investments. In return, the PNA too got a share of the rents, through share ownerships and kickbacks. It also benefited politically from the badly needed investments and job opportuni-ties that enhanced its state-building project. As we saw in Table 1.1 (Khan p. 15), economic growth was relatively high during the period 1994–2000, the share of industry was maintained at around 20 per cent of GDP, implying equivalently high growth rates in the industrial sector. These high rates of private investment were particularly impressive given the uncer-tainty of the final status negotiations.

The interests of the indigenous and expatriate capitalists were different, and so were the roles they played in the PNA's development strategy. Indigenous capitalists were generally owners of small or *very* small enterprises, typically relying on cheap labour and simple technology. Many employed only two or three workers in artisanal enterprises or repair shops. They were likely to benefit somewhat from greater integra-tion with Israel, which may have lowered the prices of some of their inputs and allowed some of them to seek higher prices for some of their products in Israel. Even if the PNA had wanted to construct a free market to help these small capitalists and informal sector traders, the externally imposed restrictions on movements of goods and labour, the territorial fragmentation of Palestine and the trade and fiscal restrictions imposed by the Paris Economic Protocol meant that this was not an attainable policy goal. At the same time, agricultural growth was constrained by Israeli control of Palestinian water sources, and to a lesser extent by trade restrictions that prevented Palestinian exports of agricul-tural commodities that could threaten Israeli producers (see Chapter 3 by Zagha and Zomlot). In this context, the PNA strategy of relying on big expatriate capitalists to drive economic growth through capital-intensive investments in service and manufacturing sectors could be defended as a promising economic strategy given the alternatives. This strategy had a number of other benefits since highly visible projects like hotels and telecommunication networks added to the prestige of the PNA, and it was easier to share rents with a few large capitalists than many small ones.

It is not surprising that there was a growing conflict of interests between smaller (mostly indigenous) capitalists and bigger (mostly expatriate) capitalists. Smaller capitalists were more likely to put pressure on the PNA for consultation and participation in policy-making, and to demand more transparent free-market policies. In contrast, expatriate Palestinian capitalists *were* capable of making concentrated long-term investments in higher technology sectors, and the PNA clearly saw them as significant agents of change. The PNA's economic policies show that the leadership was willing to create rents to attract investments from this group, even if it entailed raising prices for some critical goods and services that would hurt consumers and smaller producers in the short-run. Attracting large investments in a context of significant political uncertainty and weak state powers to protect domestic capitalists against the competition and restrictions coming from Israel required the provision of a variety of rents to these big investors. While the PNA's institutional structure left a lot to be desired in terms of transparency and accountability, it did respond to these requirements with a rent-allocation strategy that attracted a significant amount of expatriate capital in an otherwise hostile environment.

### Rents to attract investments by large expatriate capitalists

Before the Oslo Accords, Palestinian expatriate capital had shown little interest in investment in the occupied territories, given their occupied status. This changed with the Oslo agreements. Expatriate investors were not only interested, they realized that in the long-run, profits would be even greater if they could have a say in the construction of the regulatory structure, the structure of taxes, and general economic policy-making. Thus, immediately following the Oslo Agreements, a number of large expatriate capitalists offered Arafat a partnership in which they would come up with significant investments in return for involvement in policy-making from the outset. Arafat turned down the offer, apparently fearful that the expatriate capitalists would be able to play a disproportionate role in determining the structure and policies of the new state before its authority had consolidated. Arguably, allowing a small group of investors to play a prominent role in influencing regulatory structures and policies at an early phase of state formation may not have been desirable given that these investors would very likely have tried to influence the design of institutions in ways that favoured them.

It was only after the PNA had achieved a degree of entrenchment following the general elections of 1996, and Arafat had secured substantial funding from the international donor community,[22] that he contemplated developing the partnership with expatriate capital. The latter was represented by figures such as Masri, al-A'qad, Khuri, Sabagh and Shuman. By then Arafat had both the resources and the institutional capacity to allocate rents independently and to determine overall policy. Consequently, he could hope to use the expatriate capitalists to further what he believed was the national interest, rather than letting them define what the national interest was. On the one hand, the leadership clearly recognized that rents would have to be created for expatriates to encourage them to invest. Investors repeatedly identified political uncertainties as the major disincentive for investment (see for instance, Diwan and Shaban 1999). On the other hand, executive centralization ensured that these rents could not be captured by capitalists unconditionally, in other words regardless of their performance. Moreover, by then the PNA had also acquired a capacity to create other types of rents necessary for its political survival, in particular, as we have seen, to accommodate and incorporate the middle classes.

Given the very limited powers of the PNA quasi-state, the rents that it could offer potential investors were not always conventional ones. It had no control over exchange rate or interest rate policy. As Chapter 6 by Fjeldstad and Zagha shows, it also lacked an adequate fiscal base to offer any significant direct or indirect subsidies. Thus rents were allocated through such mechanisms as allowing the creation of monopolies but implicitly demanding investment and performance in exchange. Expatriate investors were granted monopoly status in some activities (such as Paltel in telecommunications, and in a number of other companies held through Padico, the Palestine Development and Investment Company). Some of these companies were natural monopolies; others were not (see Nasr, Chapter 5). In each case, monopoly rents were not taxed away by the state but could be retained provided the investment was sustained and performance was acceptable. The PNA was also ready in its tax code to grant additional tax exemptions to investors for different periods depending on the capital invested and the labour employed. This further enhanced the rents of selected larger companies dominated by expatriate capital. In addition, informal mechanisms were also reported for enhancing the rents of vital companies, such as arrangements to defer utility or tax bills, often in exchange for kickbacks, but sometimes simply in response to special pleading.

If these rents were allocated regardless of performance and without any possibility of withdrawal and re-allocation, it is unlikely that they would have had any desirable effect, whatever the intentions of the parties. The incentive to act opportunistically would be irresistible once a rent had been captured. Here, the centralization of power gave the executive some leverage to make sure that the allocation of rents did have the desired effect of attracting investments and were not just free gifts for 'cronies'. The granting of the telecommunications licence, and its subsequent re-negotiation provides an example of how this rent-allocation system was beginning to work. Shortly after Oslo, Arafat granted an American registered company (Integrated Technology Incorporated) the sole right to operate telecommunications in the WBG for 25 years, the deal being subject to American law. A person associated by marriage with Arafat headed the company. Once the deal became public knowledge, a lobby was formed by a group of expatriate capitalists to persuade Arafat to rescind the deal on the grounds that the company was unknown and inexperienced and was likely to prove incompetent or inefficient. These expatriate capitalists agreed to cover the cost of annulling the licence (reported to have been many millions of dollars) in an out-of-court settlement. Arafat eventually granted the licence to a Palestinian company formed by expatriate capital, Paltel, in which the PNA became a shareholder. Paltel went on to become the most profitable company established under the PNA and modernized in a very short time the communication system in the WBG. State-led rent-management of this type is not surprising in a centralized regime that can take a long-term view. If a single decision-maker is comparing different options, allocations that are more efficient are likely to emerge because the leadership can easily see that the more efficient can credibly offer a higher payoff over time than the less efficient. Since Arafat and the PNA understood that their political survival would ultimately depend on economic performance, they had no reason to favour clan over economics.

### Local capitalists, petty corruption and primitive accumulation

As we have seen, local capital in the Palestinian territories was dominated by very small-scale family capital, with at best a small number of medium-sized capitalists engaged in commerce, real estate and manufacturing. The privileged access to rents granted to large expatriate capital inevitably left indigenous small and medium capitalists disaffected. Most local capitalists also found that they could exercise little influence to change these economic policies. This was particularly galling because they looked at expatriate capital as having been absent while they had faced the restrictions and hardships of the Israeli occupation. And now the expatriates had apparently turned up to reap profits and privileges, arguably with no serious concern for political rights or democratic change. At the same time, expatriate capital looked upon local capital as technically backward and lacking knowledge and experience of operating in the modern world. To add to their difficulties, small capitalists most directly experienced the predatory aspects of the state apparatus, particularly at the local level. Since the leadership did not see small capitalists as critical growth leaders, and since their capital was not mobile, some amount of local extortion by tax collectors and security forces appeared to be sanctioned or at least overlooked by the centre.

These instances of petty extortion and corruption have to be clearly distinguished from much bigger processes of politically driven accumulation that we have previously described as 'primitive accumulation' (Khan, Chapter 1). Primitive accumulation describes a process involving high political and bureaucratic officials who use political power to help their own accumulation or to help proto-capitalists associated with them. Political power can be used to capture or acquire significant assets that are in the public domain, to be more or less rapidly converted into private assets. This too occurred in Palestine, as in other countries in the early stages of capitalist development. The small-scale indigenous capitalists were occasionally beneficiaries of these processes, but they were very often at the receiving end of asset transfers and politically driven accumulation that disadvantaged them. Much of the criticism and opposition to processes of primitive accumulation came once again from small capitalists and traders who were most vocal about this type of high-level corruption in which PNA officials were involved. To judge the effects of Palestinian primitive accumulation, we have to remember that primitive accumulation takes place in both dynamic and collapsing developing countries. In the former, primitive accumulation in the early stages of capitalist development takes place because a class of productive capitalists does not already exist. The collapse of pre-capitalist production enables a new emerging class to use its political power to consolidate resources and to become, over time, the new productive capitalist class. In the failed states, the capture of assets does not lead to production, but only to hoarding, conspicuous consumption and the export of assets to foreign banks.

Primitive accumulation can only lead to the development of productive capitalist enterprises if a number of conditions are met. Primitive accumulators must have the confidence to engage in long-term investments. This in turn requires that investors believe that the state has a long-term perspective and will not act in a predatory way, and that the state has the power to prevent or limit lower-level predation by its own staff. This does not mean that the state leadership will not want to tax (legally or otherwise) some of the profits of the new class. But investors must be assured that the tax will not be so big as to make their investment no longer worthwhile. The new capitalists are even more likely to remain productive if they believe that the state executive is relying on their profitability, and has the power to deprive them of their assets if poor management threatens leadership goals. It is not surprising that in countries with weak states, primitive accumulation often leads to assets leaving the country. In contrast, with strong states as in East Asian countries, primitive accumulation can lead to high rates of productive investment. Primitive accumulation in Palestine showed *some* evidence of proceeding to the establishment of viable capitalist enterprises, certainly more so than in many other comparable developing countries. A number of factors may have contributed to this: the presence of latent entrepreneurial skills, economic nationalism, and the perception that a centralized executive would not allow egregious violations that harmed the economy.

Amundsen and Ezbidi (Chapter 4) provide several examples of primitive accumulation in the Palestinian context. First, they describe how a Nablus security chief who did not have personal collateral used his political connections to get a bank loan to set up a chicken farm. In many if not most developing countries, a security chief getting a bank loan by using political connections would have set up a fictitious chicken farm at best, and the loan would be transferred to consumption or to a foreign bank, with no intention of repayment. But in Palestine, the outcome in this case was the construction of a real chicken farm that actually produced chickens for a profit. The chief made quite a lot of money, but he did so by producing chickens. Political capital in the first instance was converted into productive economic capital. They also cite other examples of primitive accumulation leading to the construction of hotels and other service sector infrastructure by politically connected individuals close to the leadership. In most of these cases, these were profitable enterprises. While Amundsen and Ezbidi are right to be critical of these processes and to point out that they could easily cause much damage, we argue that we need to compare Palestinian state performance in managing primitive accumulation with other developing countries at similar levels of development. In this *comparative* perspective, Palestinian primitive accumulation appears to have been at least partly *developmental*. The fact that so many primitive accumulators did in fact invest productively strongly suggests that while the exercise of political power for accumulation was tolerated, there were sufficient incentives for production, and disincentives for unproductive consumption. Examples of unproductive primitive accumulation are less frequently observed in Palestine. Along a spectrum of developing countries with countries like Nigeria at one end, where primitive accumulation is largely unproductive, and rapid developers like China at the other end, where primitive accumulation has been highly productive, Palestine would probably be somewhere in the middle, and possibly towards the China end of the scale. Given the very limited sovereignty enjoyed by the PNA, and therefore its very limited capacities to discipline primitive accumulation, this is a significant observation. If some amount of primitive accumulation has to happen when a pre-capitalist society is transformed into a capitalist one, the state capacities that the PNA displayed could be strengthened and institutionalized to accelerate this transition and achieve a structure of viable capitalist property rights that could then be stabilized. The PNA revealed some capacity for ensuring that primitive accumulation was consistent with a productive capitalist transformation, and feasible strategies of reform should seek to strengthen, develop and regulate these capacities in the future.

Not surprisingly, the capitalists who neither benefited from monopoly rents nor from primitive accumulation were most critical of the PNA's system of governance. These were largely the smaller and medium-sized local capitalists who felt that they were excluded from the system being constructed by the PNA. They participated instead in political activity to make the PNA more accountable and responsive to their needs. This took the form of establishing business associations and erecting coordinating structures, such as the Palestine Trade Centre or Paltrade, with the aim of voicing joint interests and demands. Small and medium capitalists were more concerned with establishing a level playing field, promoting a free market, and improving the rule of law and the quality of governance. But the vast majority of local capitalists were very small capitalists who did not even have the minimum economic resources to take part in this organizational activity. So in fact, the local capitalists leading the demands for greater accountability were of middling size and above. At the end of May 2000 Paltrade organized a national dialogue conference between the private and public sectors that came out with joint policy recommendations on issues of concern for local capitalists.[23] In December 2000, an overarching coordinating body was created that included the main sectors of indigenous capital: the Federation of Chambers of Commerce, the Federation of Chambers of Industry, Paltrade, business associations, and the Palestine Information Technology Association (Pita). In its programmatic statement, Paltrade went on to call on Arab states to take steps to support the private sector through loans, the easing of customs procedures, opening their markets to Palestinian goods and labour, and facilitating the use of Egyptian and Jordanian ports for Palestinian trade.[24] Representatives of local industry frequently and strongly demanded a transparent partnership between the private sector and the PNA in formulating a strategy supportive of local industry.[25]

Thus the political activity of small and medium capital, led mainly by the latter, was primarily concerned with getting rid of the damaging impact of market restrictions and rents. The rents being created by the PNA for big expatriate capitalists and trading monopolies (see Nasr, Chapter 5) were examples of these rents. But it has to be remembered that the most significant market distortions were caused by the restrictions on the movements of goods and labour that Israel insisted on, and by the restrictions on Palestinian fiscal, monetary and trade policies allowed under the Oslo and Paris Agreements. While domestic capital quite naturally aimed its criticisms against the PNA in the first instance, many of the rents being created by the PNA, such as the monopoly rents of the trading monopolies, were themselves responses to market distortions that were exogenously imposed. Regardless of the motivations of the PNA leadership in creating these rents, getting rid of them in this specific context would not necessarily improve the conditions even of small capitalists. Other rents, such as rents to attract investments and technologies, or those associated with primitive accumulation, are observed in almost all developing countries, and we have argued (Khan, Chapter 1) that the historical evidence suggests that development is accelerated if they are properly managed rather than if attempts are made to try to abolish them.

Partly, at least, the campaign for free markets and good governance was also driven by the global dominance of a particular version of market economics, and of the good governance agenda. These demands were strongly promoted by international donors, the World Bank and the International Monetary Fund. The absence of a significant public sector in the WBG and the fact that expatriate capitalists lacked local political voice meant that major public expressions of economic goals for society came from the local, relatively small-scale, private sector. It was also aided by the fact that the PNA itself adopted free-market doctrines without necessarily practising them, and publicly at least, acknowledged the need to limit its own role to a regulatory one.

Thus there were conflicts between the economic model desired by the local capitalists, and the rent-allocation model being used by the PNA executive to attract big blocks of expatriate capital to push development. But the conflict was often more apparent than real. Quite apart from the possibility that capitalists always find arguments to justify their own rents and to criticize the rents going to others, in the Palestinian context, significant moves towards a freer market were unattainable given the control exercised by Israel over movements of labour and goods. An immediate improvement in state accountability in the direction of an advanced economy with enforceable contracts and a sound judiciary was also unattainable, if only because of the disputes with Israel over land and resources, and the necessary centralization of power in a context of political conflict and uncertainty. As a result, much of the indigenous bourgeoisie's interaction with the PNA remained at the level of communicating aspirations. These aspirations were not alien to the top political elite, who also had an interest in the eventual emergence of a widely based and viable private sector. In the long run, they too wanted opportunities to convert some of their financial wealth into productive capital, and a more widely based capitalism would undoubtedly increase the revenues of the regime. Nevertheless, attracting big blocks of capital and expatriate expertise remained a major plank of the executive's medium-term economic strategy throughout the interim period. As we have already seen, it was only after the serious reverses of 2000 that the PNA began to dismantle some of the rent-creating mechanisms it had constructed, and we have argued that this was not necessarily a positive outcome for a future round of state formation under a client-state architecture, particularly if asymmetric containment is likely to continue.

### *A summary of the implications of the structure and organization of Palestinian capitalists*

To conclude, the relative development of the Palestinian bourgeoisie and particularly of expatriate capital presented opportunities for the PNA that were significantly different from those available to most other Arab countries. In the 'state capitalist' strategies historically observed in Egypt, Algeria, Iraq and Syria, the public sector had to be the driver of accumulation and economic management (Perthes 1995). To some extent, this could be explained by the absence in those countries of big enough blocks of private capital (relative to the size of the economy) that could drive accumulation. The PNA, in contrast, had access to relatively large blocks of private capital which it could control politically and which could rapidly bring in expertise and developmental capacity. This created strong incentives to push growth through a partnership with the private sector since the leadership could get significant benefits from such a strategy. It also created incentives to dampen predatory activities and an opportunity to resist the asymmetric containment imposed by Israel. Elements of the state-led strategy in Palestine thus had developmental characteristics reminiscent of East Asian states where the state harnessed the private sector as a partner and provided it with the incentives and resources to play a dynamic role.

Conditional rent allocation to some of the big expatriate capitalists combined with sustained pressures for greater competition from indigenous capital created an environment that may potentially have been very conducive for growth and social transformation if the inhospitable environment in terms of external conflicts could have been improved. Such an assessment does not downplay the very real observations of shortcomings in regulatory structures, of low level extortions, of some allocations of rents that were clearly inefficient, and so on. It simply points out that *some* of the underlying conditions supported a number of developmental state characteristics that could have assisted in accelerating a capitalist transformation in the Palestinian territories. Policy could have been directed to develop and consolidate these embryonic state capacities. Had progress along these lines been achieved, it would subsequently also have been feasible to strengthen the rule of law, deepen democracy and counter corruption, while institutionalizing and legalizing the rent-seeking associated with necessary rents (Khan, Chapter 1).

## Governance under the PNA and prospects for the future

Our examination of the internal and external conditions underpinning different types of rents and rent-management in Palestine shows that these conditions supported in different ways and to different extents a number of different state characteristics. The eventual outcome was therefore to a large extent an open one, and depended critically on the way in which internal developments and external pressures strengthened or changed these determining conditions. Israel appears to have supported the Oslo route as long as it believed that it could create a client state in Palestine. We have argued that there were a number of internal conditions in Palestine that were conducive for the emergence of an integrationist client state, one that could generate an acceptably rapid developmental transformation and thereby make an impact on Palestinian economic and political aspirations. But there was no support in Palestine for a client state based on asymmetric containment. However, for reasons that we have discussed in Khan (this volume), Israel was only prepared to offer a client state based on asymmetric containment.

These inconsistent aspirations fatally undermined the Oslo project, and this experience has critically important implications for the ongoing state-formation process in Palestine. The containment itself created conditions for the strengthening of predatory state characteristics within Palestinian institutions,

Table 2.2: Palestinian conditions and their implications for the consolidation of different state characteristics

| | External conditions | State capacity | Organization of civil society | Organization and capacity of capitalists |
|---|---|---|---|---|
| *Actual conditions in Palestine* | (Israeli control of critical rents, Israeli strategy of asymmetric containment, substantial donor aid) | (Strong policing capacities, centralization, capacity to discipline bureaucrats, blurred division between state and ruling party) | (Fragmented middle class, weak secular opposition, repression of Islamists) | (Low-technology local capitalists, higher technology expatriate capitalists, both politically weak) |
| *State characteristics* | *Implications of actual conditions for the consolidation of different sta te characteristics* | | | |
| *Client-state characteristics* | The PNA accepted a limited client status but *asymmetric containment* made the client state **economically and politically unviable** | The PNA's extensive policing capacity **supported** the consolidation of a client state | Weak and fragmented opposition **supported** the consolidation of a client state | Lower technology capitalists **could potentially support** an *integrationist* client state, but no capitalists supported *asymmetric containment* |
| *Predatory state characteristics* | External conditions thwarting development created **incentives** for predatory state behaviour | Arbitrary state powers **supported** predation, but high enforcement capacity **restrained** predation as state could promote and gain from development | Weak and fragmented opposition **supported** the emergence of predatory state characteristics | Expatriate capitalists with mobile capital **inhibited predation in strategic areas** but immobile, local capitalists were **exposed to predation in non-strategic areas** |

| | | | | |
|---|---|---|---|---|
| *Fragmented clientelist state characteristics* | Easy aid availability **supported** emergence of fragmented clientelist state | Effective repressive capacities meant state paralysis due to demands of competing factions was **very unlikely** | Weak factions unable to challenge state rent allocations: made the consolidation of fragmented clientelism **very unlikely** | Inefficient capitalists **could support** fragmented clientelism by buying factional support to protect inefficient rents, but factions were weak |
| *Developmental state characteristics* | Adverse external conditions created **strong incentives** for developmental interventions, but *asymmetric containment* **limited** developmental possibilities | State capacity to withdraw conditional rents from investors and political factions **supported** strong developmental rent-management capacities, but limited by weak bureaucratic structures | Weak social factions unable to protect inefficient rents: **supported** developmental rent-management | Advanced capitalists were developmental partners of state, small capitalists felt excluded: in general capitalists **supported** state strategies but **with internal conflicts** |

and to a lesser extent enhanced the possibility of a fragmented clientelist state emerging. Most important, though, was the growing recognition amongst the Palestinian leadership that the Israeli version of the client state was not going to be viable, and this must have created strong incentives for progress in the direction of developing embryonic developmental state characteristics. Table 2.2 summarizes our assessment of the conditions underlying the early state formation attempts in Palestine and helps to explain the impasse reached at Camp David in 2000 and the significant challenges facing the construction of a viable Palestinian state in the future.

The security-first route that Israel has always insisted on meant that if Palestinian state formation had to proceed at all, it would have to be achieved through the construction of a client state during an interim period and perhaps beyond. This was the implicit but critical condition under which Israel agreed to enter the Oslo peace process, and remains implicit in the 'road map' that the USA subsequently attempted to impose on the two parties following the second Iraq war. Israel's logic was that it had to maintain significant leverage over policy-making in the emerging Palestinian state to ensure that the new state gave *Israeli* security the priority Israel demanded. However reasonable such an aspiration may have been from an Israeli perspective, the attempt to construct a client state had significant implications for the viability of the Palestinian state-formation process. We have argued that the client-state strategy became unviable because despite pronouncements to the contrary by Israeli policy-makers, Israel failed to maintain, let alone deepen, its economic integration with the Palestinian economy. Instead, Israel sought to main-tain control over Palestinian policy-making through a strategy of asymmetric containment. The adverse implications of this strategy for Palestinian economic and political development meant that in the end, no amount of force could ensure the acceptance by Palestinians of the strategy we have described as *asymmetric containment*.

At the same time, partly in response to the constraints created by Israel's asymmetric containment strategy, and partly driven by its own autonomous nationalism, the PNA also pushed developmental interventions using the limited political and economic powers that it enjoyed. The availability of expatriate Palestinian capital created incentives and opportunities for the leadership to try and exploit the possibility of breaking out of its contain-ment through development. A number of internal conditions supported these moves, including, paradoxically, the centralization of power and the fragmen-tation of opposition groups in Palestinian society. But these moves remained patchy given that they were obstructed by the client-state architecture set up by Oslo and Paris, and given the absence of any international engagement in enhancing these critical developmental capacities of the PNA. We also noted some internal and external conditions that supported the possibility of state consolidation in the direction of predation and fragmented clientelism. Once again, the centralization of executive power created by Oslo, and the histor-

ical fragmentation of potentially powerful internal factions in Palestine
*limited* moves towards these negative outcomes.

Table 2.2 summarizes the key points of our analysis. Our focus on the
political necessity of many rents and of the dynamic economic effects of
others, points to the importance of governance structures that can effectively and efficiently manage rents. This sharply distinguishes our approach
from the good governance agenda. The emerging consensus that the PNA
was failing *because* of its non-adherence to the good-governance criteria is
very misleading since the good-governance framework is underpinned by the
unrealistic assumption that a rent-free economy is a precondition for
economic and political viability. Only if a rent-free economy was essential
for development would good governance reforms that attempt to create a
rent-free economy actually result in a more viable state being constructed
(Khan, Chapter 1). While our reading of economic history leads us to reject
this analysis, it may still be true that corruption or the weakness of democracy did have a role in damaging Palestinian state formation by allowing the
establishment of damaging rents. We discussed this possibility by looking at
the damaging rents underlying a client state, a predatory state, and a fragmented clientelist state and the conditions that would assist each of these to
become dominant. Our analysis of Palestinian conditions suggests that there
were indeed a number of conditions promoting damaging rents and the
associated rent-seeking and corruption associated with them. Our analytical
framework suggests that the most promising way to target the damaging
rents associated with these types of corruption is to address the conditions
that resulted in their creation and maintenance, rather than by pushing
general good governance reforms. Not only are general good-governance
reforms unlikely to be successfully implemented in developing countries,
they would at best have very limited effects for improving economic and
political viability.

Our discussion also shows that an analysis of observed governance failures must be informed by an assessment of the *hierarchy* of institutional and
political factors causing these failures. By hierarchy we mean that some
conditions and factors were more inflexible than others and their prior definition determined the operation of lower level institutions and governance
arrangements. Figure 2.1 summarizes the critical components of the causal
hierarchy that our analysis identifies. The most important institutional characteristic that could not be changed by the PNA was the architecture of
Oslo set up as a result of Israel's insistence that the route to Palestinian
statehood would be subject to Israeli security being satisfactory to a degree
judged adequate by Israel. The insistence on the prioritization of security
and the retention of controls over the emerging Palestine state so that it
delivered this security has not changed post-Oslo and is driving the subsequent 'road-map' to Palestinian statehood.

The result of Israel's security-first requirement under Oslo was the
'client state', with its critical characteristics of externally controlled rents

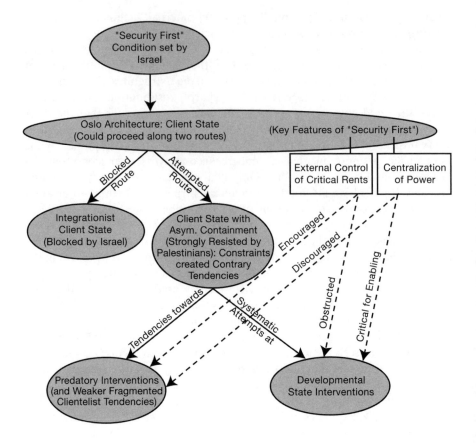

*Figure 2.1* The hierarchy of determinants of Palestinian state characteristics

and executive centralization. But even within this externally determined architecture, further progress was additionally constrained by the fact that Israel's internal considerations took it down the non-viable route of *asymmetric containment* rather than the *relatively* more viable route of *integration*. It is in this context that we have to assess the lower level governance characteristics observed in the PNA. Figure 2.1 shows that the effective blocking of development in the asymmetrically contained client state created the incentives and opportunities both for the development of some predatory and fragmented clientelist characteristics, as well as the emergence of some developmental characteristics.

A number of lessons from the 1994–2000 period are thus likely to be of critical importance for the future. First, any observer of the PNA would have found plenty of instances of maladministration and predatory behaviour at different levels of the administration, particularly at lower levels. Figure 2.1 suggests that it would be very difficult to attack these problems if we focus simply on governance within the Palestinian territories, leaving out of the analysis the higher-level architecture that created strong incentives for predation and limited developmental interventions. This does not mean that some improvements in service-delivery and administration within the Palestinian territories are not possible, but we would argue that significant improvements are unlikely as long as the higher-level constraints are not tackled.

Second, our analysis suggests that given the hierarchy of determinants shown in Figure 2.1, an uncritical application of good-governance reforms can in some instances make matters worse. Suppose the client-state apparatus and asymmetric containment remains. In this context, an attack on the rent-creating capacities of the PNA in the name of good governance can reduce its capacity to intervene developmentally and reduce its financial viability. If so, the consequences could be serious. Such reforms may strengthen predatory characteristics or the emergence of fragmented clientelism. One can, for instance, imagine scenarios where a future leadership could fragment and cynical local leaders resort to predation or aid handouts to survive. Israel may hope that if good governance reforms destroy the rent-creating capacities of the PNA, this may force the leadership to accept a client state with asymmetric containment as a better option than full disintegration. This may well be an exaggerated hope. The PNA is more likely to simply collapse, and with it the prospects of a two-state solution. It is far less likely that even if its leadership eventually capitulates and signs an agreement amounting to an acceptance of a client state with asymmetric containment that this can actually by implemented or even sold to the Palestinian public.

On a positive note, our analysis also points out there are powerful conditions within Palestinian society that could support capacity building in the direction of some variant of a viable developmental state. If an integrationist client state is not on the agenda, the only other route to a viable state is to abandon the client-state route altogether, and to immediately construct a sovereign Palestinian state. This is unlikely to happen, given Israel's historic insistence on security first, and particularly given the possibility that the client state is not just required for Israel's security but also to protect the settlements and perhaps to deal with other aspects of Israel's 'Palestinian problem' (Khan, Chapter 1). But for the historical record, it is important to establish that even the Palestinian quasi-state labouring under a client-state apparatus and asymmetric containment was still able to display significant developmental characteristics. With sovereignty, these rent-creation and rent-management characteristics could have been rapidly developed and institutionalized in a state with substantial capacities for organizing a rapid transformation of Palestinian economy and society. If a sovereign Palestinian state does not emerge, it will not be because the Palestinians lacked the ability to construct a viable state with significant transformation capacities.

# Notes

1  See Kohli (1994) for a comparison of Japanese and British colonial strategies. Kohli points out that the extreme social fragmentation which the Japanese brought about in East Asia may paradoxically have helped the subsequent consolidation of developmental states in East Asia. This is interesting for understanding the significance of the relative autonomy which Arafat's PNA enjoyed.

2  In some sectors such as construction, Palestinians formed more than 40 per cent of the Israeli labour force, but only 15 per cent in agriculture and insignificant in industry (annual Statistical Abstract of Israel for the 1970s and 1980s).

3  The Israeli budget for the occupied territories often ran a surplus, amounting to $17 million in 1992. Palestinians contributed direct and indirect taxes, and deductions for 'social security' (Diwan and Shaban 1999: 10).

4  Israel allocates some 80 per cent of the water from aquifers lying under the West Bank for its own use and sells some 31,184.3 thousand cubic metres to Palestinians.

5  See the reports of the Palestinian General Audit Department.

6  The chairman of the budget committee of the PLC was pressurized to resign because he insisted on presenting to the PLC a report highlighting irregularities in the PNA budget for 1999. The report revealed a missing sum of $126 million, apart from revenues of public investments that did not enter the treasury. The missing sums were deposited in bank accounts abroad for which various people had signing authority subject to the President's approval (Shu'abi 2000: 88–97).

7  Personal communication by an informed contact.

8  Berzeit University, Development Studies Programme, (survey No. 3), February 2001.

9  Although the speakers of the Palestine National Council (PNC) and the PLC were not appointed by Arafat, as the leader of Fateh, he had to agree to such appointments. Non-Fateh Executive Committee members of the PLO were appointed by factions in the PLO as their representatives. Independent members of the Executive Committee of the PLO had to be approved by Arafat.

10  *Wasta* can be used legally, to bypass bureaucracy (e.g. in acquiring a passport or accessing medical treatment), or semi-legally or illegally (but not always immorally) to gain an advantage over others in the competition for jobs or contracts. *Wasta* and *mehsubia* clearly favour intermediate social groups and classes. They should be differentiated from *rashwa* (bribe) which is considered illegal and immoral.

11  In 1992, the number of those employed in professional, technocratic, administrative and clerical type of occupation (excluding Arab Jerusalem) was 35,180 individuals, while the number in mid 2000 totalled (with Arab Jerusalem) some 144,675 individuals. According to the population, housing, and establishment census carried out at the end of 1997, the population of Arab Jerusalem totalled 210,209, and the total population of the WBG totalled 2,895,683 (1,873,476 in the WB, and 1,022,207 in GS). That is, the population of Arab Jerusalem (annexed unilaterally in 1967) formed 7.25 per cent of the total population of the WGS (ICBS 1993: Table 27.20; PCBS 2000b: Table 26; PCBS 1998; PCBS 2000d).

12  In 1999, employment in the local economy of the WBG was: agriculture 14.7 per cent; manufacturing and quarrying: 16.4 per cent; construction: 12 per cent; commerce, hotels, and restaurants: 17.6 per cent; transportation, storage and communication: 6.3 per cent; services and other activities: 33 per cent (MAS 2000: Table 4.2). At the same time, 57 per cent of Palestinians working in Israel and its settlements were employed in construction.

13 One result of this networking is the marginalization of institutions, including the cabinet. It made the president's office the centre of power, and those running the office more powerful than any minister (Shu'abi 2000: 88–97).

14 Ibid, p. 91.

15 In a public opinion poll carried out in February 2001 by the Development Studies Programme at Beirzeit University (survey No. 3), those interviewed with higher education (BA +) had much less confidence in Palestinian negotiators than illiterates, and a much higher support for changing the government than illiterates.

16 Before the Israeli occupation of the WBG in June 1967, there were 11 banks with 31 branches. All were closed by Israeli military orders, and replaced with 5 Israeli banks with 31 branches. Israeli banks limited their roles to commercial transactions between Israel and the occupied territories with no role in development lending. Before the PNA was established, two non-Israeli banks were allowed to operate in WBG under strict Israeli supervision (Gaza Bank in the Gaza strip, and the Cairo-Amman bank in the WB) with eight branches (Karim and Dhahir 1996; MAS 2000.)

17 On 25 September 1997, Palestinian security forces closed down about 20 offices and branches of Islamic charitable institutions suspected of being run by Hamas. In 1998 another 15 NGOs affiliated with Islamic groups were shut down.

18 Arafat was highly distrustful of NGOs, and till 1999 allowed his Ministry of Interior a free hand to control the NGOs, mainly because he saw them as diverting rents from the PNA. Early in 1999, Arafat spokespersons waged a campaign against the NGOs accusing a number of them of corruption and lack of transparency, and their heads of self-aggrandizement and using service delivery for political ends.

19 The World Bank, for the first time in its history, established in 1997 a project to support NGOs directly (the Palestinian NGO Project) without going though government channels, financed by a $10 million grant. The aim was to use NGOs as delivery mechanisms, to improve the institutional capacity of Palestinian NGOs, and to strengthen the relationship between the PNA and Palestinian NGOs.

20 According to MOPIC (1998), total governmental disbursements to NGOs for 1994–98 amounted to US $213 million, which was 79 per cent of the total (US$268), the remainder being from non-governmental sources.

21 By the early 1990s Palestinian NGOs were receiving between $140 and $240 million each year from outside sources. By 1994 (as a result of the Second Gulf War and the Oslo Accords), this assistance dropped to about $90 million, and further to around $60 million in 1995 and 1996 (World Bank 1997: 1–2).

22 Disbursements from the international donor community to the Palestinian areas between 1994 and the end of 1998 amounted to an annual average of half a billion dollars (MOPIC 1999).

23 The main recommendations were to affirm the free market model and the importance of external trade; but also to urge the PNA to oppose obstacles emanating from Israel that affected trade (*The Paltrader*, vol. V, nos. 2 and 3, May/June 2000).

24 See the interview of the director of Paltrade in the Gaza Strip, published in the daily *al-Ayyam* (Ramallah), 1 April 2001, p. 11.

25 For instance, by the president of the Federation of the Chambers of Industry in a press conference attended by the Minister of Economy and Trade, and representatives of the private sector, see *al-Ayyam*, 8 April 2001, p. 11.

## References

Abed, T. G. (1988) *The Palestinian Economy*, London: Routledge.

Amsden, A. (1989) *Asia's Next Giant: South Korea and Late Industrialization*, Oxford: Oxford University Press.

Aruri, A. (ed.) (1989) *Occupation: Israel Over Palestine*, Belmont: The Association of Arab-American University Graduates.

Diwan, I. and Shaban, R. (eds) (1999) *Development under Adversity: The Palestinian Economy in Transition*, Washington: World Bank and Palestine Economic Research Institute (MAS).

Halper, J. (2001) *The Key to Peace: Dismantling the Matrix of Control*, The Israeli Committee against House Demolitions *Mimeo*.

Heiberg, M and Øvensen, G. (1993) *Palestinian Society in Gaza, West Bank, and Arab Jerusalem*, Oslo: FAFO.

Hilal, J. (1998a) The Effect of the Oslo Agreement on the Palestinian Political System in Giacaman, G. and Lønning, D. J. (eds) *After Oslo: New Realities, Old Problems*, London: Pluto Press.

—— (1998b) *The Palestinian Political System after Oslo*, Ramallah: Muwatin, The Palestinian Institute for the Study of Democracy and Beirut: The Institute of Palestine Studies.

—— (2002) *The Formation of the Palestinian Elite*, Ramallah: Muwatin, The Palestinian Institute for the Study of Democracy and Amman: Al-Urdun Al-Jadid Research Centre.

ICBS (Israeli Central Bureau of Statistics) (1993) *Statistical Abstract of Israel* (44).

IMF (International Monetary Fund) (2003) *West Bank and Gaza: Economic Performance and Reform Under Conflict Conditions*, Washington: IMF.

Karim, N. A. and M. Dhahir (1996) 'Views on an Integrated Strategy for Reconstructing the Palestinian Financial Sector', (in Arabic) *Palestine Policy* 3 (11): 110–35.

Kimmerling, B. and Migdal, J. S. (1994) *Palestinians: the Making of a People*, Cambridge, MA: Harvard University Press.

Khan, M.H. (2000) 'Rent-Seeking as Process', in Khan, M.H. and Jomo, K. S. (eds) *Rents, Rent-Seeking and Economic Development: Theory and Evidence in Asia*, Cambridge: Cambridge University Press.

Kohli, A. (1994) 'Where Do High Growth Political Economies Come From? The Japanese Lineage of Korea's "Developmental State"', *World Development* 22 (9): 1269–93.

Maliki, M. *et al.* (2000) *Internal Migration and Returnees in the West Bank and Gaza Strip* (in Arabic), Ramallah: MAS.

MAS (Palestine Economic Policy Research Institute) (2000) *The Economic Monitor* (7).

—— (2001) *The Social Monitor* (4).

MOPIC (Ministry of Planning and International Cooperation) (1998) *First Quarterly Monitoring Report of Donor Assistance*, Ramallah.

—— (1999) *First and Second Quarterly Monitoring Report of Donor Assistance.* Ramallah.

Okuno-Fujiwara, M. (1997) 'Toward a Comparative Institutional Analysis of the Government-Business Relationship', in Aoki, M., Kim, H-K. and Okuno-Fujiwara, M. (eds) *The Role of Government in East Asian Economic Development: Comparative Institutional Analysis*, Oxford: Clarendon Press.

PA (Palestinian Authority) (2000) *Economic Policy Progress Report,* Report of the Palestinian Authority in collaboration with the Staff of IMF.

Pappé, I. (ed.) (1999) *The Israel/Palestinian Question*, London: Routledge.

PCBS (Palestinian Central Bureau of Statistics) (1998) *Population, Housing and Establishment Census Preliminary Results 1997*, Ramallah.

—— (2000a) *Labour Force Survey*, Second Quarter, Ramallah.

—— (2000b) *Labour Force Survey*, Annual Report, 1999, Ramallah.

—— (2000c) *Water Statistics in the Palestinian Territory*, Ramallah.

—— (2000d) *Census of Labour Force (April–June 2000)*, Ramallah.

Pederson, J. and Hooper, R. (eds) (1998) *Developing Palestinian Society: Socio-Economic Trends and their Implications for Development Strategies*, Oslo: Fafo Institute for Applied Social Science. Available online at <http//www.fafo.no/pub/rapp/242/Kap2b.htm> (accessed December 2002).

Peres, S. (1993) *The New Middle East*, London: Shaftesbury.

Perthes, V. (1995) *The Political Economy of Syria under Asad*, London: I.B. Tauris.

Rubin, B. (1999) *The Transformation of Palestinian Politics: From Revolution to State-building*, Cambridge, MA: Harvard University Press.

Shlaim, A. (2000) *The Iron Wall: Israel and the Arab World*, London: Penguin.

Shu'abi, A. (2000) 'A Window on the Workings of the PA: An Inside View', *Journal of Palestine Studies*, XXX (1): 88–97.

UNSCO (United Nations Special Coordinator's Office) (2000) *Report on the Palestinian Economy, With a Special Report on Palestinian Merchandise Trade*, Gaza.

Wade, R. (1990) *Governing the Market: Economic Theory and the Role of Government in East Asian Industrialization*, Princeton: Princeton University Press.

World Bank (1997) *The Palestinian NGO Report Project, Public Discussion Paper*, al-Ram, West Bank.

# 3 Israel and the Palestinian economy

## Integration or containment?

*Adel Zagha and Husam Zomlot*

Our assessment of the Palestinian state formation process depends critically on the economic arrangements with Israel that underpinned the economic and political freedoms of the emerging state. In this chapter, we examine the formal economic arrangements that underpinned the Oslo period. This analysis underlines our analysis of the contradictory moves towards integration and containment that characterized Israeli policy in this first phase of Palestinian state formation. The broad framework that defined the economic constraints facing the Palestinian quasi-state were enshrined in the provisions and limitations set out in the so-called Paris Economic Protocol (PEP)[1] signed shortly after the Oslo Accords. The Paris Economic Protocol circumscribed the financial viability of the PNA and was open-ended enough to allow Israel to interpret its provisions in particularly damaging ways from the perspective of the Palestinians. It allowed Israel to develop aspects of both integration and containment, with features of containment having particularly adverse effects on Palestinian economic development and political viability, as discussed in Chapter 2 by Hilal and Khan. In particular, tax collection and restrictions on trade were used in ways that gave the Israelis asymmetric power over the PNA, and these powers were rapidly used to exert containment when the need arose. Second, the creation of the PNA had huge and negative implications for Palestinian employment in Israel and in Israeli-controlled areas. Once again, Israel used the creation of the Palestinian quasi-state to erect controls over labour movements with immediate effect. In the sphere of labour movements, Israeli strategies attempted to combine integration with containment, by ensuring that labour movements were only allowed after systems had been set up to allow day to day monitoring and control. This not only inflicted huge costs on the Palestinian economy, it also increased its political dependence since closures were increasingly used as a political weapon. Finally, we look at what the Paris Protocol and the interim agreements did not allow. In particular, a Palestinian currency was ruled out. Although a Palestinian currency may not have been economically viable in the interim period, its absence had serious implications for the future as far as the management of the Palestinian economy was concerned and its economic and political sovereignty. In addition to this, the Palestinian quasi-state was prevented from negotiating its own trade and customs treaties with other countries beyond the limited provisions laid out in the Protocol. These provisions helped Israel to develop its containment strategy. We will see in other chapters, particularly Chapter 2 by Hilal and Khan and Chapter 5 by Nasr, that the types of governance institutions that developed under the PNA were often second-best arrangements that developed to deal with unreasonably harsh economic constraints. Moreover, an evaluation of the political and economic viability of the PNA route to state formation has to distinguish between problems due to its own internal governance institutions and those due to external constraints. These issues are further discussed in Chapter 2 by Hilal and Khan.

## The Paris Economic Protocol

Following the Six Day War in 1967, control of the West Bank and Gaza Strip (WBG) had passed from Jordan and Egypt, respectively, to Israel. Since then, the economies of the WBG had become closely integrated with that of Israel. The WBG traded intensively with Israel, and their labour markets came to be intimately linked to Israeli labour demands. At peak times, almost one third of the gainfully employed residents of the WBG came to be employed in Israel, accounting for 7 per cent of total employment in Israel and contributing one quarter of the gross national product (GNP) of the West Bank (WB) and two fifths of that of the Gaza Strip (GS). The Oslo Accords and the PEP marked a significant break in this process of economic integration by introducing control mechanisms that had a serious negative economic effect on Palestinians living in the Occupied Territories.

During the period of military occupation, Israel imposed a *customs union* on the WB and GS together with the following additional elements.

First, limited movements of labour and capital between Israel and the Occupied Territories were allowed. In particular,

- Palestinian workers were allowed to commute on a daily basis to Israel, and
- Israeli capital was allowed to invest in the Palestinian territories. This was mainly in the form of building settlements for Israeli settlers and the related infrastructure and industries. These 'capital flows' were imposed by force and at the expense of Palestinian rights over land. There was a limited amount of subcontracting to Palestinians in certain sectors such as the apparel industry.

Second, the Israeli shekel became legal tender in the Occupied Territories together with the Jordanian dinar and the US dollar. Thus the economy of the WBG was integrated with the Israeli economy on Israeli terms after the ties of the Palestinian economy with its Arab neighbours were cut off.

From the Palestinian perspective, and certainly from the perspective of the PNA, the Oslo Agreement was a gamble that had to deliver a significant change in the relationship of dependence and occupation if the 'peace process' was to succeed. But the road map to independence was by no means clear. The interim period was to be governed by a series of agreements, of which in the economic sphere, the most important was the Paris Protocol on Economic Relations between Israel and the PLO,[2] signed in Paris on 29 April 1994. This covered an interim period defined as the period from 1994 to May 1999. However, because the terminal point of the Oslo Agreements was not well-defined, there was an enormous incentive on the part of Israel to interpret the Interim Agreements as a much more long-lasting arrangement than the Palestinians could envisage. In fact, even after the interim period was technically over, its provisions remained in force because no other arrangements emerged. The main provisions of the PEP were as follows:

- The PEP formalized the *de facto* Customs Union between the WBG and Israel that had come into existence during the period of Israeli military control after 1967. The existing Israeli tariffs continued to serve as the common external tariff (CET) with a few exceptions. But at the same time, quantitative restrictions on the movement of specific agricultural products exported by the WBG were imposed.[3] The quotas were supposed to be annually relaxed until they were supposed to have been phased out by the end of 1998.[4]
- The PEP allowed for a partial opening of the WBG's trade with Jordan and Egypt, and with the rest of the world through these two countries. There were three positive lists (A1, A2, and B) which spelt out items that could be imported from or through Jordan or Egypt at tariff rates different from the CET, and in specific quantities according to the assessment of Palestinian needs as agreed upon between the Palestinian representatives and the Israeli representatives in the Joint Economic Committee (JEC).
- The PEP allowed the PNA to have its own income and corporate tax system but continued to impose the Israeli value added tax (VAT) system allowing a margin of variation of 2 per cent, from 17 per cent to 15 per cent. The argument for imposing the Israeli VAT system on the Palestinian territories was ostensibly to prevent illegal trade flows motivated by tax avoidance.
- Since borders with the outside world were controlled by Israel, the PEP provided a tax-clearance system, according to which Israel collected and transferred to the PNA taxes and customs duties imposed on Palestinian imports from or via Israel. The system required vouchers to

clear the revenues due to the PNA if it could be shown that areas under its control were the place of final destination. A similar tax-transfer system was set up to rebate income taxes collected from Palestinian workers working in Israel.

- The New Israeli Shekel (NIS), the Jordanian dinar and the US dollar were recognized as legal tender in the WBG. The issue of a Palestinian currency was postponed indifinitely, and the PNA agreed that it could not issue a currency of its own unless Israel gave its assent. This in itself resulted in a significant loss of seignorage revenue for the PNA.[5] Furthermore, a limit was set on the PNA's ability to convert shekels at the Bank of Israel (BOI) into foreign currency. A complex equation was established to determine this limit. Furthermore, the BOI was not obliged to convert in any single month more than 1/5 of the semi-annual amount.[6]
- Finally, the PEP recognized that Palestinians would continue to seek employment in Israel. But it did not guarantee them unlimited access to the Israeli labour market. In fact, the PEP explicitly gave the employing side (Israel) the *'right to determine from time to time the extent and conditions of the labor movement into its area'*.[7]

Despite the fine words of the Preamble of the PEP and the justification of these provisions in terms of reciprocity, the document is a peculiar one. Although it was negotiated over a period of six months, its provisions were very often ambiguous in their wording. From the Israeli perspective, vagueness was an advantage as their negotiators were more aware of the range of rents a state could generate through trade and monetary arrangements and they were happy to leave open questions that could be later interpreted in a way favourable to Israel. On the other hand, ambiguity was highly damaging for the Palestinian side because the PEP failed to say anything about working procedures, processes of arbitration or of enforcement that the JEC would follow in case of disagreements.

Given the balance of power between Israel and the PNA, the incompleteness in the arrangements was advantageous for Israel as the meaning of particular clauses or the response to changed circumstances could be interpreted by Israel in line with its strategies at that time. This is why in agreements on economic cooperation, such as the European Union and other free-trade organizations, the interests of weaker countries are often protected by giving them more weight than their relative economic power, and even the power of veto in some cases (Arnon and Weinblatt 2001: F301). In contrast, under the PEP, the JEC was supposed to resolve disputes, but in fact because of the balance of power between the two sides, it eventually played no role in resolving problems. Instead, Israel always had the political and military dominance to impose its interpretation of the Protocol on the Palestinian side.

The JEC was in turn subordinated to the Joint Civil Affairs Co-ordination and Co-operation Committee (CAC). The latter was founded with the mandate to oversee the transfer of responsibilities from the Israeli Civil Administration (the administration that ran the Occupied Territories after 1967) to the PNA. But instead of being a temporary body, the CAC turned out to be a permanent fixture of the 'transition period'. The JEC was composed of economic experts and civil servants from the relevant Israeli and Palestinian Ministries. The CAC was composed of members from the Palestinian Ministry of Civil Affairs and the Israeli Ministry of Defence. It is clear who held the upper hand in this body, and moreover, the Israeli defence establishment was hostile even to the one-sided arrangements in the PEP from the beginning. It is not surprising that despite the PEP identifying the JEC as the vehicle for implementing its provisions (Article II), the JEC proved to be singularly impotent. The JEC rarely assembled and was totally incapable of rectifying either non-implementation or issues of contention between the two sides. Moreover, the lack of regular communications and contacts between the two sides and the vacuum that this created, led to a disempowerment of the JEC with highly negative results. The JEC did not meet regularly and no official minutes for the JEC sessions exist. The JEC lost ground systematically in its first few years and economic matters, closely connected with the implementation of the Protocol, were taken over by other committees, essentially security committees. An examination of the way in which the ambiguous provisions of the Paris Protocol were interpreted and implemented by Israel will illustrate how containment rapidly dominated integration as a description of the relationship between the two economies.

## Israeli rebates of Palestinian taxes

With respect to its fiscal position under the PEP, the PNA was fatally dependent on Israeli rebates of customs and income taxes as described above. However, the PNA shortly discovered that Israel would interpret 'imports' into Palestine in a peculiarly restrictive way. They would only count as imports those goods that were directly imported by *Palestinian* companies via Israel and *not* those imports into Palestinian territories that were first imported by an *Israeli* company for onward shipment to Palestinian territories. Thus products which were initially imported by Israeli companies and then re-exported to the Palestinian territories, were, according to the Israeli interpretation of the PEP, not eligible for the re-claiming of customs duty. The bulk of imports into Palestine came via Israeli companies given the security concerns (not necessarily always justified) that could be used to delay at the ports any imports directly organized by Palestinian companies. Palestinian indirect imports through Israel were estimated to be 60 per cent of all imports from Israel (Shaban and Jawhary 1995: xxvi). According to Shaban and Jawhary (1995: xxxiii) the foregone revenue on indirect imports as a percentage of GDP was about 6 to 7 per cent. It follows that Israel's interpretation of the PEP, which the Palestinian side could do nothing to overturn, resulted in significant revenue loss for the PNA. More significantly, it made the PNA even more dependent on the tax revenues that Israel agreed to remit. The tax issues will be discussed further in Chapter 6 by Fjeldstad and Zagha on the PNA's tax system.

Israel's narrow interpretation of what constitued an import came as a surprise to the PNA, since they justifiably expected imports of foreign goods via Israeli importers to be 'proper imports' given Israel's control of external borders. Therefore, all import charges paid on goods which came into the WBG as indirect imports were actually collected by Israel but not refunded to the PNA. There are also many examples of Palestinian merchants who, in order to avoid delays and complications in Israeli ports (as well as to evade income taxes), disguised the true final destination of their imported goods with the connivance of Israeli traders and customs officials. The consequence was that the PNA lost some of the import taxes that it could have collected from Palestinian importers as well. A related and significant source of fiscal leakage was Israel's refusal to refund to the PNA the relatively high purchase taxes, excise duties and surcharges which were imposed on some locally produced Israeli products exported to the WBG and consumed by the Palestinians. These included *tama*: a mark-up that was applied to all imports, over and above the purchase tax and other tariffs, and *harama*: a kind of *tama* applied only on imports of raw materials.[8] The Palestinian Ministry of Finance estimated the foregone revenues to be around $380 million per year. Approximately $25 million of that total was lost on cigarettes alone. The annual lost revenues represent some 78 per cent of the actually refunded amount in 1997 which was $484.1 million and constituted 59 per cent of the total budget revenues.[9] The Palestinians lost not only the import taxes due to the purchase of Israeli products but also the ability to purchase cheaper products from abroad. The Palestinians had an obvious interest to limit this trade diversion and to favour imports from abroad over Israeli products, but the PEP restricted their ability to do this.

In response to this fiscal leakage, the PNA attempted to capture a larger share of customs revenue by requiring that certain goods for sale in the Palestinian market must be imported through licensed agents to ensure that the imports were recorded as direct. Although these efforts had some success, it was argued (Diwan 1999: 87; Shaban and Jawhary 1995) that customs revenue yield could be increased by several percentage points of GDP if the revenue-sharing formula were abandoned in favour of a presumptive macro formula. The latter would be based on an estimated share of imports into Israel intended for final use in the WBG. There was obviously no scope of negotiating this within the framework of the PEP.

Direct trading through Jordan or Egypt might also partially have helped to solve the problem of fiscal leakage. However, and in spite of all measures to encourage this, non-Israeli foreign trade remained trivial. There was some increase in imports through Jordan and Egypt but it did not exceed 2 per cent of total imports, whereas imports from Israel averaged 75 per cent of aggregate Palestinian imports during 1995–2000 (MAS 2001: 127).

If the unexpected reduction in the PNA's tax base was not bad enough, from the very beginning, Israel inflicted significant costs on the PNA first through delaying and then by periodically freezing the transfer of tax revenues collected for the Palestinians by Israel. Both were used to demonstrate to the PNA that its survival depended on Israel, an essential feature of a containment strategy. The freezing of tax rebates first happened in the summer of 1997 during Netanyahou's government. This was *prima facie* a violation of the PEP, but once again there was no recourse available for the PNA through arbitration or through the JEC. In fact, even before the freezing of its revenues was actually implemented, the PNA was obviously well aware that this was a real possibility and had to take countervailing measures. We see in Chapter 2 by Hilal and Khan that this had significant effects for the PNA's internal governance. Ironically, far from making the PNA more docile, these actions made it more willing to defy Israel in the end.

Israel's interpretation of PEP also had an effect on the PNA's ability to raise *direct* taxes in the Palestinian territories. The articles outlined in the PEP on direct and indirect taxes on local production were replaced by new subarticles in Washington on 28 September 1995. The most important feature of the new article (V, 5b) on direct taxation was that '*no tax shall be deducted at source on income derived by an Israeli from transportation activities, if the point of departure or the point of final destination is in the areas under Israeli tax responsibility*'.[10] This prevented the PNA from taxing a very wide range of economic activities in its territories if any part of the activity could be shown to have originated in Israel. We know now that under the threat of security closures against Palestinians, almost all transportation activities between Israel and the WBG were carried out by Israelis. This is because Israeli transportation was more likely to get through checkpoints, but as a result the PNA lost the ability to tax the income associated with this trade. Even under 'normal' circumstances it could not tax the income generated by tourist agencies and buses operated by Israelis for tourists visiting archeological or religious places in the areas under PNA jurisdiction, simply because their point of departure was Israel or because they were going back to Israel as their final destination. As the political situation deteriorated, more and more trade had to shift to Israeli-based businesses simply to get through checkpoints, with obvious effects on Palestinian revenues.

## Access of Palestinian labour to Israeli labour markets

The effect of the Oslo interim agreements on Palestinian employment in Israel had equally important effects for the Palestinian economy. Israel's policy of trying to immediately establish the principle of physical separation had hugely negative effects on the Palestinian economy. Once again, it is important to recognize that the border closures began long before the eruption of Al-Aqsa *Intifada* in September 2000. In fact, even before the establishment of the PNA, Israel had begun to impose the restrictions on labour movements that would be formalized and extended during the state formation process. The PEP outlined no procedures for determining what an adequate degree of labour market access during the interim period would be from the Palestinian perspective, or how to achieve redress if Israel behaved unreasonably. Given the restrictions on autonomous Palestinian development, labour employment in Israel remained a critical component of Palestinian Gross National Income.

Policies of labour separation were first introduced by Israel during the First Palestinian *Intifada* and these were strengthened following the Gulf War in 1991.[11] It was at this time, in the early 1990s, that the Israeli policy that we describe as containment began to evolve in embryonic form. Before that time, Israel's policy was one of open borders following the 1967 occupation of WBG, as Israel attempted to absorb the territories into the Israel state. The demographic balance eventually persuaded them that this was not a policy consistent with the maintenance of Zionism. Israel's signing up to the Oslo Agreement has to be seen in this context, but its actions following the Agreement show that instead of conceding sovereignty to the Palestinian territories, it saw the Agreement as an opportunity to deepen and perpetuate the containment strategy that was already in place.

Contrary to what was sought by the Oslo Accords and the subsequent PEP,[12] WBG employment in Israeli Controlled Areas (ICA), that is Israel *plus* the settlements, faced new and dramatic restrictions during the Oslo Extended Interim Period (OEIP) which commenced in 1994. These restrictions were part of a *restructuring and separation* of labour markets that transformed the WBG work force working in Israel into a tool that could be manipulated to control the Palestinian territories and place pressure on the Palestinian Authority.

Historically, the separation of Jewish from Arab workers in the Palestinian labour market had been one of the core principles of the Zionist project. Since the onset of the Zionist colonization of Palestine beginning early in the last century, the then newly established Jewish entities or *yishuv*[13] imposed non-market restrictions on employment through formal and informal institutions. This method was intended not only to close off Jewish enterprises to indigenous Palestinian labour but also to ensure a maximum subsidy to newly arriving Jewish workers who might otherwise have left the economically unattractive new colony (Shafir and Peled 2000). Segmentation, exclusivism and the separation of the *yishuv*, and later all of Israel, from the indigenous Palestinian population characterized and shaped the nature of early economic and labour relationships.

The Israeli occupation of the WBG in 1967 was a turning point in this established pattern of labour-market segregation. This was a period of economic boom in Israel, with a growing demand for cheap unskilled labour, particularly in the construction sector. There was also a perceived need to pump cash into the pockets of the captive population in the

Occupied Territories. Thus began a period of relatively free movement of labour from the WBG to Israeli labour markets (Shafir and Peled 2000; Shalev 1992; Arnon *et al.* 1997). Consequently, there was a jump in WBG employment in Israel from 11 per cent of total WBG labour force in 1970 to 38 per cent by 1988.[14]

This rapid integration of the WBG work force into Israel fostered a steep rise in WBG aggregate and per capita income during the 1970s and part of the 1980s.[15] Nevertheless, this was not necessarily a positive outcome for the Palestinian economy. In a context of quite deliberate Israeli policies to undermine production capacities in the WBG, the export of one-third of its unskilled low-paid workers pushed up wages and left the fragile domestic sectors of the WBG economy unable to compete with Israeli products. The decline of agriculture[16] and the stagnation of manufacturing further intensified the dependence of the WBG work force on the Israeli labour market. Finally, the growing Israeli demand for manual and unskilled labour generated a *deskilling* process since WBG workers found it unnecessary to acquire further education or training (Roy 2000). Unskilled workers could often earn more in Israel than skilled workers who were excluded from Israeli labour markets through informal mechanisms and could not find employment within the Occupied Territories because of the absence of indigenous industrialization.

Despite this pattern of labour-market integration being advantageous to Israel, there was a growing realization that Palestinian population growth posed a demographic threat to Israel's Zionist state. The Oslo Agreements can be seen from the Israeli perspective as a response to the demographic threat and it is not surprising that the Interim Period marks yet another turning point in Israel's attitude to the Palestinian labour market. Once again we see a reversion to the policies of separation reminiscent of the early days of Zionism, prior to the expulsions of Palestinians and large-scale Jewish immigration, when Jews were a small minority in a largely Arab entity. Despite the open-ended statements in the PEP on labour-market access, Israel's implementation of labour-market policies during this period was instead consistent with its early history when the Jewish minority could only use Palestinian labour by simultaneously maintaining separation, control and the ability to punish, in other words, asymmetric containment.

The share of WBG employment in ICAs dropped from more than one-third in the pre-Oslo period to an average of 19 per cent in the post-Oslo period. This ratio was particularly low in 1995, 1996 and 1997, that is immediately following the signing of the Agreements, averaging 16, 14 and 17 per cent respectively. It then increased to an average of 22.5 per cent in 1998, 1999 and 2000, which was still significantly lower than in the pre-Oslo period. During this period, the Palestinian labour force was also growing rapidly. Before Oslo, 30 per cent of the Palestinian labour force (and of the Palestinian employed population) worked in Israel. After Oslo, only 16 per cent of the workforce and 19 per cent of the employed population worked in

Israel, the discrepancy reflecting the high unemployment in WBG over this period.[17]

The biggest impact of the new policy was on the Gaza Strip. The latter had a defined and controlled geopolitical boundary and could therefore be easily controlled, while Israel's map of the WB's boundaries was less defined and there was a heavy presence of Israeli settlements here. The evidence showed a significant decline in the GS work force dependent on the Israeli labour market during the OEIP, while in the WB, integration into Israeli labour markets persisted. This was because a higher concentration of Palestinian workers in Israeli settlements and industrial zones was possible inside the WB compared to the GS. This appears to be part of a deliberate Israeli policy of shifting the needed unskilled work force from Israel proper to Israeli enterprises in settlements and border industrial zones. One could also detect a high degree of volatility in the WBG labour flows to ICAs during the OEIP, going up and down in line with Israel's political conflicts with the Palestinian Authority.

Figure 3.1 shows the magnitude of the employment shock that followed Oslo, particularly in Gaza, where it was relatively easier to impose controls on labour movements. Less than 3 per cent of total WBG workers in ICAs came from the GS during April to June 2001 as compared to an average of around 40 per cent during the pre-Oslo period (1967–93). While this exceptionally low share of GS workers can be attributed to the tighter Israeli blockade of the GS compared to the WB during the second quarter of 2001,

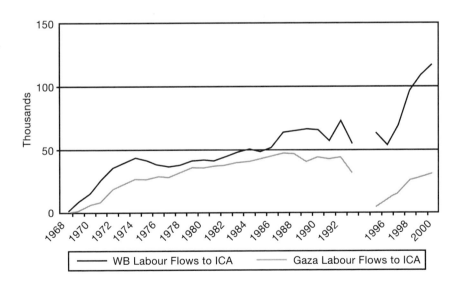

*Figure 3.1*  WBG labour flows to Israel and Israeli-controlled areas (1968–2000)

Table 3.1  WBG employment in domestic and Israeli labour markets (1970–2000)

| Year | Total WB employed | | | Total GS employed | | | Total WBGS employed | | |
|---|---|---|---|---|---|---|---|---|---|
| | Domestic | Israel | Total | Domestic | Israel | Total | Domestic | Israel | Total |
| 1969* | 101.5 | 8.4 | 109.9 | 51.8 | 1.1 | 52.9 | 153.3 | 9.5 | 162.8 |
| 1971 | 91.4 | 25.7 | 117.1 | 51.9 | 8.3 | 60.2 | 143.3 | 34 | 177.3 |
| 1973 | 88 | 38.9 | 126.9 | 46.3 | 22.6 | 68.9 | 134.3 | 61.5 | 195.8 |
| 1975 | 92.3 | 40.8 | 133.1 | 47.6 | 26.1 | 73.7 | 139.9 | 66.9 | 206.8 |
| 1977 | 92.4 | 35.8 | 128.2 | 50.7 | 27.8 | 78.5 | 143.1 | 63.6 | 206.7 |
| 1979 | 93.2 | 40.2 | 133.4 | 46.8 | 34.8 | 81.6 | 140 | 75 | 215 |
| 1981 | 94.3 | 40.4 | 134.7 | 48.2 | 36.5 | 84.7 | 142.5 | 76.9 | 219.4 |
| 1983 | 98.1 | 47.5 | 145.6 | 45.9 | 39.3 | 85.2 | 144 | 86.8 | 230.8 |
| 1985 | 103.7 | 47.5 | 151.2 | 49 | 41.9 | 90.9 | 152.7 | 89.4 | 242.1 |
| 1987 | 114.7 | 62.9 | 177.6 | 54.1 | 46 | 100.1 | 168.8 | 108.9 | 277.7 |
| 1989 | 115.4 | 65.4 | 180.8 | 59.2 | 39.5 | 98.7 | 174.6 | 104.9 | 279.5 |
| 1991 | 123.8 | 55.9 | 179.7 | 65.9 | 41.8 | 107.7 | 189.7 | 97.7 | 287.4 |
| 1993 | 147.7 | 53.6 | 201.3 | 84.4 | 30.4 | 114.8 | 232.1 | 84 | 316.1 |

| | | | | | | | | |
|---|---|---|---|---|---|---|---|---|
| 1995** | 245.8 | 62.2 | 308.0 | 105.4 | 3.6 | 109.0 | 351.2 | 65.8 | 417.0 |
| 1996 | 262.7 | 52.3 | 315.0 | 104.8 | 9.2 | 114.0 | 367.5 | 61.5 | 429.0 |
| 1997 | 283.4 | 68.6 | 352.0 | 114.8 | 14.2 | 129.0 | 398.2 | 82.8 | 481.0 |
| 1998 | 304.0 | 96.0 | 400.0 | 124.9 | 24.1 | 149.0 | 428.9 | 120.1 | 549.0 |
| 1999 | 309.7 | 108.3 | 418.0 | 143.3 | 26.7 | 170.0 | 453.0 | 135.0 | 588.0 |
| 2000 | 351.2 | 116.1 | 467.3 | 163.8 | 29.8 | 193.6 | 515.0 | 145.9 | 660.9 |

Source: Bank of Israel and the Palestinian Central Bureau of Statistics (PCBS), Labour Force surveys, various issues.

Notes: *Data for the pre-Oslo period (1969-93) are from Bank of Israel and Israeli Central Bureau of Statistics (ICBS).

**Data for the post-Oslo period (1995-2000) are derived from the various PCBS Labour Force Surveys.

***There are a number of caveats in comparing numbers of Palestinian workers in Israel. On the one hand, the ICBS and Bank of Israel who provided the first set of data, underestimated the Palestinian population and consequently the Palestinian workers in Israel. According to Sha'ban (1993) there was a 12.5 per cent underestimation. On the other hand, Israeli data excluded Palestinians in East Jerusalem working in Israel while the PCBS subsequently included them. Palestinian workers from Jerusalem are believed to be in the range of 10 to 15 per cent of the total Palestinian workforce (UNSCO 2001). The underestimation by Israeli sources coupled with the addition of workers from Jerusalem by Palestinian sources might balance out. Nevertheless, the data should be interpreted cautiously.

data from previous years show the same trend. Workers from the WB accounted for 95 and 85 per cent of total WBG employment in ICAs in 1995 and 1996 respectively, and an average of 80 per cent during 1998–2000.

Table 3.1 shows a gradual increase in West Bank Palestinian employment in Israeli Controlled Areas in the period following the Oslo Accords. Since labour movements to Israel proper were being constrained during this period, as evidenced by the Gaza data, the West Bank labour flows reflect growing Palestinian employment in Israeli settlements and industrial zones *within* the WB during this period, rather than in Israel proper. Unfortunately, there are no accurate statistics on Palestinian workers working in settlements pre- and post-Oslo. Israeli sources did not provide separate numbers of workers in settlements and industrial zones, nor did the Palestinian Central Bureau of Statistics for the post-Oslo period.[18] However, available data suggests that WB workers in Israeli settlements account for more than 30 per cent of WB workers in 'Israel' while in the GS the figure is in the range of 5 to 10 per cent according to UNSCO estimates.[19] The expansion of Israeli settlement-building during this period required more employment particularly in the construction sector and this together with greater restrictions of labour flows to Israel itself are the most important factors behind this trend.

This partly explains an apparent paradox in these trends, since we also observe a surge in WBG labour flows to ICA in the third-quarter 2000 – just before the eruption of the Second *Intifada* on 28 September 2000. The number of WBG workers in ICA grew from a low of 61,500 workers in 1996 to 116,000 in 2000 (excluding around 30,000 Palestinian workers from East Jerusalem). Thus by 2000 Palestinian employment in Israel was higher compared to the pre-Oslo period (when the average employment was 76,400 during 1968–93) and even higher than the 115,600 peak reached in 1992. But the aggregate figures should not be confused as evidence of growing integration. Some of the employment growth was, as we have argued, due to the recording of employment within the occupied territories in settlements and industrial zones that now counted as ICAs. But in addition, Israel interpreted and implemented the PEP in such a way that allowed it to set up an extensive network of checkpoints and virtual borders. Over time, this gave it the ability to stop labour movements *at any time* while allowing labour movement on a daily basis at its convenience. Once this new labour control structure had been established, labour mobility on Israeli terms was allowed, but now with a great deal of uncertainty and vulnerability on the Palestinian side. This was clearly demonstrated by the almost total closures that Israel could inflict at short notice following the outbreak of the Second *Intifada* in September 2000. WBG labour flows to ICAs came to a virtual halt in the first weeks of the Al-Aqsa *Intifada* and increased to only 74,000 by 2001, of which 32,000 were from East Jerusalem and only 2,000 from GS, according to the PCBS labour force surveys.[20] Thus with respect to the labour market, the PEP continued to maintain the dependent status of the Palestinian terri-

*Table 3.2* Population and labour in the West Bank and Gaza Strip

| Year | Population (in thousands) | Labour force | Total employed persons | Employment in Israel (%)* | Unemployment (%)** |
|------|------|------|------|------|------|
| 1970 | 969.9 | 181.4 | 173.6 | 11.9 | 4.1 |
| 1975 | 1092.3 | 209.1 | 206 | 32.5 | 1.0 |
| 1980 | 1172 | 222.7 | 217.6 | 34.9 | 1.3 |
| 1985 | 1323 | 251.2 | 242.1 | 36.9 | 3.6 |
| 1990 | 1563 | 307.8 | 296.5 | 36.3 | 3.6 |
| 1993 | 1800.3 | 338.5 | 315.8 | 26.6 | 6.7 |
| 1996 | 2630.8 | 563.5 | 432 | 14.2 | 23.8 |
| 1997 | 2783.1 | 584.8 | 467.2 | 17.1 | 20.3 |
| 1998 | 2897.5 | 623.3 | 533.6 | 21.7 | 14.4 |
| 1999 | 3019.7 | 671.6 | 591.1 | 22.8 | 11.8 |
| 2000 | 3150.1 | 695.2 | 595.2 | 18.8 | 14.1 |

Notes: (*) As a percentage of the Palestinian labour force, there is little difference if we look at Palestinian employment in Israel as a percentage of the total Palestinian employed population.

(**) Unemployment rates are the official figures.

Source: For 1970-93: ICBS 1996: Table 3.2. For 1996-2000: MAS 2001: xvii.

tories, and allowed significant restructuring and separation on Israeli terms that increased the vulnerability of Palestinian labour. Without taking into account these details, it is difficult to explain why Palestinian dissatisfaction and anger was increasing at a time when ostensibly the Israeli labour market was becoming more receptive of Palestinian labour in the early 1990s.

The employment figures on their own do not give an accurate account of the pressures on the Palestinian labour market since one of the important characteristics of the Palestinian territories had been a dramatic growth in population. Table 3.2 shows that the population *tripled* between 1970 and 2000. The release of the latest census conducted in December 1997 by the Palestinian Central Bureau of Statistics presents reasonably accurate figures on the Palestinian population and labour force. According to the census, the Palestinian population of East Jerusalem, West Bank and Gaza were 210,000 1,600,100 and 1,002,207 respectively (PCBS 1998). A youthful population and a rapid growth rate characterize the Palestinian demography. Almost half of the Palestinian population is under the age of 15, which explains the remarkably high 1:5 dependency rate in the WBG.[21] Between 1997 and 2000, the Palestinian population in the WBG grew at an annual rate of 4.2 per cent, one of the highest growth rates in the world (PCBS 1999). The unemployment rate reached a peak in 1996 with almost a quarter of the labour force actively seeking work. Paradoxically, unemployment reached its lowest level in the third quarter of 2000 when only 10 per cent were unemployed.[22] Clearly there is a link between growing Palestinian political unrest and the institutionalization of the labour control and separation architecture.

## Economic effects of Israeli security closures

Closely related to the policy of labour separation described above was the system of security closures that Israel constructed during the Oslo period. Starting from March 1993, the very beginning of the Oslo period, Israel started a systematic policy of closing off Palestinian areas partially or totally. Closures not only prevented Palestinian labour moving to Israel, but very often also prevented movements *within* the Palestinian territories. On average the number of days of closures (with some variations between WB and GS) increased from 20 days in 1993 to 140 days in 1996. It then began to decline, reaching a low of 10 days in 1999 but rose again to reach 60 days in 2000 (MAS 2001: 9). The border closure after the outbreak of the confrontation between the PNA and Israel in September 2000 was the worst of these and had devastating effects on the Palestinian economy.

One of the core problems was the distinction in the Interim Agreement (to which the PEP is attached) between 'functional jurisdiction' and 'territorial jurisdiction'. The PNA had both jurisdictions only in area A (mainly limited to urban areas in the WBG) but only 'functional' jurisdiction in areas B and C (which separate the urban concentrations into isolated pockets) – therefore, it had no territorial jurisdiction in areas B and C. The problem was that the execution of some of the 'functional' jurisdictions stipulated in the PEP were severely hampered by the lack of territorial jurisdiction over the borders and passages (area C) connecting the Palestinian areas. For instance, the PEP guaranteed free trade to the PNA without allowing the PNA any jurisdiction over borders and passages. A host of security measures hindered trade both internally and externally, and these got worse precisely at moments when growing tensions required an easing of economic constraints. These security measures in effect constituted Non Tariff Barriers. They included permits, import licenses, security checks and delays, the stipulation of (Israeli) import agents, clearing/shipping agents and insurance agents, and so on. These measures resulted in high transportation, storage, insurance and clearance costs with obvious economic effects.

The border closure policy affected both the flows of people (mainly workers), but also of goods and services. We can identify three basic categories of losses for the Palestinian quasi-state directly caused by the border closure policy. First, there was an impact due to the loss of employment. This in turn can be broken down into the loss of income tax generated on the employment of Palestinian workers in Israel, the steep impact on unemployment in the Palestinian areas, and the need to redistribute part of the

PNA's own rents to large numbers of unemployed persons and their families to cushion the impact of the closure on them. Second, there was the effect on trade. We have seen that the PNA lost significant amounts of VAT and import duties because closures induced trade diversion. Imports into the Palestinian areas increasingly had to be carried out through Israel, implying both a loss of revenue and a growing dependence on relatively expensive Israeli products.

Finally, closures had an impact on the integration of the West Bank economy with the Gaza Strip. This meant not only the loss of revenues that could have accrued to the PNA from more trade and integration of the WB and GS. It also forced a disadvantageous integration between enclaves of the Palestinian economy and the Israeli economy that amounted to a loss of control by the PNA over economic policy-making. Trade between the West Bank and Gaza had to transit through Israel. This trade could have been documented, checked and let through in either direction without any threat to security. However, no provisions were explicitly made in the PEP to facilitate transit trade. This allowed the Israelis to virtually choke off trade between the two Palestinian enclaves. The Palestinian Ministry of Trade and Economy estimates that internal trade between these two areas declined by one-third during 1994–2000. A devastating effect of this decline was that investment in internal trade declined sharply from $7.6 billion in 1994 to *minus* $2.4 billion in 1999 implying disinvestment in internal trade in the WBG.[23] Not surprisingly, trade with Israel, and the trade deficit, increased sharply. Palestinian exports to Israel increased from 90 per cent of total exports in 1995 to 94 per cent in 2000, while imports from Israel increased from 75 per cent of total imports to 79 per cent over the same period (MAS 2001: 127–8).

These trends put more pressures on the PNA and limited its power to generate rents and revenues from internal trading. At the same time, they deepened the dependence of the Palestinian economy on Israel. Moreover, Israel found itself in a comfortable position in terms of the revenues it collected on behalf of the PNA which it could directly appropriate to pay debts of the Palestinians to Israeli public firms like the water company MECOROT and the Israeli Electricity Company. This further limited the autonomy of the PNA to influence the allocation of resources.

The effect of security measures including inspections, passes and transport arrangements that directly inhibited trade could not be addressed at all within the JEC. One of the major problems of the PEP was that it was a protocol attached to other agreements. This made the implementation of the PEP conditional on the 'security' arrangements as stipulated in these agreements. However, the way in which Israel tried to achieve its security in the context of the interim agreements imposed harsh costs on the Palestinian economy and made it even more difficult for the PNA to deliver security to the Israelis. Once again, there was no mechanism to negotiate in a balanced way the inter-dependence between security and economic issues. The result was a steady worsening of economic constraints in the Palestinian territories brought about by Israel's self-defeating attemtps to achieve a one-sided improvement in security.

Finally, there were other, less important examples of problematic interpretations of PEP that resulted in significant disadvantages for the Palestinian side. For instance, Article III, 12 which was concerned with the importation of petroleum products, allowed importation from Jordan, provided the petroleum met Jordanian standards. However, the caveat in the text that Jordanian standards should meet average EU or US standards made matters difficult. The paragraph was so confusing that it was not clear whether petroleum products that met Jordanian standards were allowed to be imported only from Jordan or also from other countries. Perhaps not surprisingly, in the eight years or so after the signing of the PEP, petroleum products were exclusively imported from Israel.

In general, Israeli standards and specifications are stricter than international norms and serve to protect the Israeli market. As far as Palestinians are concerned, these are simply trade barriers disguised as product specifications; making it virtually impossible for the underdeveloped Palestinian economy to compete with standards that are even higher than international ones. Moreover, such regulations pushed the Palestinians to import from Israeli producers in order to ensure that standards are met and additional costs of failing to comply are avoided. These standards, combined with the harassment of potential investors particularly from the Palestinian diaspora were used to hold back potential investments in the WBG and thereby limited the production base of the economy. At the same time, these restrictions limited the PNA's power to generate rent from these potential investors because many of them postponed their investment plans till a future date when the investment climate became conducive to long-term investments.

Another example is that Israel and a number of other countries insisted that imports to the PNA areas must be organized through Israeli import agencies for no obvious reason.[24] Similarly, insurance of imported products had to be organized through Israeli insurers despite the fact that the PEP stipulates symmetrical treatment.[25] Thus Palestinian import agencies, insurance companies and the Palestinian trucking and transportation industry were all excluded from benefiting from the flow of imports.

Ultimately, the major flaw in the PEP was its failure to address the issue of Palestinian sovereignty. The establishment of a customs union with Israel based on Israeli trade regulations and the imposition of arbitrary trading restrictions, Israeli control of labour flows, the lack of direct access to international trade borders with the rest of the world, and the lack of a domestic Palestinian currency, imposed severe limitations on the Palestinian economy and reflected the absence of even minimal political sovereignty. Far from being a framework that would allow the development of greater economic integration, the evidence suggests that the PEP allowed Israel to formalize its attempts to construct an institutional framework for containment. Since the PEP and the interim framework in general was framed in an open-ended way, it allowed Israel as the dominant power to interpret the agreements in ways that deepened Palestinian economic dependence and allowed Israel to use this dependence as a political tool. This was possible because the PEP was an incomplete contract between the PNA and Israel, which left the question of interpretation open, thereby giving the stronger party (the Israelis) an advantage given their superior bargaining power. While in the short-term this was of great advantage to Israel, it is paradoxical that the failure to transfer sovereignty to the PNA rapidly and meaningfully may have had devastating long term effects not just for Palestinian state formation but for the future of Israel as well.

## Notes

1  The PEP was first signed in Paris in 1994 and was amended in Washington in September 1995.
2  See the Israeli–Palestinian Interim Agreement on the West Bank and the Gaza Strip, Washington DC, 28 September 1995, Annex V: Protocol on Economic Relations, (JMCC 1996). This document will also be referred to as the PEP as it is an extension of the initial agreement.
3  The products were poultry, eggs, potatoes, cucumbers, tomatoes and melons. All these products were overproduced in the WBG in relation to domestic consumption, therefore the surplus had to be disposed of in the only nearby market, i.e. Israel.
4  They were only relaxed in 1999. However, with the eruption of the September 2000 *intifada* and the subsequent closure and siege policy against the Palestinians, new quotas were imposed on many Palestinian exports from month to month depending on the security conditions.
5  Fisher (1982) argues that seigniorage represents a siginificant source of government income especially for less-developed countries where the currency-to-GDP ratio is typically high. There were different estimates of the potential seigniorage that the PNA could have captured. Estimates range from 4 per cent of GNP (Hamed and Shaban 1993: 133), 4.5 per cent of GDP per year in the period immediately after the introduction of the currency declining to 1 per cent to 2 per cent of GDP afterwards (Arnon and Spivak 1996: 4) and more recently between 3.62 per cent to 5.72 per cent of GNP per year which translates into 13–20 per cent of the PNA's revenues (Schiavo 2000: 174) These amounts would be sufficient to cover the total deficit in the PNA's budget. Zagha (1996: 259) estimated that a once-and-for-all withdrawal of the NIS from the WBG would have provided the PNA with $537.8 million (about 45 per cent of 1991 GDP), an amount sufficient to rebuild the infrastructure of the area without having to wait for donors' assistance or having to cope with the priorities of their agenda.
6  See the PEP Article IV on 'Monetary and Financial Issues' items 15–18, (JMCC 1996: 157–8).
7  See the PEP Article VII, 1 on 'Labour' (JMCC 1996: 163).
8  In 2001 Israel abolished purchase taxes on a variety of imported goods, including electrical appliances shortly after agreeing to transfer the revenue from these taxes to the PNA. The move was taken without any consultation with the PNA as was stipulated for in the PEP. The result of this move was a reduction of the revenue that should have been transferred to the PNA. However, we do not have enough information to estimate such a loss.

9  These are estimates of the IMF resident mission in the West Bank and Gaza Strip.
10  See the PEP (JMCC 1996: 159). Italics and underlining are added.
11  This policy was first introduced in Gaza in 1989 when Israeli authorities prevented workers from entering Israel without a valid Israeli ID and a magnetic card. The post-1991 period, however, witnessed tighter measures that applied the same requirements to workers from the West Bank and further required work permits for all Palestinians intending to commute to Israel for work. According to UNSCO (1997), there have been 469 comprehensive closure days during the period 1993–99 that disrupted 16 per cent of normal workdays.
12  The PEP sought to maintain the status quo of customs union and free movement of goods and containment of labour mobility between Israel and the Palestinian administered territories.
13  Jewish communities in Palestine before the declaration of the state of Israel in 1948.
14  Israel and Israeli controlled areas include Israel, Israeli settlements in the WBG and border industrial zones that are controlled by Israel, for example the Irez Industrial zone in the northern Gaza border with Israel.
15  Per capita GNP growth rate averaged 7.1 per cent during the 1970s and 1980s (World Bank 1993: 17).
16  For example, agricultural share of WBG domestic employment fell from 31.6 per cent in 1970 to 16 per cent in 1987. See Roy (2001: 213).
17  Labour force participation rate in the WBG increased from 39 per cent in 1995 to 41.6 in 1999 and declined to 37.5 per cent in 2000 due to the severe and extended closures during the fourth quarter of the year when the Second Palestinian *Intifada* started. Data on unemployment also shows a historically high rate, reaching as high as 24 per cent in 1996 and averaging 18 per cent in the period 1995–2000. Population growth rate did not fall beyond the 4 per cent during the OETP. See PCBS *Annual Report*, 1999 and various PCBS *Labour Force Surveys*.
18  Palestinian workers tend not to report such work following the PNA's decision to prevent Palestinian labour flows to settlements. The PNA considered working in Israeli settlements in the WBG to be illegal and penalized those who did so after 1996.
19  According to UNSCO, the daily average of Palestinian labour flows to Israeli settlements and industrial zones (ISIZ) was 12,000 in the period prior to September 2000. UNSCO's estimates of labour flows to ISIZ showed less volatility as compared to flows to Israel proper. (See UNSCO *Economic and Social Conditions in the West Bank and Gaza* and *Report on the Palestinian Economy*, various issues.) UNSCO relies on Israeli sources, as Palestinians do not provide data on this category for political reasons. We believe that Israelis significantly underestimate flows of Palestinian workers to ISIZ. An upward trend in employment in ISIZ would reflect Israeli settlement expansion and would embarrass the PNA.
20  See PCBS, *Labour Force Survey*, (April–June 2001). This survey added a new category to distinguish Palestinian workers from the WB who hold an Israeli ID or a foreign passport and are working in Israel. This category mainly consists of Palestinians from East Jerusalem working in Israel and accounts for around 45 per cent of total WB workers in Israel (32,000) in the second quarter of 2001.
21  The labour force, which includes all persons over 15 years of age who are working or searching actively for work, represents only 22 per cent of the total population (a total of 633,000 in (1999). This means that every working Palestinian sustains five persons. In case of unemployment, five persons are without a source of income.

22 PCBS *Main Indicators* and PCBS *Labour Force Survey: Main Findings* (July–September 2000), published November 2000.
23 The decline was sharper in the WB than in the GS. See MAS (2001: 112).
24 Few Palestinians were able to become direct import agents for international brands. Therefore, for the majority of imports, Palestinian agents were sub-agents for Israeli import agents.
25 This is another example of how the PEP is an incomplete contract. For more on incomplete contracts see Hart (1995).

## References

Abed, G. (1988) *The Palestinian Economy: Studies in Development under Prolonged Occupation*, London: Routledge.
Arnon, A., Luski, I., Spivak, A. and Weinblatt, J. (1997) *The Palestinian Economy: Between Imposed Integration and Voluntary Separation*, Leiden: Brill.
Arnon, A. and Spivak, A., (1996) 'On the Introduction of a Palestinian Currency, *The Middle East Business and Economic Review*, 8 (1): 1–14.
Arnon, A. and Weinblatt, J. (2001) 'Sovereignty and Economic Development: The Case of Israel and Palestine', *The Economic Journal*, 111 (472): 291–308.
Bank of Israel (various years) *Annual Reports*, Jerusalem.
Diwan, I. (1999) 'International Economic Relations: Access, Trade Regime and Development Strategy', in Diwan, I. and Shaban, R. A. (eds) *Development under Adversity: The Palestinian Economy in Transition*, Washington: The World Bank and MAS.
Farsakh, L. (1999) *The Implementation of Labour Related Articles in the 'Protocol on Economic Relations Between Israel and the PLO': A Critical Assessment*, Ramallah: MAS.
Farsakh, L. (2001) 'Palestinian Labour Mobility and the Redefinition of Economic Boundaries between Israel and the West Bank and Gaza', Paper presented to the Middle East Economic Association and School of Oriental and African Studies conference: 'Global Changes and Regional Integration: The Redrawing of Economic Boundaries in the Middle East and North Africa', London, 20–2 July.
Fischer, S. (1982) 'Seigniorage and the Case for a National Money', *Journal of Political Economy* 90 (2): 295–313.
Hamed, O. and Shaban, R. A. (1993) 'One-sided Customs and Monetary Union: The Case of the West Bank and Gaza Strip under Israeli Occupation', in Fisher, S., Rodrik, D. and Tuma, E. (eds) *The Economics of Middle East Peace: Views from the Region*, Cambridge: MIT Press.
Hart, O. (1995) *Firms, Contracts, and Financial Structure*, Oxford: Clarendon Press.
ICBS (Israeli Central Bureau of Statistics) (1996) *Statistical Abstract of Israel*, issue 1012.
JMCC (Jerusalem Media and Communication Centre) (1996) *'Israeli–Palestinian Interim Agreement on the West Bank and the Gaza Strip', Washington DC, 28 September 1995, and the 'Declaration of Principles on Interim Self-Government Arrangements', Washington DC, 13 September 1993*, Jerusalem: JMCC.
MAS (Palestine Economic Policy Research Institute) (2001) *The Economic Monitor*, Special Issue 1994–2000, December. Jerusalem.
PCBS (Palestinian Central Bureau of Statistics) (1998) 'Population Census: Main Findings', Press release.
—— (1999) *Population Projection for 1997–2000*, Ramallah: PCBS.

—— (various issues) *Labour Force Survey*, Ramallah: PCBS.

Roy, S. (2001) *The Gaza Strip: The Political Economy of De-development*, 2nd edn, Washington DC: Institute for Palestinian Studies.

Schiavo, S. (2001) *The Rationale for a Palestinian Currency, in Israel/Palestine Center for Research and Information (IPCRI) The Strategy of Palestinian Monetary Policy: Introducing A New Currency*, Jerusalem: IPCRI.

Shaban, R. A. and Jawhary, M. (1995) *The Palestinian-Israeli Trade Arrangements: Searching for Fair Revenue Sharing*, Jerusalem: MAS.

Shafir, G. and Peled, Y. (2000) *The New Israel: Peacemaking and Liberlization*, Boulder, CO: Westview Press.

Shalev, M. (1992) *Labour and the Political Economy in Israel*, Oxford: Oxford University Press.

UNSCO (United Nations Special Coordinator's Office) (various) *Economic and Social Conditions in the West Bank and Gaza*, Quarterly Reports, Autumn 1996, Spring 1997, Summer 1997, Spring 1998, Autumn 1998, Spring 1999 and Summer 2000, Gaza.

—— (1997) *Special Report on Israeli Closure Policy*, Gaza.

—— (2001) *Report on the Palestinian Economy*, Gaza.

World Bank (various issues) *The West Bank and Gaza Update*, The World Bank Group: Quarterly Publications of the West Bank and Gaza Office.

—— (1993) *Developing the Occupied Territories: An Investment in Peace*, 6 vols, Washington DC: World Bank.

—— (2000) *The Impact of Prolonged Closures on Palestinian Poverty*, Special Report from the West Bank and Gaza Office, November.

Zagha, A. (1996) 'A Monetary Alternative for the Palestinian Economy: A Palestinian Currency', *Middle East FORUM*, Issue 1: 253–63.

—— (2000) 'Permanent Status Trade Relations between the State of Palestine and the State of Israel', in Benhayoun, G. *et al.* (eds) *Regional Cooperation in a Global Context*, Paris: L'Harmattan.

# 4 PNA political institutions and the future of state formation

*Inge Amundsen and Basem Ezbidi*

The state formation process in Palestine that started in 1993 with the Oslo Agreements came to an almost complete halt with the collapse of the Camp David talks. The onset of the Second *Intifada* in late 2000 and the Israeli reoccupation of most of the West Bank and Gaza in 2002 marked a significant setback to this process. From its establishment to the eruption of the Second *Intifada*, the Palestinian National Authority (PNA) carried out several transformational initiatives as part of a complex state formation process. A Palestinian state apparatus with political mechanisms was established and steadily enhanced. This happened despite the fact that the Oslo Agreements gave the PNA only partial control of national governance, despite the fact that the status of the territory remained unsettled, and in the face of political, social, and economic challenges common to, and often more serious than, those in other emerging states.

Based on and modulated primarily from the Palestinian Liberation Organization (PLO), this rudimentary state developed a presidency, a number of ministries and other executive and administrative bodies, as well as an elected legislative body and a judiciary branch. As a system of governance with formal as well as informal structures and mechanisms of authority, the PNA was developing institutional and decision-making characteristics that pointed towards contradictory tendencies in terms of the state type and political system that was emerging. These characteristics were paradoxical in terms of their extent and direction, as well as in terms of their impact on the nature of the emerging state and on its potential to evolve into an efficient, developmental polity (see Chapter 1 by Khan and Chapter 2 by Hilal and Khan).

The observed and perceived tendencies gave room for contradictory interpretations regarding the nature and possible future developments of the Palestinian state. The Palestinian–Israeli conflict over territory and sovereignty tremendously influenced the structures and functions of the PNA, and this made some commentators argue that a client state – of Israel and of the donor community – was being created in Palestine (Samara 2000). This view asserted that the PNA was only able to secure and allocate externally generated resources and rents in exchange for accepting and guarding the peace process with Israel. There were others who primarily considered the internal factors, who tended to see the PNA as an extension of the PLO, and saw mixed and not very positive trends in terms of democracy, transparency and accountability. And there were commentators who considered the PNA as a quasi-state paving the ground for a clientelist/neopatrimonial state.[1] They based their assessment on the argument that the PNA was allocating property rights and distributing generated rents to powerful and important groups (such as PLO bureaucrats, capitalists and the security chiefs), in exchange for stability and legitimacy (Brynen 1995). While some commentators went as far as to conclude from the conflicting and contradictory trends that a predatory quasi-state was being developed, we argue that the outcome was open and there were tendencies in different directions.

The Palestinian process of state formation also included a number of characteristics that bode well for a developmentally oriented state that could ensure the transformation of Palestine into an economically and politically dynamic and viable entity; a developmental state. Indeed at the outset, the PNA seemed to have the capacity, i.e. the coherence, coordination, legitimacy and political will necessary to bring about deep social, economic and political transformations. However, the obstacles were almost insurmountable and certain factors came to point in the opposite direction: the fragmentation of its territory, the competition over scarce resources and the use of state resources to buy the support of factions and groups in society. This was necessary for political survival in the short run, but our main argument is that this was probably detrimental to the state's developmentalist capacities in the long run.

First, we will give a short overview of the Palestinian political system and its main institutional characteristics in order to scrutinize the political and organizational structure and capacity of government under the PNA. Second, we will assess the scope, direction and extent of the utilization of coercion and control and the way this may have impacted upon the political system. Third, we will attempt to assess the political will to redistribute resources to productive forces that are beneficial to society. Analysis of these elements will allow us to assess relevant points of strength and weakness of the developmental state model in Palestine. However, any analysis of these tendencies has to be qualified by the fact that the first phase of Palestinian state formation was very brief. It lasted from mid-1994, when PLO cadres returned from exile and the PNA was established on parts of the occupied territories of Gaza and the West Bank, to the Second *Intifada* and the Israeli reoccupation in late 2000. Because of this, and because much vital information is lacking, we cannot be sure whether the Palestinian state would have become a developmental state or not. For instance, we cannot establish the extent to which the PNA had the capacity to regulate rents and rent-opportunities in a way that ensured economic dynamism, but we can draw attention to some background factors, in particular, to the capacity and the will of the PNA to do so eventually. We thus hope to enrich the debate by pointing to the strengths as well as the weaknesses of the political and governance apparatus, and some of the structural factors behind these strengths and weaknesses.

## Capacity: presidentialism and rapid transformation

In order to make the social and economic transformations necessary for development, any developing state needs critical state capacities. As noted by Khan in Chapter 1, state capacity in developmental terms includes a state's ability to allocate resources to dynamic and productive classes and groups and away from property holders who no longer play a productive role. It also includes the proper management and regulation of access to resources, such as property rights, credits, and opportunities for rents, in order to ensure growth and stability in the developing economy. The state's capacity includes the power to discipline those who capture rents and resources, in order to make sure that damaging rents do not proliferate and necessary rents are used productively and not plundered or wasted.

The political and institutional power of a state rests partly on formal institutional arrangements, that is, on the way power is constitutionally concentrated and distributed. The degree of power concentration will, for instance, be reflected in the formal structures of the state, in the division of power between the executive, the parliament, and the judiciary, and between political and administrative bodies. Furthermore, it will be reflected in the structure of the party system, the electoral system, and in the way power is concentrated (or distributed) in territorial terms.

## The Palestinian Authority

The Palestinian political system (1994–2000) was formally a mixed type of government with presidential and parliamentary elements existing side by side. The presidential element was apparent through the president who derived his legitimacy from the people through direct election and was represented in the form of the office of the presidency. The parliamentary element was manifest in the presence of an elected council (the Palestinian Legislative Council (PLC)) with the authority of enacting laws and guiding public policies. Next to these institutional powers stood, of course, the judiciary.

Although the Palestinian political system was formally a mixed type of government, it was closer to the presidential mode of government, with a high degree of power concentration. The executive branch enjoyed in formal terms almost unrestricted powers, with few countervailing and balancing institutional powers compared to counterparts in other polities. Despite an increasing pressure from inside as well as outside for democratic reforms, and despite certain reforms carried through and more on the agenda, efficient and institutionalized checks and balances never fully developed.

Represented mainly by the presidency, the executive supervised the various political, economic, financial, administrative and semi-diplomatic fields in addition to the supervision of negotiations and the implementation of the various agreements and treaties with Israel and foreign countries. Furthermore, occasionally through the cabinet, it supervised the administrative organs, prepared and approved the annual budget before its presentation to the PLC, initiated and proposed legislation to the council, and issued secondary legislation, including orders, decrees, and regulations. It signed the legislation enacted by the PLC, set up the courts and appointed judges, and granted pardons and commuted sentences.

The structure of the executive branch was rather intricate because of a direct overlap of PNA and PLO institutions (Sayigh and Shikaki 1999). One of the clearest examples was that on the one hand there was the PLC and its Executive Authority (government), and on the other hand there was the Palestine National Council (PNC, the PLO parliament-in-exile) and the PLO Executive Committee. The PNA cabinet and the PLO Executive Committee were hardly distinguishable and largely overlapping, both in functions and membership. Furthermore, there was a 'Palestinian leadership', a loosely defined group of PNA ad PLO officials. This body was designed to handle the negotiations with Israel, but it also dealt with internal affairs, operating in a crisis management style. In fact, meetings of this organ replaced the cabinet for all practical purposes. Dominated by the PLO, the policy decisions of this body were not subject to accountability to either the PLC or any other PNA body (Sayigh and Shikaki 1999; Rubin 1999).

While the PNA was the official governing body, much of the actual authority rested with the PLO. Note that the PLO did not recognize the PLC as the sole representative of the Palestinians, because the PLC constituency covered only the estimated 2.7 million inhabitants of the occupied territories (in 1996) and not the estimated 3.5 million Diaspora Palestinians. The PNC, on the other hand, considered itself as the representative of all Palestinians, both in the occupied territories and in the Diaspora. While in formal terms the PNA had the authority of administering the internal affairs of the occupied territories, it had no authority in the spheres of foreign relations, peace negotiations or in signing agreements. These tasks were the responsibility of the PLO and were performed by the Arafat-appointed 'Palestinian leadership'.

The authority and mandate of the elected PLC was scattered and limited, geographically and functionally. The Oslo Agreements restricted it from legislating on a wide range of issues left for final status negotiations. Furthermore, the Oslo framework provisions were amended with PLO Executive Committee specifications that concentrated considerable power in the hands of the president, who became bestowed with a US-style veto over the legislature. Constitutionally, the executive branch needed the approval of the PLC for its major policies, but in reality the most important political and economic policies were formulated, implemented, and assessed by the executive authority alone, without PLC approval. The PLC passed important laws, but under the existing model, with the lack of a clear constitutional order, not all laws adopted by the PLC found their way to the president's desk for signature. Of the 95 laws submitted to the executive by the PLC since the foundation of the council in 1996 until October 2002, only 31 were ratified by the President (PLC 2002). The laws that were ratified were endorsed only after they had been reformulated to meet the president's expectations. Moreover, the executive disregarded many PLC decisions and laws in the areas of democracy, human rights, administration and budgets.

Furthermore, the executive power and its security apparatus occasionally obstructed the work of the PLC and its committees. For example, the council was deprived of information, such as insight into documents requested to facilitate investigation of suspected corruption and other violations. Ministers were neither helpful nor forthcoming towards PLC requests for hearings regarding various charges. They were slow to reply, when they did not completely withhold documents and information from the council. Finally, findings of commissions of inquiry set up by the executive authority, such as the Presidential Anti-Corruption Commission, were not released to the PLC (let alone the public) (Sayigh and Shikaki 1999).

The executive completely monopolized the negotiations with Israel. It refused to submit the Hebron Protocol before the PLC for discussion and approval; it did not comply with the PLC's decision to put the negotiations with Israel on hold in the aftermath of the Jewish settlement activities on Abu-Ghnaim mountain; and the executive branch disregarded the PLC's decision not to hold further negotiations until the Israeli government fully executed the first and second phase of redeployment of its troops from the West Bank. This situation left the PLC endowed with few constitutional sanctions to enforce executive compliance, depriving it of the right to insist on oversight, and without any power to efficiently control decision-making on broad policy issues. Thus, the council was unable to supervise the decisions of the president and unable to hold the executive accountable.

The executive also monopolized other parts of the public arena. It extended its dominance to include the judiciary, where the president enjoyed the power of appointing the members of the Supreme Court and the Attorney General, and of issuing decrees to establish local and regional courts. Moreover, several court decisions were simply ignored by the presidency and no follow-up action was taken, like on rulings regarding corruption in various public agencies and institutions, and on decisions regarding the violations of human rights and civil liberties committed by security forces. For example, in 1997 the Attorney General ordered the release of 11 student detainees held for up to two years without charge or trial. They were released but immediately re-arrested by the Preventive Security Forces. This manoeuvre undermined the status of the Attorney General who later resigned because of continuous intervention by the minister of justice and by heads of the various security forces (*Al-Siyasa Al-Filastiniyya* 1998).

Lack of independence of the judiciary seriously hindered the rule of law in Palestine. The executive preferred to rule by decree and to use the existing range of legal codes selectively. In fact, there were Ottoman, British, Jordanian, Egyptian and Israeli regulations in force, contributing to the weak and irresolute legal basis of Palestine. According to Palestinian lawmakers, the president used the power accorded to him by international agreements in order to issue primary legislation in the guise of secondary legislation, so that it did not need PLC approval (Sayigh and Shikaki 1999).

In political terms, the judiciary was in a permanent state of deliberate political marginalization and in practical terms in a state of operational crisis, as there were shortages of judges, prosecutors, court administrators and other staff, and an extreme task overload. As a result, citizen's civil and political rights were often violated, usually in the name of security. The security forces made arrests with no clear charges and prisoners were subjected to harsh captivity conditions and a number of them died in detention. In addition to this, the special State Security Court revived and utilized a wide range of emergency laws and often passed harsh and speedy sentences.

The executive controlled the budget of the Palestinian Authority and as a result, the division between the PNA and the PLO was blurred. According to an American audit report, early budgets prepared by the Palestinian Authority showed that certain PLO expenses were transferred to the new civil administration, like salaries of former PLO militia members hired by the PNA to join its police force, martyr family payments, pensions, and supplementary civil servant salary costs. On the other hand, certain 'public' expenses were covered by the PLO outside of PNA budgets. For instance, more police were hired than the 9,000 policemen foreign donors were willing to finance. At the same time, several traditional PLO revenue sources (like the Palestinian Liberation Tax Fund receipts and private donations) were not included in the PNA budgets (GAO 1995: 4–6).[2] The problem was not just that the interest of the PLO was being served in this way, but that that these decisions were being made directly by the president. It was not just the PLO that was undermining transparent financial transactions. According to some news reports, Israel transferred tax money owed to the PNA into a Tel Aviv PLO bank account controlled by the president himself and one other PLO officer, thereby colluding in the circumvention of proper accounting procedures (*Telegraph*, London, 5 December 1999; *Ha'aretz*, Tel Aviv, 2 February 1997; Schwartz 1997).

Apart from these allegations of financial impropriety, there was also the question of power of the PNA being concentrated in one person. This was due to the overlap of executive functions and responsibilities of the president. Arafat was not just the chairman of the PLO and the interim president of the PNA. He was the president of the strongest PLO member organization, Fateh, and held the leadership of various security and semi-military groups (Legrain 1999). Consequently, the chairman's powers (and legitimacy) were not just based on his electoral success as the popularly elected PNA president in 1996, but from his collection of positions and legitimacy as leader of the national movement. This overlap in responsibilities and the concentration of power in one person placed the president above any checks and balances, and allowed him to bypass representative bodies.

## State capacities

The formal concentration of power in the hands of the president and the 'Palestinian leadership', with few institutional checks and balances, together with the informal arrangements such as the overlap between the PNA and the PLO explains why the PNA had the potential institutional capacity to carry out social and economic transformations. In the face of the demands of the national struggle and the peace process, the command system was set up without the luxury of multiple layers of command, institutionalized representation and cumbersome mechanisms of participation, control and checks and balances. In other words, the constraints to Palestinian executive powers were not *institutional*.[3]

While this strength was probably sufficient in order to transform Palestine into a viable and perhaps even a dynamic entity, it was nevertheless threatened by fragmentation, non-productive investments and clientelism. Much of this was due to the extreme conflict situation with Israel over territories and resources. Thus, – and this is our basic argument – the authoritarian tendencies that on the surface suggested strengths and capacities for social transformation, represented political weaknesses as well, and some dangers for future state capacities. One of the dangers of extreme power concentration is that power can be used to protect and defend the power holders. If there are no institutional guarantees, a benevolent, nationalist or developmentally oriented state may not remain so in the long run. Unchecked powers tend to spend increasing resources, both political and economic, to resist institutional checks and balances and to maintain their monopoly.

In Palestine, there were some tendencies in this direction. For instance Amnesty International criticized the use of security forces against internal opposition (Amnesty International 2000), new elections were not held, and even when the PLC members enjoyed parliamentary immunity, they were subject to harassment by both Israeli and Palestinian security. The following incident is a telling example of how the executive misappropriated its power to protect its standing. In late 1998, a special budget and oversight committee of the PLC issued a report that revealed a number of governance failures. These included the abuse of public positions for financial gain in state monopolies, the winning of tenders by companies using connections with public officials, nepotism in the appointment of officials, the granting of permits and tax cuts based on personal relations, and the use of public properties for personal benefit (Shuaibi 1999; Rubin 1999: 41; *Al-Majlis Al-Tashri'I* 1998: 4–5, 21). The government-controlled Palestinian media ignored this investigation, and the president cautioned the lawmakers that they could face punishment for their offending statements. This was a clear indication that checks and balances did not work in the PNA.

## Coercion: control and transformation

In order to push the social and economic transformations necessary for development, a developing-country state needs to have appropriate state capacities, and these include coercive capacities. As noted by Khan in Chapter 1, state capacity depends on the state's ability to manage the emergence of new productive classes, maintain political stability and manage developmental rents to accelerate technology acquisition. This capitalist transformation can be socially very disruptive, with winners and losers, and the state needs a coercive capacity both to control and discipline those who gain monopoly rights, property rights, preferences, state grants or credits, and to manage social conflicts.

A successful developmental state will depend on a ruler with strong control on economic decision-making, the security to recruit and back a cohesive economic policy implementation team, and the political authority to override bureaucratic and political opposition to policy changes. Without a minimum degree of political stability and coercive efficiency, the situation may run out of hand. While in the long run, any regime will have to have a minimum of legitimacy in order to survive, a developmental regime will probably be able to create and redistribute the resources necessary to gain its legitimacy. In the short run, however, a regime needs the coercive capacity to overcome temporary crises. Coercive power includes a state's military, paramilitary, security, and police units, the armaments of these, and its infrastructure facilities. Military strength depends upon the command structure, upon military and logistic hardware, upon support from outside, and last, but not least: upon the willingness to use force.

## Coercive capacity in Palestine

The PLO leadership had always promoted a strong state in Palestine, in full control of political powers and state institutions in the national interest, because of the enduring conflict with Israel. Furthermore, Israel and the Western powers emphasized 'security' for Israel through the Oslo Agreements and made this an issue more important than democratic institutionalization in Palestine. At the beginning of the Oslo process, there were few common interests between the Israeli and the Palestinian side. However, the desire to foster a strong executive power was such a commonality, since the agreements clearly favoured Israeli interests and many of the arrangements had to be implemented despite some strong objections by Palestinian opposition forces.

An important area of interest for the PNA was policing, surveillance and the maintenance of internal order, because of the internal and external needs for 'security' and its various implications. The PNA had to prove that it was able to deal with security (this was one of the reasons it was allowed to emerge in the first place), and the PNA was given substantial material and practical support to do this, with the backing of Western donors. Security forces came to play a considerable role in keeping the emerging entity intact, and they came to impact substantially on the various spheres of life under the PNA.

Very soon, there emerged in the West Bank and Gaza a wide range of security forces, all of which were directly under the president's command (Luft 1999). They enjoyed such a degree of power and influence that they could not be ignored by any other powers in Palestine. Elected representatives, local and central authorities, members of the opposition, rivals and any influence seeker among the dominant elites, be it politicians, bureaucrats or business figures, had to take the security forces into account.

When the PNA was established, the security groups were concentrated around the Police Force, which was assigned the task of maintaining security and protecting the PNA as a whole. Other branches like the Preventive Security Forces were added, in the form of specialized units, where each branch had its own leadership, line of command, sources of financing and alliances. The Preventive Security Forces were recruited primarily from activists of the First *Intifada*. In practice, they were involved in crime prevention, tax collection and other duties, and they came to be the strongest among the security groups.

Further fragmentation of the security apparatus, with separate lines of command in parallel branches of the respective security force units, became necessary due to the separation of the West Bank and the Gaza Strip and the division of the Palestinian territories into areas A, B, and C. Thus, security agencies existed in proliferation, all of the different branches being placed directly under the president's command (Luft 1999). These forces consisted of (about) 12 agencies, where the police force alone employed about 30,000 people (Luft 1999; Sayigh and Shikaki 1999). They were present in the various districts and areas of the West Bank and the Gaza Strip, and their composition entailed former PLO guerrilla units, returned Palestinians, and former *intifada* activists.

In theory, the security groups were subordinate to the Higher Council of National Security, a body that was comprised of the heads of all security groups and was assigned the task of providing advice on internal security issues. They were to report to the central command in each area, as the local Governors of the districts were officially the representatives of the PNA at the local level. However, the effectiveness of the Higher Council was hampered by the fact that it was lacking clarity of rules and procedures and its mandate, missions and responsibilities remained vague and informal. Among the various groups, divisions of labour and exact duties and responsibilities were either unclear or fragile, and there was a paucity of coordination, at times among the various units within the same group. This confusion and overlap of functions weakened those proper rules and legal procedures that did exist. Finally, all security groups were founded and remained closely controlled by the president. Formally, the PNA president was himself the head of the Higher Council of National Security, and in practice the security forces all reported to him, separately and directly. There was also an overlap between various security forces and local strongmen, persons of influence in society, be it for political, economic or social reasons. Security chiefs tended to unite with Fateh chapters and influential clans. Heads of security agencies always sought the support and approval of the governor and of the Fateh faction in their local area in order to be able to function.

The 'security first' considerations legitimized a concentration of national resources in the coercive apparatus, in security, police and paramilitary forces, an aspect that bode well also for the prerogatives of the Palestinian national struggle. But one of the undesired results was that political freedom and social equality were underdeveloped, and the freedom of the press was restricted through an extensive self-censorship (CPRS 1999; Sayigh and Shikaki 1999; Amnesty International 2000). The coercive strengths of the PNA seemed sufficient to secure the regime's ability to undertake social and economic transformations, for example to transfer property rights to new productive classes while maintaining political stability. However, unchecked powers were obviously also a problem. The security and police forces were solely under the command of the president and potentially could be misused. The growth of security units and spending on them were also unconstrained by any other social interests.

The portion of the general budget spent on security agencies represented the single biggest item of PNA recurrent expenditure, accounting for over 30 per cent of the general budget (Sayigh and Shikaki 1999:74). At the same time, the Palestinian security agencies had their own budgets independent from the ministry of finance and were thus insufficiently subjected to Ministry and PLC oversight and control, and to external audit. In addition, each security group secured some of its own finances, using a wide range of means that sometimes went beyond the legal. In their pursuit of power and resources, security group officials committed human rights violations, practised corruption, and were involved in undeclared commercial activities as well as unauthorized tax collection. Furthermore, personal rivalry worsened the internal environment of the security groups, and security chiefs sometimes viewed their agencies as power bases and used these to further their own ends.

Although it strengthened and reinforced the Palestinian quasi-state's coercive credit, the overall impact of the unchecked coercive capacity of the security units (accompanied with a weak legal infrastructure) was that it raised the level of agitation and disturbance among the population, reduced the legitimacy of the state, and may have adversely affected badly needed investments. This in turn harmed and ultimately lessened the state's capacity to become an efficient developmental catalyst in the process of transformation.

## Political will: the organization of transformation

The political will to push a successful developmental transformation depends on the incentives for state leaders that are structurally contingent on factors like regime security, bureaucratic competence and coordination, the distribution of organizational and political power in society, and external factors.[4] In addition to the political will to regulate the economy and to redistribute resources to productive forces, there also needs to be a political will to do this in a way that is beneficial for society, rather than only for the regulators and rent-appropriators. A broad redistribution of the benefits is essential in order for the regime to gain political legitimacy and support. Furthermore, the political will to follow the costly and risky route of a developmental transformation also depends on whether other, less strenuous options are available for the leadership, even if these are less beneficial for society.

The composition of the ruling elite in social (class) terms and in terms of culture and ideology partly determines its political will. Who is ruling is relevant for understanding the interests the state represents. Internal elite cohesion can also determine the firmness of political will. The question is to what extent the state elite behaves as a unitary and rational actor, i.e. the degree of unity or fragmentation of the state at different levels of the state institution. This is reflected in the composition of the ruling elite and by the composition of ruling elite subgroups and coalitions.

## Political will in Palestine

Initially, the PNA had considerable legitimacy and did not seem to be just a transitory stage in the course of developments. There was a high degree of unity and autonomy within the state leadership (based as it was on the PLO). Both leaders and led shared a large degree of national pride and willingness to make sacrifices for the purpose of reconstruction in Palestine. This provided the PNA with a large degree of popular support, and it displayed the capacity to implement some of the basic policies and reforms necessary for development. Most important was that the PNA had strong incentives to develop the productive economic base of Palestine.

First, the PLO through the Oslo Agreements was recognized as the sole representative of the Palestinians (while the PLO on its side recognized the right of Israel to exist). The PNA was further strengthened in its internal and external legitimacy through the 1996 elections (even though the boycott by most opposition groups meant that its internal legitimacy remained contested and unsettled). There is no reason to believe that the Palestinian leadership was short-termist. Even the USA seemed to protect it against direct threats to its security by supporting its police force, and threats to its existence by recognizing its president and by opposing Israel's plans to dispose of him.[5] Second, there was no alternative for the PNA but to strive for a stronger economic backbone. The 'savings' of the PLO were running out, the contributions from the Arab world dropped substantially after the Gulf War, and the aid levels from the Western world could not be trusted to be 'sustainable' (see Chapter 7 by Hanafi and Tabar on the donors for more on this). Third, the new ruling elite emanated from the 'extra-territorial' PLO with a political agenda, specific interests, organizational structure and internal cohesion of its own. For one thing, the PLO brought in a populist national ideology. The 'nationalist' cause dominated and the PNA adopted a state-led development project with a major role for the private sector (Rubin 1999: 8, 192).[6]

The PLO also exhibited distinctly democratic elements. Being an umbrella organization covering a number of different member organizations, it was accustomed to accommodating differing opinions. However, in times of crisis it had learnt the discipline, command and authority necessary for a guerrilla organization engaged in an armed conflict with Israel, when it operated according to the 'Fakehani Rules', the rules of loyalty and treason that the PLO leadership and cadres had learnt when in exile in Beirut from 1971 to 1982. When it was first organized in 1994, the people who formed the nucleus of the PNA were mostly PLO cadres. On the ground, in May 1994, PLO chairman Yasser Arafat, a small group of PLO leaders, the Tunis-based PLO bureaucracy, and nine thousand Palestinian guerrillas moved in from Tunisia and several other Arab countries, and replaced the retreating Israelis. In moving the exiled PLO civilian and military headquarters to Gaza City in the Gaza Strip, Arafat established, according to plan, a new headquarter and took the title and prerogatives of President.

Thus, the PNA institutions came to be manned initially by people with a strong personal loyalty and dependence on the Chairman and the PLO, people who had undergone military training and been under his political and 'military' command. Many of these people (but not all) had been in exile for years and came to be called 'returnees'. It was a flexible rather than rigid organization, adapted to quick decision-making and efficient execution.

While regulations regarding public recruitment were weak, and since there were no clear criteria and guidelines that defined the tasks, budgets and actual personnel needs of specific operational institutions, the pattern of recruitment adopted by the PNA was dominated by considerations regarding informal ties, political loyalty, personal relationships and other patrimonial logics. This came to be at the expense of the meritocratic principle of hiring based on level of education, experience and efficiency. A sophisticated system of internal balancing was developed, accommodating important individuals and factions, partly in order to meet the expectation of many among the returning PLO personnel who hoped to acquire positions comparable to their previous posts, and partly to secure the cooperation of important individuals among the local West Bank political and economic elites.

While the most important administrative positions in the PNA were basically filled with people from the PLO apparatus in exile and by others who had proved their political loyalty to the PLO and its leader, further down the administrative apparatus had a greater representation of 'insiders' from the West Bank and Gaza in a rather haphazard manner. For instance, whenever the Israelis (usually after negotiations and American pressure) were releasing Palestinian prisoners from custody, most of these people were in need of jobs. And since these were people who had proved their loyalty to the 'cause' and to the PLO, nothing seemed more natural than to give them jobs in the Palestinian public administration, which also secured their continuing loyalty. Appointment was utilized not only to secure loyalty but also to revive traditional ties. For instance, the PLO's Executive Committee was enlarged in order to accommodate, among others, members of traditional families (Al-Agha, Al-Khoudari, Al-Husseini, Al-Sheka'a). The Al-Qawasmi clan and its web of relatives and friends dominated most of the high positions in the ministry of transportation and its various regional offices.

The political pressures determining resource allocations inevitably affected public services. In addition to this, several sectors were understaffed, especially those requiring specialized or highly qualified personnel (such as specialized physicians in public hospitals), while at the same time other sectors were overstaffed, in particular at the management levels of appointment. The numbers in public employment expanded rapidly, with over one fifth of the work force in the WBGS (668,000 in 2000) and about 40 per cent (of the active work force) in Gaza on the public payroll (Abu-Shokor 2002; Sovich 2000). The combination of a desire to ease unemployment with political and personal factors reflected the fact that public hiring was a means of rewarding political loyalty and maintaining stability.

By employing fighters and political activists and including traditional elements, the PNA was able to stabilize a tense internal environment, but at a cost. It is likely that sometimes, qualified persons were not hired to accommodate unqualified individuals. Despite the fact that 'excessive' employment was politically important, even required for political stabilization, the norms and rules thus established for the civil service, such as reliance on the state for employment and the compromise of efficiency and merit, were likely to have undesired consequences in the longer run. Political employment left the PA with a high proportion of the labour force in public employment; it caused bureaucracy to be slow and inefficient, and burdened an already weak economy with additional expenses.

The overall efficiency of the public administration in the PA was low. Officers were inexperienced, their mandates were in many cases weak and unclear, and without a basic law and procedural principles the administration's organizational evolution was rather haphazard. There were competing chains of command, insufficient delegation of authority, excessive compartmentalization in certain respects, and a lack of departmental autonomy in others. Besides, there were inadequate formal procedures, insufficient flows of information, and inadequate audits and internal controls. These led to serious rivalries between functioning civil servants and political appointees in the bureaucracy. These problems may have destabilized the state apparatus in the future if moves towards formalization remained slow.

Furthermore, while the 'insiders', the locals who had led the First *Intifada*, had organized from below and tried to create territory-wide representative institutions (and threatened to some extent the exiled PLO leadership), the PLO favoured the Diaspora organization as the core building block of the new PNA. As a result, the local command remained subordinate (Frisch 1998; Sovich 2000). This state building from the 'outside' allowed the leadership to retain control and dominance, but reduced its ability to secure grass roots support and true internal consensus on divisive issues, such as issues related to national reconstruction and negotiations with Israel.[7] The problems and shortcomings of the civil service, coupled with some widely discussed corruption scandals, came to jeopardize the PNA's political and institutional standing in society.

Adding to the rift between the 'insiders' and 'outsiders' was the fact that the major opposition groups, Hamas and Al-Jihad, were rooted 'inside' and they disputed the PLO's mandate to represent all Palestinians. While the PLO embarked on a process established by the Oslo arrangement, the Islamic opposition groups actively, sometimes even violently, boycotted that process. The tension between the two groups affected the process of national reconstruction, and came to weaken the competence of both sides to efficiently manage the affairs of the *intifada*, with severe internal and external consequences.

## Strengths and possibilities

Palestine had a number of prerequisites for a strong and developmentally oriented ruling elite and state apparatus. The basis of the PNA – the PLO – was coherent, experienced and coordinated. There were no indications that the regime was impatient, insecure or short-termist. The PNA had no alternatives other than embarking on an economic developmental course based on pushing the development of capitalism, and the PLO changed its ideology accordingly. As there was a weak economic base and a low level of industrialization, there was no rapid way of financing the regime and its survival. There were no easily exploitable natural resources, no large import–export businesses to tax, and even when donor money was abundant in the first years, this resource was not sustainable.[8]

But while the PNA had strong incentives to push development, its means were not always entirely appropriate, and it had other pressing agenda. In addition to the conflict with Israel, there were internal groups and interests to accommodate, and in this situation of executive dominance under precarious circumstances, opportunities opened up for personal and political interventions in administrative matters, and for rewarding political loyalty through favouritism and clientelism. The enduring conflict with Israel demanded a military command organization at the top, but one cannot easily determine whether such an organization was the most appropriate administration for formulating and implementing long-term developmental policies. While we are looking at a brief time span during which the PNA faced very adverse conditions, it is possible that more progress could have been made to institutionalize formal procedures of recruitment and improve representation, participation and accountability. What we do know is that the PNA employed clientelist methods of recruitment and political stabilization. These clientelist inclusion and co-optation strategies were quite successful in reducing any bureaucratic hostility towards government priorities (in fact, there was national pride and a strong commitment to the policies of national reconstruction in all state agencies), and there were no signs of any substantial or influential resistance from within the administrative apparatus.

However, two dangers were present. First of all, positions were filled according to political considerations of employing political allies, supporters and loyalists, the need to co-opt and pacify rivals and contenders, and to reduce unemployment. Second, as a result, public resources were often used unproductively in public administration, which endangered not only the quality of the public administration, but also ultimately its legitimacy. In a situation of inconsistent, unstable and unpredictable rules and regulations, public officials had the opportunity to demand bribes, to take 'fees' for delivering services that were inadequately codified or even known to the public, and to demand commissions for all kinds of services (for example for licences, permits, exemptions, deductions and releases).

From the time the PLO based Palestinian Authority started to operate and develop, and in particular since 1997, accusations, revelations and scandals of corruption increased in number and intensity. According to various reports, such as that of Sayigh and Shikaki (1999) and the PLC special budget and oversight committee report (1998), there was high-level political corruption in the presidency, involving high-ranking political figures and PLO officers, and widespread bureaucratic corruption within several administrative bodies. Although Yasser Arafat was not personally criticized, corruption was said to be systemic in Palestine and alleged to have reached the highest circles, including the president's office. Public opinion polls show that in the public's *perception* corruption existed in the various Palestinian institutions, including the president's office. While perception measures are known to be subject to serious biases, perceptions can affect popular support for a regime. A poll taken in June 1999 revealed that 80 per cent of the public believed that high levels of corruption existed in the various ministries and government; 75 per cent believed that corruption existed in the security organizations; and over 41 per cent per cent of the public believed that the president's office was involved in corruption. Resentments were especially strong in the economically struggling Gaza Strip where many people believed that corruption stifled the kind of business activity that could help lift them out of poverty, and the Police Force was perceived as the most corrupt (CPRS 1999).[9]

There was competition among PNA institutions for donor assistance. However, there were indications of too slow a progress in the institutionalization and legalization of resource transfers, and of too slow an economic redistribution to broader segments of the population. The latter was definitely due to the fact that there was not much to redistribute and because deliberate Israeli policies hindered economic development in Palestine (the 'security closures' being especially efficient in this respect, see Chapter 3 by Zagha and Zomlot, and Chapter 6 by Fjeldstad and Zagha on this issue). Nevertheless, when opportunities for participation and voice were restricted in Palestine, the regime was met with harsh criticism not only from the outside, but also from the inside.

Given the PNA's weak administrative capacity and its mixed record on democracy, Western donors' efforts, aided by internal popular pressures for accountability and transparent public conduct, were able to push the leadership to adopt a reformist programme. These pressures focused on administrative and political spheres and pushed for a better finance and tax administration, transparency, increased judicial management and improvements in the electoral laws and procedures. And gradually, the PNA's capacity in planning and prioritization did improve a good deal as the Ministry for Planning and International Cooperation gradually assumed the central role in these matters, and as the Ministry of Finance extended its jurisdictional authority and took over control over all levels of public finance.[10]

However, if external factors and Israeli strategies had allowed the emergence of a sovereign and developmental Palestinian state, there would still be dangers with the institutional structure that was developing. An authoritarian regime (or a democratically elected regime with special constitutional provisions and centralized executive authority) can be more efficient in pushing rapid and extensive social and economic transformations, but such regimes have, unfortunately, few institutional or other guarantees that they will stay developmentally oriented. The prerogatives needed to implement economic transformations partly contradict other principles of stabilization, legitimacy and democratic consolidation.

Legitimacy and stability in the long-run require inclusion, participation and redistribution, but (newly) established political and economic interests may block this.[11] A centralized executive authority may become too independent from and unrestricted by other social forces.[12] There is always a danger that regimes with a marked relative autonomy in the initial phase can become too preoccupied with their own interests (securing life-long tenure of power and predation), unless restricted and counterbalanced by other forces in society.

## Clientelism: favours and resource transfers

The rapid transformation model is not necessarily characterized by a fair redistribution of resources. The danger is that pressing political concerns might overshadow distributional issues necessary for political legitimization. Political stability normally implies the accommodation of powerful groups, critical factions and clients, and their support is usually secured through state resource allocations. The groups and clients who benefit from these resources and rents are typically not the poorest groups in society, but well-organized and politically important groups. The political balancing act is to accommodate certain groups for political reasons and other groups for economic reasons: to strike a balance between political and economic logics.

Some of the dangers of this political accommodation strategy we have seen: contested political legitimacy, weakened public administration, overspending on staff and in particular, security staff. Other dangers are well known. A political leadership taking a direct interest in the profitability of enterprises may end up creating politically supported monopoly rents. When the political leadership owns shares in enterprises, when enterprises are created and supported as state-owned or partly state-owned, the distinction between national and private interests can become blurred, to put it mildly. Clientelism and patronage can also develop into a self-reinforcing system. Groups that are co-opted and given preferential treatment will do whatever they can to reinforce their position and demand even more resources. Strategic alliances are hard to break up, once established. A regime that for some time has been going down the road of clientelism and patronage can be hard to turn around in a modernizing process of institutionalization and rationalization. The logics of clientelism are strong and persistent. The longer the clientelist resource transfers go on, the more difficult it may be to withdraw established favours from these groups. The benefactors of monopolies, state-created rents and subsidies are likely to defend their positions in the future. These tendencies are even more dangerous when the legal framework is weak and institutional checks and balances are nonexistent. Successful businesses, without legal protection in a well-functioning state, are prone to predation by the ruling elite.

## Clientelism in Palestine

Hilal and Khan (Chapter 2) point out that the PNA demonstrated both a will and a capacity to allocate rents to promote investment and development, to correct mistakes in the allocation of rents, and to overcome factional interests. At the same time, there were also contrary tendencies with dangers for the future. On the one hand, the PNA had the political strengths necessary in terms of capacity, organization and will to push a social transformation, but on the other hand, it had to accommodate certain groups in society by giving them access to resources ('a piece of the cake'). In the politically precarious situation, there was a political necessity to create allies and make alliances. Given the fact that the route of democratic participation and voice was not institutionalized, these groups had to be accommodated directly, through resource transfers.

At the outset, the PNA quasi-state seemed dominant, partly because of a seriously fragmented Palestinian society with an underdeveloped middle and capitalist class. Hilal and Khan, in Chapter 2, demonstrate how key administrative positions during Israeli direct rule (the period of occupation from 1967 to 1994) prevented the development of these classes. When in addition large parts of the population were internal and external refugees, one can easily see how the bases for internal political organization were held back. The local (indigenous) capitalist sector was also small in real terms and dominated by small-scale capital, family-owned and family-run firms (see Chapter 5 by Nasr on this). Thus, there were no internal strategic partners for the state in its capitalist development strategy.

The PNA did what it could to attract investors from abroad, in particular the Diaspora Palestinians and expatriate capital. Expatriate Palestinian capitalists had funds to invest combined with entrepreneurial experience, and through generous support mechanisms (tax exemptions, state-guaranteed loans and partnerships, limited entry and guaranteed rents) and through sheer nationalism, many expatriate Palestinians did invest in Palestine under the PNA, despite the very insecure conditions for their investments. Note however, that privileged access to rent granted to expatriate capital inevitably left indigenous small and medium capitalists further marginalized. And more importantly: investments of some size were dependent on state protection and privileges, and were made by people with close ties to the political leadership. In the precarious political situation (with an unclear legal framework and weak legal protection of property rights), maintaining good relations with the political leadership was a necessary expense for protecting investments.

Even when there were some signs of productive capitalists emerging in Palestine, there were also signs of politicians, state officials and their clients capturing resources, subsidies and credits to enrich themselves in ways that sometimes harmed the common good. When transparency is non-existent and private–corporate–political interests overlap, there is space for secret allocations through patron–client networks. In the 1997 PLC report, it was concluded that PNA officials used their powers, such as the power to grant licenses and subsidies, to profit their own businesses, that some of Arafat's advisors represented the PNA in dealings with companies they partly owned, and that security officers intervened in economic matters for their own benefit (Rubin 1999: 40). Khan and Hilal make the point that even when the president made appointments, in most cases for political reasons and co-optation purposes, he likewise retained the right to dismiss these state officials and could thus correct any mistakes. These corrections sometimes happened but the incentive to push development and the power to correct mistakes may not be a sufficient guarantee for society. Who, other than the leader, truly determines what constitutes a 'mistake', and who defines the criteria of success? Are the dismissed officials the ones who commit the mistakes, or the ones who renounce such processes? Can or will individuals appointed for political reasons, be dismissed for mistakes? In the long run institutional processes have to be set up to ensure that public policy remains in the public interest.

One incident may be indicative of a pattern. In late 1998, the special budget and oversight committee of the PLC issued a report that revealed severe economic mismanagement and corruption in the PNA. The Committee recommended that the cabinet be dissolved and a new cabinet formed in which none of the ministers stated in the report were included. The result was that a new cabinet was established, but virtually all of those ministers accused of corrupt practices were back in place – only with a different portfolio. Subsequently, two ministers who had not been cited in the report resigned from the cabinet because of the lack of proper political action to deal with the corruption charges and the lack of administrative reform (Shuaibi 1999; Rubin 1999: 41; *Al-Majlis Al-Tashri'I* 1998). One could argue that the demand or the expectation of firing all officials involved in corruption is unrealistic in a context where significant rents exist together with necessary discretionary powers for the executive. Indeed, no developing country political system has achieved the eradication of corruption. Officials and business leaders in all developing countries are likely to be involved in one way or another in corruption and corruption itself can be associated with all types of rents in developing countries. In the Palestinian case, however, the public was highly disappointed with the decision to keep most or all of those ministers accused of corrupt practices, even if there was no guarantee that some other group of officials would have been less corrupt.

In terms of immediate impact, corruption negatively affected the standing and credibility of the PNA in the broader society. In addition to weakening the competitiveness of the economy, corruption must have discouraged some foreign investments and contributed to the lower quality of social services, in areas such as health, communications, and fuel, primarily harming low-income groups. The long-term impact of corruption, however, is more difficult to assess. The damage caused by specific types of corruption is hard to appraise in a short period of time, particularly since the process of state building was collapsing for other reasons as well.

In such an uncertain economic climate, the use of political power to assist private accumulation did deliver results, but also created new challenges. The chairman, a number of his closest political friends and allies, a number of prominent PLO figures, ministers and top-level bureaucrats, and many members of the PLO and PLO-affiliated organizations were involved in various businesses in Palestine. For instance, PLO figureheads owned the two most prestigious hotels in Palestine, the Oasis Hotel and Casino in Jericho, and the Grand Park Hotel in Ramallah. The Grand Park was frequently used for state visits, and the Oasis hotel in Jericho was particularly interesting for Israelis and Jordanians who are forbidden to gamble in their home countries.

Another example was the request made to the Israeli side by the Palestinian minister of civil affairs, asking for the closure of the Allenby Bridge, the border crossing to Jordan, in order to stop imports of cement for a period. This helped the PNA's trading monopoly in cement. The PNA cement monopoly was criticized not only because it eliminated competition and raised costs for the vital construction sector, but also because it created a powerful coalition against the development of a Palestinian cement industry. This closure action assisted the minister's son in monopolizing the cement market through the Al-Karmel Cement Company he partly owned (but see also Chapter 2 by Hilal and Khan, and Chapter 5 by Nasr, who argue that even in this case, a number of less venal factors were also driving the creation of the Palestinian trading monopolies). Less defensible was the hiring of a consultant firm called Teem by the Ministry of planning and international cooperation, which was owned by the minister himself, to carry out most of training and consultancy work in the ministry (according to the hearings by the Oversight Committee of the PLC in 1997/98).

These examples demonstrate that political power can be used to organize primitive accumulation that can in turn result in productive investments. The obvious danger is that these processes can easily go wrong, and in the Palestinian case, the profits earned have been neither subjected to institutional oversight nor fully disclosed. Thus, although most of these were apparently well-working enterprises, an accurate assessment of their efficiency is difficult, especially now that the order itself has entirely collapsed.

The groups and factions that enjoyed preferential treatment for political reasons were likely to be sometimes unproductive, but more seriously, some were armed. We are primarily referring to the proliferation of security forces and to the politically driven job creation in the public administration, but also to some traditional and local elites. The traditional Palestinian elites had been declining for some time, and the remaining traditional hierarchies and patronage relations were fragile. But the PNA needed to enlarge the regime's political base across regional, kinship, and other traditional solidarities, and it did this by allowing to some extent, privileged access to resources on the basis of clientelism. Traditional elites thus entered into 'modern' spheres both because they had a 'right', and because they were co-opted. In the PLO Executive Council, for instance, there were people representing regions (like Gaza, Nablus, Hebron and Jerusalem) and to a lesser extent people representing influential families, and in one case a religious group, the Palestinian Christians (Legrain 1999).[13] Although it is doubtful whether this practice reinforced traditional elites, at least it preserved and legitimated them.

The separation of the West Bank and the Gaza Strip and the division of the Palestinian territories into areas A, B, and C forced the PNA to form parallel commands and branches, and this fragmented the security apparatus. Besides, the Security Council lacked clarity of mandate and regulations, and its missions and responsibilities remained vague and informal. Among the various groups, divisions of labour and exact duties and responsibilities were either unclear or nonexistent, and there was a lack of coordination among the various groups. All this led to a proliferation of security groups and created the danger of an eventual fragmentation of the territories into fiefdoms.

Some security forces and government departments were involved in tax collection, and in the turbulence of the times often spent these taxes locally without remitting them to the Ministry of Finance. This could lead to misappropriation as well. The general prosecutor of Jericho collected large sums of money as taxes from businesses, and kept it in his private bank account without informing the Ministry of Finance. Allegedly, he amassed over four million NIS. It was alleged that taxpayers were occasionally coerced to extract larger sums (an allegation made to the hearings of the Oversight Committee of the PLC in 1997/98). There were occasional bitter struggles between various security services and alliances not only over the patronage allocations from the central government, but also over the taxation of local resources.

A number of case study examples can illustrate some of these processes. We are not indicating that these were general operational principles, only that some instances of these types were observed. Our first example is an incident that took place in a refugee camp near Nablus. In the aftermath of the Wye Plantation Agreement in 1999, a factional conflict broke out in the camp over the confiscation of weapons. The groups involved were the PNA police force, the respective Fateh branches of the camp and the town, representatives from the municipality, and the governor of Nablus. The main line of conflict was between the central and the local authorities, with the Arafat nominated governor on the one hand, and the locally elected mayor on the other. It was the governor's clan (the Al-'Aloul family) against the mayor's clan (the Al-Sheka'a family), and the struggle was on the control over a refugee camp that received considerable economic support from outside. This provided a typical example of internal struggles due to unclear responsibilities and a bitter fight over influence and control.

On the whole, the Nablus municipality was well run with an efficient administration, achieving rapid modernization, in particular in infrastructure and economic development. At the same time, for reasons that have been discussed throughout this book, there was limited accountability and oversight, which allowed the mayor to create a personal power base. Neither central government nor locally elected bodies checked its financial dealings or watched over the spending of the money provided by donors and other foreign agencies. Due to the lack of accountability, the mayor was able to allocate some of this money to strengthen his influence and to expand his web of supporters. He gave monthly salaries to selected individuals and armed a small militia that received orders from him only.

The head of the local police force was also personally indebted to the mayor, since he was reinstalled in this position after he had been once fired for illegal business transactions. He had previously served as the head of the intelligence division in Nablus, when in 1997 he was fired after being caught smuggling and dealing in stolen goods (personal computers). For whatever reasons, the general director of the National Police Force appointed this individual as the director of the police department in Ramallah, and in 1998 he was brought back to Nablus.[14] Another example is how the Nablus branch of the National Guard raised extra money. It had 550 names registered on paper as members, while only 350 were on duty. The remaining 200 names were fictitious, but remained on the payroll. This was however, not a unique incident. There was the so-called 'Fateh Quota' that consisted of 60 fictitious names, which was sometimes granted to prominent Fateh leaders as an additional source of revenue. In 1998 the Oversight and Human Rights Committee of the PLC released a report that revealed another case regarding fees Palestinian travellers had to pay when passing through the border to Jordan and Egypt. Each traveller paid 121 NIS as travel fees but got a receipt for 117 NIS only. The sum seems insignificant, but is estimated to sum up to about 1 million NIS annually. The report included the names of each person involved, including officials in the security forces, bureaucrats and politicians.

A last example is the local chief of the National Guards in Nablus, who obtained a personal bank loan by using his institution as collateral. The money was invested in four chicken farms. Dozens of National Guard members served as workers on these farms, the product was sold to the supplies department of the National Guard and then landed on the soldiers' dinner plates. The person in charge of supplying the local branch with foodstuff was a close relative of the local chief. As the returns from these transactions went into the chief's pockets, he came to own several houses and businesses in the West Bank and Gaza.

## What kind of entity was developing in Palestine?

These examples indicate a state with relatively positive prospects for becoming a developmental entity. It showed a strong political will to embark on a developmental economic course, which was its only option. The state displayed sufficient coercive strength and administrative capacity to support its economic and political policies. However, the very strength of the PNA that could have made it into a 'late developer' was also a burden. The developmental capacity of Palestine was not only undercut by Israeli encroachments, but also by internal struggles, clientelism, corruption and a hesitation to open up the system for further participation, enhancing human rights, rule of law and so on. Instead of reinforcing its legitimacy and authority through inclusion and participation, its strengths were partly used to fight internal battles, to pay off or discipline opponents, and to buy political support.

Given the precarious strategic situation with the movement towards statehood stalled by Israeli demands for 'security', and the critical challenges coming from fundamentalist groups, the PNA had sufficient reasons to protect its authoritarian and security-oriented policies. While the PNA had the political strengths necessary in terms of capacity, organization and will to push a developmental transformation, it had to accommodate unproductive groups in society. Rents were created and distributed to satisfy three core groups on which the PLO-dominated governing elite depended, namely the security apparatus, the nominated public officials and bureaucrats, and local strongmen. Although the PNA seemed to be (and probably was) the stronger partner in this relationship, clients tended to accumulate resources, and to slowly strengthen their bargaining position.

We do not believe the time-span (of six years) was long enough to determine whether the Palestinian state would have failed for internal reasons or could have developed into a developmental state. Moreover, we have only looked at *some* of the internal political aspects of this problem. For other economic and social aspects, we will have to refer to other chapters in this book. However, we believe that some unproductive client groups were being considerably strengthened in powers and influence.

The excessive job creation in the public administration and the proliferation of security forces was costly in terms of unproductive consumption. These clients were mainly unproductive, and the resource transfers might well have led to a fiscal crisis and diminished prospects for sustained economic development, if the trend was to continue. More seriously, some of these client groups established their own revenue generating mechanisms, and some were armed. Thus, despite good prospects for a developmentalist entity, we have seen several indications that the Palestinian quasi-state developed traits congruent with the neopatrimonial/clientelist type of state displaying its core characteristics of presidentialism (personalized power) and patrimonial logics (the use of state resources for political purposes).

Now, when the process of state deformation continues through the current reoccupation, and the deliberate marginalization of the PNA, some of the established local strongmen will probably increase their powers further, at the cost of the central authorities. In the scenario of a complete

Israeli reoccupation of Palestine, it is likely that the next stage of Israeli strategy may be the granting of some local autonomy to certain larger cities (where the bulk of the Palestinian population live), to co-operative and friendly local strongmen as direct clients of Israel. The likelihood, in other words, is of a rapid acceleration of the 'bantustanization' of Palestine. Were this to happen, the construction of a viable Palestinian state would be fatally compromised.

## Notes

1  Neopatrimonialism is defined in the African context by Bratton and van de Walle (1994) as a combination of presidentialism, clientelism, and the use of state resources for political legitimation.

2  According to the GAO report: 'We were able to determine (…) that some of PLO's administrative, military and social welfare expenses have been subsumed under the Palestinian Authority's budget. At the same time, we found that several traditional PLO revenue sources were not included in the Palestinian Authority's budget' (GAO 1995: 2). Note also that according to the Rocard report, the PNA Ministry of Finance 'drew its senior officials and most of its institutional culture from the PLO's Palestine National Fund and Fateh's Financial Department. Neither body had real experience preparing a public budget, nor subjecting it to debate and review by public bodies'. (Sayigh and Shikaki 1999: 54).

3  The major constraints on the Palestinian executive powers were external, as evident from the siege of the presidential compound in Ramallah by Israeli forces and the house-arrest of the Palestinian president, from June 2002.

4  This latter point will not be discussed here as our focus is on internal factors (see Chapter 2 by Hilal and Khan, for an extensive discussion of the external factors). We completely agree, however, that for political, strategic and religious reasons, Israel did not seem to want a developmental state in Palestine; only a subservient client state to serve the security needs of Israel.

5  At least this was the situation until the eruption of the second intifada and the attacks on the USA on 11 September 2001, and the ensuing American war on terrorism. Now the USA seems to adopt the Israeli views on the PNA and its leadership.

6  According to Rubin, the PLO had a state-oriented ideology with roots in socialism, because some of the PLO member organizations adhered to a revolutionary Marxist ideology and the biggest party Fateh and its leader could be placed in the socialist camp. However, in the early years, the PLO was a genuine coalition of guerrilla groups, and the groups' programmes were mostly rooted in bourgeois nationalism. Some claimed to be Marxist, but their ideas came more from Mao Zedong than from Karl Marx or Lenin. Others followed the 'Arab Socialist' ideology of the Ba'ath parties. Arafat and the Fateh leadership held more closely to the traditions of the Arab revolution and the strong influence of the Algerian struggle. Nevertheless, Fateh and all the Palestinian factions recognized their connection with the anti-imperialist uprisings in the Portuguese African colonies, in South Africa, in Northern Ireland, and most importantly, in Vietnam.

7  Frisch notes a striking difference between Zionist and Palestinian state building. The state apparatus of Israel was built upon a territorial leadership, supported by the Diaspora, while the Palestinian administration was built upon the Diaspora PLO organization, with support *and* opposition from the territories (Frisch 1998: xii).

8  Easy access to natural resource rents can reduce incentives for developmental strategies, and also allow groups that capture state power to monopolize it for long periods using military might.
9  Public Opinion Polls were carried out by the Center for Palestine Research and Studies (CPRS), the Palestinian Center for Public Opinion (PCPO), and by Birzeit's Development Studies Program. See also Rubin 1999: 67.
10  In mid 2002, after donor pressure, Mr Salam Fayyad was handpicked as Minister of Finance. He had served eight years in the IMF in Washington, and he had been the IMF resident representative in Palestine for five years.
11  Haggard and Kaufmann (1995: 10–11) make this distinction between the early and later stages of economic reform. Initially, centralized executive authority can be important to overcome bureaucratic and political opposition, and this strength is usually based on the ruler's personal control over the coercive and party apparatuses. Likewise, in new democracies newly elected leaders will normally enjoy a 'honeymoon' period during which economic reforms may be implemented rather easily, because new leaders enjoy strong popular backing and the old regime is discredited and opposition disorganized. In the longer run, however, reforms must appeal to a new coalition of beneficiaries in order to be legitimate, sustained and consolidated.
12  In distinguishing between modern rational, productive, and/or industrial capitalism, and various other forms of capitalism like commercial, political, booty, adventurous, traditional or patrimonial capitalism, which could well be labelled together as 'parasitic capitalism', Max Weber argued that modern (industrial) capitalism would only develop where the right balance was made between strong states and strong markets. Karl Marx's notions on the relation between labour and capital, and Adam Smith's emphasis on the central role for trade and the market are necessary, but not sufficient elements for developing capitalism. Weber pointed to the important relationship between the central state and the autonomous cities (with their bourgeoisie), a relation of counterbalancing powers where neither could turn to the easy way of parasitic accumulation (Weber 1981: 83).
13  For political reasons, the Islamic opposition kept itself out of the PNA and PLO institutions.
14  According to an interview with a high official who prefers anonymity.

# References

Abu-Shokor, A. (2002) *The Impact of Government Spending in the Palestinian Territories*, Nablus: Center for Palestine Research and Studies.

Ades, A. and Di Tella, R. (1996) 'The Causes and Consequences of Corruption: A Review of Recent Empirical Contributions', in *IDS Bulletin*, 27 (2): 6–11.

*Al-Majlis Al-Tashri'I* (1998) Periodical published by PLC Public Relations Department (in Arabic). Issue no.6.

*Al-Siyasa Al-Filastiniyya* (1998) (Palestine Policy). Nablus: Center for Palestine Research and Studies (in Arabic) no.18.

Amnesty International (2000) *Annual Report: Palestinian Authority*, available online at
http://www.web.amnesty.org/web/ar2000web.nsf/countries/7dae741e5b9afed58025 68f200552959 (accessed 11 August 2000).

Amundsen, I. (1999) *Political Corruption: An Introduction to the Issues*, Working Paper no. 7, Bergen: Chr. Michelsen Institute.

Baker, J. (1999) 'Resigned to the PA', *Palestine Report*, 6 February 1998. Available online at <http://www.jmcc.org/media/report/98/Feb/1d.htm> (accessed 15 February 2004).

Ben Efrat, R. (1997) 'Corruption Under Arafat: The Legislators Speak', *Israel Resource Review*, 8 September; available online at http://www.israelvisit.com/BehindTheNews/Sep-08.htm (accessed 23 January 2003).

Bratton, M. and van de Walle, N. (1994) 'Neopatrimonial Regimes and Political Transitions in Africa', *World Politics* 46: 453–89.

Brynen, R. (1995) 'The Neopatrimonial Dimension of Palestinian Politics', *Journal of Palestine Studies*, 25 (1): 23–36.

CPRS (1999) *Public Opinion Polls*, Public opinion polls carried out by Center for Palestine Research and Studies CPRS, the Palestinian Center for Public Opinion PCPO, and Birzeit's Development Studies Program.

Frisch, H. (1998) *Countdown to Statehood: Palestinian State Formation in the West Bank and Gaza*, Albany: State University of New York Press.

GAO, United States General Accounting Office (1995) *Foreign Assistance. PLO's Ability to Help Support Palestinian Authority Is Not Clear*, Report to the Chairman, Committee on International Relations, House of Representatives: GAO/NSIAD-96-23, B-270066. Washington DC, November 1995. Available online at <http://www.gao.gov/archive/1996/ns96023.pdf> (accessed 23 January 2003).

Haggard, S. and Kaufmann, R. R. (eds) (1995) *The Politics of Economic Adjustment*, Princeton: Princeton University Press.

Immanuel, J. (1997) 'Palestinian Activities: Kidrah Fired For Corruption', in *The Jerusalem Post*, 9 June.

Karre, J. (1999) *Statehood and the Palestinian Authority: Considerations on Stability*, Uppsala: University of Uppsala.

Legrain, J-F. (1999) 'The Succession of Yasir Arafat', *Journal of Palestine Studies* 28 (4): 5–20.

Luft, G. (1999) 'The Palestinian Security Services: Between Police and Army', *Middle East Review of International Affairs*, 3 (2): 47–63. Available online at <http://www.biu.ac.il/SOC/besa/meria/journal/1999/issue2/jv3n2a5.html> (accessed 24 August 2000).

Mazawi, A. E. and Abraham Y. (1999) 'Elite Formation under Occupation: the Internal Stratification of Palestinian Elites in the West Bank and Gaza Strip', *British Journal of Sociology*, 50 (3): 397–418.

Médard, J-F. (1995) 'La Corruption politique et administrative et les différenciations du public et du privé: une perspective comparative', in Borghi and Meyer-Bisch (eds.) *La Corruption l'envers des droits de l'homme*, (Actes du IXe Colloque interdisciplinaire sur les droits de l'homme à l'Université de Fribourg, 3–5 février 1994). Fribourg: Editions universitaires.

Paldam, M. (1999) 'The Big Pattern of Corruption. Economics, Culture and the Seesaw Dynamics', *Working Paper* no.11, Department of Economics, University of Aarhus.

Palestinian Legislative Council (2002) *Bulletin* September.

Robinson, G. (1997) *Building a Palestinian State: The Incomplete Revolution*, Bloomington: Indiana University Press.

Rubin, B. (1999) *The Transformation of Palestinian Politics. From Revolution to State-Building*, Cambridge, MA: Harvard University Press.

Samara, A. (2000) 'Globalization, the Palestinian Economy, and the "Peace process"', *Journal of Palestine Studies*, 29 (2): 20–34.

Sayigh, Y. and Shikaki, K. (1999) *Strengthening Palestinian Public Institutions. (The Rocard-Siegman report)*, New York: Council of Foreign Relations, Independent Task Force. Available online at <http://www.cfr.org/pub3184/henry_siegman/publications_about.php#10> (accessed 15 February 2004).

Schwartz, M. (1997) 'A Secret Account in Tel Aviv Funds Arafat's Oppression, Hand in Glove', *Challenge*, 43, 27 February 1997. Available online at <http://www.mideastfacts.com/arafat_account.html> (accessed 15 February 2004).

Shuaibi, A. (1999) 'Elements of Corruption in the Middle East and North Africa: The Palestinian Case', *Paper presented to the 9th International Anti-Corruption Conference*, IAAC, Durban, South Africa, 10–15 October 1999. Available online at <http://www.transparency.de/iacc/9th_papers/day1/ws5/d1ws5_ashuaibi.html> (accessed 14 August 2000).

Sovich, N. (2000) 'Palestinian Trade Unions' *Journal of Palestine Studies*, 29 (4): 66–79.

Tamari, S. (1994) 'The "Masses" and Power: Between Democratic Discourse and Elite Action', in Abdel-Hadi, Halibi and Tamari (eds) *National Institutions, Elections, the Public and the State*, Ramallah: Muwatin.

US Department of State (2000) *1999 Country Reports on Human Rights Practices: The Occupied Territories (Including Areas Subject to the Jurisdiction of the Palestinian Authority)*, Bureau of Democracy, Human Rights, and Labor, US Department of State, Washington, 25 February 2000. Available online at <http://www.state.gov/www/global/human_rights/1999_hrp_report/occterr.html> (accessed 11 August 2000).

Weber, M. (1981) *General Economic History*, New Brunswick: Transaction Books.

# 5 Monopolies and the PNA

*Mohamed M. Nasr*

The implications of public and private monopolies in the West Bank and Gaza Strip (WBGS) have raised concerns amongst donors and international organizations, and within Palestine, amongst political groups and the private sector. These concerns have focused on how clientelism and rent-seeking may have induced the Palestinian National Authority (PNA) to participate in the creation of harmful monopolies. As a result, the PNA has been accused of granting monopoly concessions on the basis of personal contacts, favouritism and kickbacks rather than efficiency considerations, and of establishing public import monopolies at the expense of the private sector. If true, such an analysis suggests that the monopolies and rent-seeking sustained by the PNA wasted resources, retarded private investment and must have been at least partially responsible for the poor performance of the Palestinian economy.

There are two problems with this simplistic interpretation of the role of monopolies in Palestine. First, the economic effects of rents that appear to be monopoly rents can be quite complex in reality. There are a number of economic conditions that may make apparent monopolies less malign in some contexts and even positively beneficial in others. The PNA was operating in a context where political and economic instability, among other factors, retarded private investment. Some of the monopoly concessions that the PNA granted to the private sector were specifically to induce investments in large developmental projects, especially infrastructure projects such as electricity and telecommunications. In a context of deep political instability, these rents could be judged to have played a useful role in attracting much-needed investments into what was essentially a conflict zone.

Second, a closer examination of the Palestinian context suggests that in some sectors, the external constraints were such that realistic alternatives to the operation of Palestinian monopolies were not immediately present. The imports of strategic commodities such as cement and petroleum were regulated by the terms of the Paris Economic Protocol in terms of quantities allowed and the clearance of revenues in ways that effectively gave Israel a monopoly position in the supply of these goods to the Palestinian market. In such a context, the creation of counterpart Palestinian import monopolies by the PNA at least had a rationale as it allowed the PNA to capture some of the monopoly rents that would otherwise have gone to Israel. The Paris Protocol was also important in creating an almost total fiscal dependence of the PNA on Israel. This in turn created a desperate need on the part of the PNA to generate independent revenues, and in particular, off-budget revenues that could be used in a discretionary way to manage an extremely volatile and unpredictable political context. While rent-seeking by individuals and groups undoubtedly drives the creation of all monopolies, an evaluation of the *effects* of specific monopolies must consider the context, and in particular, whether the competitive alternative would be feasible in this conflict zone facing unique external constraints.

This analysis is not meant to suggest that monopolies were not problematic in the Palestinian context. The reality was more complex. Some monopoly rents were indeed damaging, others were benign or had positive implications for Palestinian development, while others still were second-best responses to external constraints. This suggests that an attempt to generalize the problem of monopolies is likely to be misleading. Instead, the different factors motivating the existence of monopoly rents need to be identified if appropriate policies are to be devised in the future. In the absence of an explicit economic strategy and an effective regulatory structure for promoting and monitoring particular monopolies, some Palestinian monopolies were inevitably economically damaging, and were sustained by rent-seeking and clientelism exactly as standard economic theory suggests.

We start by discussing the possible economic effects of monopoly at a very general level. We then examine the development of Palestinian business, the problems confronting the Palestinian business community, and the political context within which business was operating during this period. We then analyse and try to explain the PNA's attitude towards different types of monopoly and towards the rent-seeking behaviour associated with these monopolies. In particular, we distinguish between state-created private monopolies and state import monopolies, and discuss the differences in the motivations behind these two types of monopolies and their effects. Finally, we conclude by discussing some of the implications for policy.

## Monopolies and economic development

Economists have traditionally criticized monopolies on the grounds that they result in a lower net output for society. This is also described as allocative inefficiency since resources are being misallocated if society's net output falls. The social cost of allocative inefficiency is measured by the deadweight welfare loss (DWL) which measures the net value of the output lost when the monopolist cuts back production to raise prices and profits. While there are very few true monopolies, any group of firms that has the market power to control production or sales to raise prices can have a monopoly-type effect in lowering net output, and can generate a deadweight welfare loss for society in exactly the same way. Harberger (1954) attempted to estimate the deadweight welfare loss associated with all the reductions in output due to monopoly-like market power in the United States economy in the 1920s. He found, under restrictive assumptions, that this loss did not exceed one tenth of one per cent of the US GNP during that period. This is negligibly small, implying that the concern with monopoly was misplaced. There have been many criticisms of Harberger's study in terms of both his assumptions and methodology. Subsequent studies argued that the DWL in the US economy was as much as 8 per cent of US GNP (Kamerschen 1966; Cowling and Mueller 1978).

Allocative inefficiency is not the only economic effect of monopolies. Another adverse effect associated with monopoly is internal inefficiency due to production costs rising when competitive pressure is weak or absent. Leibenstein (1966, 1978) called this phenomenon 'X-inefficiency'. He argued that when competitive pressure is weak, firms may tolerate and indeed maintain extra costs, such as the purchase of more inputs than necessary, lower effort by employees, wasteful perks for management, and so on. There is evidence that this type of inefficiency exists in many advanced economies including those of the USA and Europe. For example, a study by Primeaux (1977) on the cost structure of electricity utilities in the USA showed that the existence of competition reduced the cost of a kilowatt-hour of electricity by almost 11 per cent. Data on other countries (such as Britain and Sweden) and on specific firms (such as Du Pont, IBM, General Motors, AT&T, Boeing) indicate that X-inefficiency is widespread (Scherer and Ross 1990: 668; Shepherd 1997: 106–7).

Despite the traditional arguments against monopoly, a special case is often accepted as an exception, namely, the natural monopoly case. Natural monopolies exist when there are increasing returns to scale such that it is more efficient to have a single firm (monopoly) in the industry producing at lower cost than to have many competing firms each with much higher costs. The classic examples of natural monopolies are utilities such as electricity, gas, water, telephone, and so on. The smaller the size of the internal market, the more likely that utilities will be natural monopolies. Many countries have allowed these utilities to exist as public sector firms, other countries have allowed them as private monopolies subject to regulation.

Even in countries where such firms are part of the public sector, there is an increasing trend to privatize these firms on the assumption that government should stay out of business. However, allowing private sector monopolies to exist without effective regulation may be no better than, and could be even worse than, public ownership. But what type of regulation is required for privately owned natural monopolies?

Free-market economists likely Demsetz (1968) have suggested minimalist regulatory frameworks such as 'competition for the field'. Here firms are allowed to bid for the right to be the natural monopoly in the industry, and if the competition is open, the government is able to extract all the

monopoly rents in advance and get the benefit of private sector management. In theory, the most efficient management would bid the highest price
to get the franchise. However, this may not be the case if there are only a
few bidders who are able to collude to put in low bids. In other cases, the
bidders may bid too much, making the subsequent enterprise unviable. As a
result, in practise, there is no alternative to ongoing regulation of natural
monopolies even when they are in the private sector. The task of the regulator is not only to set prices such that the natural monopolist does not
make excessive profits, but also to create incentives for technical progress
and price reductions over time, given the absence of competition in the
sector. Effective regulation is very difficult to achieve, and regulatory
capacity is often weak in developing countries. Even in advanced countries,
regulators can often be 'captured' by particular interests or by the industry
being regulated (Stigler 1971). This industry-capture approach to regulation
says that groups who have powerful concentrated interests seize the opportunity to use the regulatory process for their own benefit, generally to
obtain some sort of monopoly rents (Crandall 1983; Maloney and
McCormick 1982; Pashigian 1984; Ross 1984; Nasr 1986). These concerns
are often justified, but there is no alternative to the construction of effective
regulatory structures with sufficient political autonomy such that regulators
are able to carry out their work.

In addition to allocative and X-inefficiencies, economists identify a
further impact of monopoly that is related to income redistribution associated with monopoly profits. In general, profits represent a transfer of
wealth from consumers and workers to owners or shareholders of the
monopolistic firms. Comanor and Smiley (1975) estimated the distributive
impact of monopoly in the USA over the period 1890–1962 and found that
monopoly power increased the inequality of wealth distribution. Whether
such redistribution is socially acceptable or not is a political issue, but it is
plausible to argue that in many cases, redistribution to the rich would
reduce social welfare.[1]

The most important recent contribution to the study of monopoly has
come from rent-seeking theory, which has argued that the conventional
measures of the social cost of monopoly have hugely underestimated the
true cost of monopolies. These theorists argue that the really substantial
cost of a monopoly is the series of expenses that are incurred by would-be
and existing monopolists to acquire or preserve their rents. With a restrictive
set of assumptions, the early rent-seeking theorists argued that rent-seekers
would collectively spend an amount equal to the potential rents that the
monopolies generated to persuade the state to grant them the monopoly
(Tullock 1967; Krueger 1974; Posner 1975; Colander 1984; Scherer and Ross
1990: 672; Henderson 1993: 762). Since the monopoly rent is typically much
larger than the deadweight welfare loss, if rent-seeking theory is correct, the
total social cost of a monopoly would be many times larger than conventional theory identifies. The (simple) theory of rent-seeking has been

challenged on a number of grounds. First, the amount spent on rent-seeking can vary significantly depending on the institutional and political conditions under which rent-seeking is taking place. Second, and even more significantly, the institutional and political context is particularly important for explaining what types of rents are created through rent-seeking. Since not all rents are value-reducing, this explains why some societies perform much better than others despite rent-seeking being a common feature of virtually every society (see Chapter 1 by Khan and Khan 2000).

## The development of the Palestinian business sector

An evaluation of monopolies and of rent-seeking in the contemporary Palestinian economy needs to begin by considering the development of the Palestinian business sector over the last few decades. The Palestinian economy is predominantly characterized by small, family-owned and family-run firms, with limited capital coming mainly from family resources. It would be wrong to conclude that this firm structure reflects the relative efficiency of small firms in Palestine without looking at the effect of almost three decades of Israeli occupation of the WBGS since 1967. Various Israeli policies and procedures helped to constrain the expansion and/or entry of Palestinian business firms during that period, including restrictions on granting permits for industrial projects, heavy taxes, restraints on the imports of raw materials needed for industry, restrictions on the exports of Palestinian goods other than to Israel, closure of Arab and foreign banks, negligence of needed infrastructure, and restraints on the development of public institutions (World Bank 1993; Nasr 1994). These policies and procedures imposed barriers to entry and growth, increased political uncertainty, and slowed down investment, exacerbating the limitations of poor natural resource endowments and the small size of the local market.

During the occupation period, a number of Palestinian firms engaged in subcontracting activities for Israeli businesses, especially in the textile and footwear industries. Some of these firms performed well as subcontractors, others progressed from subcontracting to independent production for local and export markets, especially in the leather and shoe industries, soft drinks, cigarettes and confectioneries (World Bank 1993: v. 3, 41). But the majority of firms remained small not only in absolute terms but also relative to the size of the market. Almost 90 per cent of industrial establishments in 1991 employed 7 employees or fewer, most of them were sole proprietorships generally financed by owners, family members or friends (Nasr 1994).

Israeli policies and measures played a key role in keeping the Palestinian private sector weak and fragmented. According to a World Bank mission (World Bank 1993: v. 3, 31), there were no market leaders or signs of industry consolidation or of oligopolistic formations. The mission estimated the four-firm concentration ratio in most industries in the 10–20 per cent range. Only in a few industries (cigarettes, soft drinks, and cardboard packaging) were there single firms that accounted for 25–50 per cent of the market.

Despite the optimism that accompanied the peace process since 1993, there has been little improvement in the Palestinian economy due to the Israeli siege and closure policies that continued during this period. The PNA made progress in some areas, such as institution building, rehabilitation of infrastructure and legal reforms, but most of these efforts were hampered by the lack of economic development. It is estimated that the cost of the Israeli closure policies during the 1993–96 period was around $2.8 billion, which was about the size of one year's GDP and nearly twice the sum of disbursed donor aid over the same period (Baunsgeard 1998: 16).

The impact of Israeli policies and measures on investment has been significantly negative. First, part of the donor assistance, which was originally intended to finance public investment projects, was converted into public consumption (to finance emergency job creation programmes to alleviate the suffering caused by closures). Second, the perception of high political risk associated with these policies discouraged the influx of capital into the Palestinian economy and made entrepreneurs reluctant to invest in the WBGS. In a survey by the World Bank (Sewell 2001: 3), 77 per cent of the respondents from the private sector cited instability and uncertainty as the biggest constraint to their operations and growth. According to that survey, much of the uncertainty that adversely affected business planning in the WBGS was the result of Israeli security procedures including restrictions on the movement of people, vehicles and goods.

These policies increased the cost of doing business in the WBGS and reduced the competitiveness of Palestinian products, further constraining the expansion of Palestinian business firms. As a result, the size structure of business firms did not change much after the PNA assumed responsibility in 1994. The Palestinian economy remained dominated by small, family-owned firms. In 1998, 76 per cent of firms in the WBGS were sole proprietorships, and more than 56 per cent of the people working in these establishments were owners and unpaid family members (UNSCO 1998). In the industrial sector, more than 90 per cent of firms in the WBGS employed less than 10 workers, only 20 establishments hired more than 100 people and very few industries had just one or two sellers in the market (PCBS 1998: 42–6).

Nevertheless, with the arrival of the PNA, many business and trade organizations emerged and began to play an increasingly important role in protecting the interest of various groups within the business community. These included the industry union, the hotel union, and others. These associations were completely new players and though they had little immediate impact on the decision-making process, they pointed to the rapid emergence of articulated business interests. Paltrade (the Palestinian Trade Centre) became one of the most influential private associations, getting strong support from government offices and international organizations. It sought to promote the interest of private businesses through cooperation with the public sector. This association, however, had high entry barriers in the form of registration and membership fees and it represented mainly large businesses. In May 2000,

Paltrade held the first National Trade Dialogue Conference (NTDC), which provided an opportunity for a dialogue between the leadership of the business community and senior government officials to address general problems facing the private sector. One of the main topics discussed in the conference was the publicly owned or endorsed monopolies and their relationship with senior public officials. The conference declared that it opposed all forms of monopoly, whether owned by government or by the private sector, except where there could be 'general economic or national justifications'. Even in these cases, private and public monopolies should be prevented from expanding their activities and using their position to become active in other areas. In the cases where monopolistic privileges to private companies could be justified, the conference demanded that the bid should require the winning company to register as a general shareholding company in accordance with Palestinian law. In that context, the conference demanded that a law regarding monopolies and privileges be established to prevent monopolistic enterprises abusing their power (Paltrade 2000: 23–4). The conference also demanded that the private sector should participate in the formulation of this and other economic laws, express its opinion on the final status negotiations, especially on economic issues, and participate in formal missions to other countries to discuss economic cooperation. This conference has been seen by many observers as an early attempt by local capital to exercise its influence.

## The economic challenge

The PNA had realized from the beginning the challenges and constraints it would be facing, especially in terms of financial and technical needs. An early effort by the PLO office in Tunisia estimated the cost of rebuilding and reconstructing the Palestinian state to be around $11.6 billion (PLO Economic Department 1991). Three sources of financial assistance were of special importance to the PNA: the donor countries, the wealthy Palestinian Diaspora and foreign direct investment. All these source were immediately called upon for help.

Shortly after the signing of the Oslo Accord, the donor countries pledged $2.1 billion to aid the Palestinian people during the transition period identified as 1994–98. Part of this aid was offered as technical assistance, especially for institution building. In 1996, the PNA, with the assistance of the World Bank and the IMF, prepared and presented a document to donor countries summarizing the Palestinian Development Strategy for the medium term (PNA 1996). According to that document, four areas were identified as urgent need areas, namely physical infrastructure, business development, financial systems and the legal and regulatory framework. The document also states that the PNA would support an open, export-oriented, private-sector led market economy.

The private sector could not be easily convinced to invest in the WBGS at that early stage of the transition period despite the steps that were undertaken by the PNA to improve the business environment, including rehabilitation of infrastructure, regulatory reforms and institution building. The PNA and President Arafat repeatedly called upon the Palestinian Diaspora and foreign entrepreneurs to come and invest in the WBGS, to help reconstruction and to build the emerging Palestinian state.

A few large groups did respond to President Arafat's call. In 1993, a group of wealthy Palestinians established a holding company called the 'Palestinian Development and Investment Co. Ltd' (PADICO) with a declared capital of US$1 billion and a subscribed capital of US$172 million. The objectives of the company were 'to attract investment that will help rebuild the economic infrastructure of the Palestinian economy, create jobs, (and) encourage the private sector to contribute in all sectors' (the Jordanian *Al-Rai* Newspaper 24 March 1994). President Arafat described the founders of the firm as the tigers of the Palestinian economy who were expected to play a major role in building the Palestinian state. The company established subsidiaries in various sectors, including telecommunications (Paltel), tourism (JIT and PTIC), real estate (AQARIA), industry (PIIC), industrial estates (PIEDCO), electricity (PEC), poultry (PPC), electronics (PEEC), plastics (PPIC) and the security exchange (PSEC). Another group of investors who responded to President Arafat's call to invest in the WBGS formed 'The Arab Palestinian Investment Co. Ltd' (APIC), which was part of the Al-Akkad group. This company also established many subsidiaries in various sectors including consumer goods (UNIPAL), medical services (MSS), car distribution (PAC), aluminum (NAPCO), food (SINIORA), cold storage (APCS) and shopping centres (APSC). APIC also has investments in other companies such as Paltel, PEC, and the Arab Islamic International Bank.

In addition to these two groups, there was a rush by foreign (and local) investors to establish commercial banks in the WBGS. The Israeli military had closed down all Arab and foreign-owned banks after its occupation of the Palestinian territories in 1967 and replaced them with Israeli Banks. In 1981, the Bank of Palestine reopened in Gaza and, in 1986, the Cairo-Amman Bank reopened in the West Bank. There was little competition in the provision of banking services during this period due to Israeli restrictions, creating huge rents for the incumbents. A number of local investor groups had applied to the Israeli authorities for licences to open new banks, but without success (World Bank 1993: v 3, 77). After the arrival of the PNA, the banking sector expanded substantially from 2 banks with 13 branches at the end of 1993 to 22 banks with 120 branches by the end of 2000. Of these 22 banks, only nine were locally chartered, the rest were considered foreign banks. The Diaspora Palestinians wholly or partially owned most of these foreign banks (MAS 1997). Similar but less dramatic changes occurred in the insurance sector. Until 1993 there was only one insurance company in the WBGS, the Arab Insurance Co. headquartered in Nablus, together with agents of Israeli firms. After the arrival of the PNA, four new insurance companies were established in the WBGS, in addition to branches and agencies of foreign companies.

Smaller foreign entrepreneurs also visited the Palestinian territories, especially in the early period immediately after the PNA assumed responsibility over parts of the WBGS, to explore the opportunities available for investment. Some of them started businesses, others preferred to wait. Most of those who started businesses focused on areas of low risk and/or large rents, especially in real estates and services. Long-term productive investments were limited due to the high degree of uncertainty over the permanent status negotiations. The Law of Encouragement of Investment, which was passed in 1995 and modified in 1998, was intended to provide incentives, mainly tax breaks, to local and foreign private entrepreneurs but had a limited effect in promoting productive investment. Critics argued that the law was not effective because it ignored small-scale businesses, which represented the majority of Palestinian enterprises. It was claimed that the Law was biased toward large firms and thus promoted monopolies for politically influential groups in the Palestinian economy. This is partially true. But the PNA could explain its bias towards large firms in terms of efficiency and growth. Whenever there are economies of scale, such as in infrastructure projects, large firms can be expected to be more competitive, have superior technology and create more jobs. If large firms are inefficient, theory and evidence suggests that this is because there are artificial barriers to entry, and not because of large size per se (Stigler 1968: 69; Demsetz 1968). It is true that the Law of Encouragement of Investment was not entirely successful in attracting foreign (and local) direct investment, but this was not due to its perceived bias towards large enterprises. It was more likely to have been because of other factors including political, economic and legal instability in the area.

Given the limited success of conventional incentive packages such as the Law of Encouragement of Investment, the PNA was faced with a dilemma. It wanted the private sector to invest, especially in large infrastructure projects, which would promote the development process and reduce the financial burden on the PNA. But the private sector was reluctant to do so due to severely hostile conditions. To overcome this problem, the PNA followed a number of parallel strategies. First, the PNA granted monopolistic concessions to private investors in large infrastructure projects such as telecommunications and electricity to make investment more attractive. Second, in some cases it went into partnership with private firms in business activities such as hotels, casinos, cigarettes and flour milling. Finally, in yet another set of cases, the PNA monopolized the imports and distribution of certain strategic products such as cement and petroleum. Each of these strategies involved discriminatory support for large firms. It is not surprising that the PNA came under heavy criticism for clientelism, rent-seeking and corruption, and for supporting monopolies.

Criticisms of PNA policies came from many groups, not least the Palestinian Legislative Council (PLC) itself, but also the World Bank, the

IMF, international organizations, donor countries, the business community, opposition leaders outside the Palestinian territories, and local and international media. Even the Israelis used these activities to claim that the PNA and Arafat were corrupt.[2] Since the causes, consequences and justifications of private monopolies in Palestine are different from those of public monopolies, our subsequent discussion will treat these separately.

## Private monopolies

The rehabilitation of infrastructure was given top priority in the PNA's strategic plans due to its importance for the economic development of the Palestinian economy. Most of the early infrastructure projects were implemented by the public sector (largely by the Palestinian Economic Council for Development and Reconstruction (PECDAR)) using donors' funds. However, while the conditions of Palestinian physical infrastructure were extremely poor due to prolonged negligence during the occupation period, donor funds, allocated for this purpose, were limited. To alleviate this situation, the PNA tried to motivate private investors to provide infrastructure services, and one of the ways in which it did this was by limiting entry and thereby guaranteeing rents for investors. Projects involving private-sector participation where evidence of such a strategy can be found included the Gaza Water and Sanitation Service Project, the Electricity Distribution and Management Project, the Palestine Industrial Estate Development and Management Company (PIEDCO), and the Palestinian Telecommunications Co. (Paltel). The PNA also awarded a 20-year build–operate–transfer contract to a private company for the development of a power generating plant in Gaza, under which the company would ultimately provide 2.5 MW of power. Other private monopolies and oligopolies were established in other sectors, including commercial banks, insurance companies, import monopolies, etc. In all these cases, it is possible to argue that instead of reducing the value of net social output, the creation of rents by limiting and controlling entry increased the value of net output by inducing investments in a context of instability. These were therefore potential examples of rents that served to induce investments and enhance social output (Khan 2000: 22, 40–53).

The Palestinian Telecommunication Co. (Paltel) can be taken as a case study to illustrate this situation. The company has drawn much attention as one of the early private monopolies in the WBGS due to the size of the firm, the nature of its activities and the names of its major shareholders. Paltel was established as a public shareholding company in May 1995 with an initial authorized capital of US$ 63 million (Jordanian Dinars (JD) 45 million), in accordance with an agreement signed between the PNA and a group of private investment companies and institutions. Major shareholders accounted for 68 per cent of the company, with the remaining 32 per cent being owned by individuals. The major shareholders were the Palestine

Development and Investment Company Ltd (23.29 per cent), the Palestinian Commercial Services Company (6.78 per cent), the Arab Bank (7.78 per cent), the Arab Palestine Investment Company Ltd (5.93 per cent) and the Cairo Amman Bank (3.99 per cent). In November 1999, the company raised its capital by 50 per cent to US\$ 95 million (JD 67.5 million) through a rights issue. Paltel was granted a licence from the PNA for a 20-year period to operate, maintain and manage the telecommunications sector in Palestine. This licence covers both voice and non-voice, fixed and cellular networks. A separate subsidiary called Palcel provided Mobile GSM services, and was 65 per cent owned by Paltel and 35 per cent by the PNA. Branded as Jawwal, this service began operations in October 1999.

There is no doubt that Paltel managed to achieve remarkable results within a few years of being established (in terms of services, numbers of lines and employment generation). But it has also been subject to much criticism, including accusations of misuse of monopoly power, clientelism and rent-seeking. Local firms and households complain that Paltel does not collect telephone bills from ministries, governmental establishments, major shareholders and officials, and that it redistributes these costs to other customers in the form of higher charges. As expected, the company denies charges of clientelism and rent-seeking, and insists that 'most' of the government ministries and officials pay their bills. The company claims that prices of local calls have dropped many times and prices of international calls have dropped by between 20 and 58 per cent since it took over. This might be true, but it does not mean that the company's prices were competitive or that it was efficient. Lower prices in neighbouring markets (e.g. Israel) and the considerable profits of the firm since the first year of its operations, suggest that at the very least, the claims of rent-seeking and clientelism have to be investigated further.

Criticisms were also raised regarding the way in which Paltel was awarded the exclusive rights contract. Although Paltel claims that it was awarded this agreement by bidding fairly on the project and winning the contract on competitive terms, a PLC Special Committee report (1997: 21) claims that the process was non-transparent and criticizes the agreement because it was not submitted to, or approved by, the PLC. The World Bank (2000: 3) also criticized the agreement because the scope of the exclusive rights of Paltel is uncertain and the legal and regulatory framework needed to ensure fair play is inadequate. According to the World Bank, 'as long as there is no independent, trusted regulator in WBGS, there will be a suspicion of favoritism (or worse) among investors. Whatever investment may come is likely to be based on relationships not competitiveness. This type of investment will not be able to compete outside WBGS and … will remain dependent on its connections, not its competitiveness to protect its Palestinian market.'

Another issue that relates to rent-seeking is the report that the Peace Technology Fund (PTF) has purchased 3.3 per cent of Paltel's shares for \$9 million (*al-Ayyam* Newspaper, 25 May 1999). The argument that rents are just a transfer of income and that they do not represent a waste for society as a whole has been questioned here since the Peace Technology Fund (PTF) is not a Palestinian institution. Paltel has made profits of around JD10 (around $14) million in 1997, JD8.6 (around $12) million in 1998 and JD6.4 (around $9) million in 1999 (Paltel 1998 and 1999 Annual Reports). Part of these profits was distributed to foreign shareholders, such as PTF, and this is arguably a drain or 'waste' for the Palestinian economy. It is doubtful whether the purchase of these shares by PTF added any new productive capacity in the Palestinian economy and clearly, the rents collected by PTF have not been reinvested in the WBGS. The issue, in this particular case, has an added importance because the fund, which is often called Peres Fund after Israel's foreign minister, is in practice controlled by Israel, which increases the dependency of the Palestinian economy on Israel, contrary to the declared Palestinian strategy.

The PNA defends its policy of granting exclusive rights to private firms by arguing that monopolistic contracts for large infrastructure projects, such as electricity and telecommunications, were granted to the private sector on economic grounds. Even in advanced market economies such as the USA and Europe, it is quite usual to see large private firms in the utilities sector with significant potential market power to earn monopoly profits, but these large firms are justified in terms of their greater efficiency. In Palestine, according to the PNA, large projects would not have been established had the PNA not given exclusive rights and other concessions to private investors.

Not many people dispute the economic justification of granting effective monopolies to firms in infrastructure projects. In a small country like Palestine, with a limited market size and low level of economic activity, it may not be feasible to have more than one telecommunication company or more than one electricity company. In fact, one of the recommendations of the PLC report (1997: 49) was to speed up the establishment of the 'Palestinian Electricity Company' as a public shareholding company, with the participation of municipalities, energy authorities and the private sector. The private sector also recognizes the necessity of 'granting privileges in some fields for limited periods' to private monopolies, but has expressed concerns over the lack of transparency and a legal framework (Paltrade 2000: 52). Instead Paltrade demanded that these monopolies should be prevented from extending their activities to monopolize other downstream areas (such as the monopolization of Internet services by Paltel).

The solution is clearly not to break up these natural monopolies. Even the World Bank (2000: 3) argues that instead of breaking up monopolies, it is important 'to define clearly and openly the exact scope and duration of a monopoly over any particular segment of the market…to establish a National Regulatory Authority…and to enact a competition law'. These measures are needed not to eliminate monopoly rents or exclusive rights to monopoly, but rather to regulate private monopolies in terms of price and quality and to increase efficiency in the economy as a whole. In this way, the allocative and X-inefficiency problems of monopolies can be reduced without losing the economies of scale. In addition, in the Palestinian context, it may be that there would be no investments at all without substantial rents for investors.

An interesting aspect of many private monopolies in Palestine is that not only are they supported by the PNA, in many cases, the PNA is part owner of these monopolies through complex holding companies. Attempts at public scrutiny of the PNA began very early on with the first report of the Palestinian Public Monitoring and Audit Department (PMAD) for 1996, published on 23 May 1997. The report focused on various administrative, financial and legal violations by PNA ministries and public institutions, and discussed government monopolies in this context. The report was debated by the PLC, and received wide coverage in the press, in public discussions and in donor countries. The PNA responded to the PMAD report with a statement addressed to donor countries and presented to the Ad Hoc Liaison Committee meeting in Washington DC on 5 June 1997. The statement denied any serious violations or mismanagement, and argued that these violations were minor and the result of inexperience on the part of new institutions in running a system that was not fully established.

However, this was not the end of the matter because the PLC set up a Special Committee to investigate the PMAD report and to submit its conclusions and recommendations to the Council. This PLC Special Committee submitted a lengthy report that included a detailed discussion of various issues and pointed to different types of mismanagement and violations, including public monopolies, government interventions in the market, and government participation and shareholding in private enterprises. The PLC report cited many examples of firms owned either totally or partially by the PNA, such as the Petroleum Public Commission, Al-Bahar Company, the Tobacco Commission, Palestinian Commercial Services Company (PCSC), the Radio and Television Commission and the Palestinian National Company for Economic Development (PNCED). The PLC report indicated that these institutions were not monitored by PMAD and that the revenues collected by them were not included in the government's budget. It was finally in response to this report and to pressure from donor countries that the PNA published a document titled 'West Bank Economic Policy Framework: Progress Report' prepared in collaboration with the IMF and dated 31 May 2000. The Progress Report provided a list of the PNA's investments in commercial operations through the PCSC, which was fully owned by PNA. Table 5.1 lists these investments, and shows that at the end of 1999, the PCSC reported equity holdings of around $292 million.

These figures did not cover the total asset ownership of the PCSC. The total assets of the PCSC reported at that time amounted to $345 million; in a later estimate in 2003, this was revised upwards to $633 million (IMF 2003: 101). Nevertheless, the figures give us an indication of the range and

*Table 5.1* PNA equity holdings as of December 1999

| Company name | Estimated market value ($ million) | Percentage of equity |
|---|---|---|
| Jericho Resort (hotel and casino) | 60.0 | 30.0 |
| Cement Company | 50.0 | 100.0 |
| Palcell | 50.0 | 35.0 |
| Paltel | 32.2 | 8.0 |
| Arab Palestinian Investment Company | 16.0 | 20.0 |
| PADICO | 15.0 | 8.0 |
| Various real estates | 14.0 | 100.0 |
| Bioniche Lire Sciences Inc. | 9.0 | 10.0 |
| The United Company for Storage and Refrigeration | 8.5 | 30.0 |
| Peace Technology Fund | 6.2 | 34.0 |
| Qaser Jaser Hotel (Intercontinental) | 5.0 | 25.0 |
| Palestinian Flour Mills Co. | 4.1 | 47.0 |
| Palestinian Electricity Co. | 2.6 | 6.0 |
| Palestinian Investment Bank | 2.3 | 8.0 |
| Bethlehem Convention Centre | 2.0 | 45.0 |
| Coca Cola | 1.5 | 15.0 |
| Gaza Insurance Co. | 1.5 | 14.0 |
| Al-Ahlia Co. | 1.4 | 50.0 |
| National Aluminum Profiles Co. | 1.3 | 16.0 |
| Grand Park Hotel | 1.2 | 25.0 |
| Steel Co. | 1.2 | 15.0 |
| Vegetable Oil Co. | 1.0 | 7.0 |
| Palestinian-Qatar Fund | 0.9 | 33.0 |
| Al-Motakhasesa Investment Co. | 0.9 | 15.0 |
| Gaza College and School | 0.7 | 40.0 |
| Al-Ahlia Industrial Co. | 0.7 | 15.0 |
| Al-Salaam International Co. | 0.5 | 5.0 |
| Al-Mara'i Co. | 0.5 | 00 |
| Glass Cutting Co. | 0.4 | 40.0 |
| Palestinian Cigarettes Co. | 0.3 | 80.0 |
| Logo Company | 0.3 | 28.0 |
| Al-Tekania Engineering Co. | 0.2 | 30.0 |
| Jordanian Specialized Co. | 0.2 | 50.0 |
| 1st Choice Management | 0.1 | 30.0 |
| Sub-total | 291.6 | |

structure of PCSC equity holdings in ostensibly private enterprises. This ranged from less than 5 per cent to 100 per cent, in enterprises wholly owned by the PCSC. In most cases, the holdings were minority holdings, so these companies counted as private monopolies or oligopolies. Nevertheless, a few were effectively public monopolies and will be considered separately in the next section. In the case of the public–private partnerships, Khaled Salam, also known as Mohammad Rasheed, economic advisor to President Arafat, Chairman of the Board and General Manager of PCSC, argued that the PCSC was an ideal partner for the private sector. He argued that business people themselves approached PCSC and expressed a willingness to be partners in some projects (interview with Khaled Salam, *Al-Ayyam* Newspaper, 6 November 1997). This might be true because private entrepreneurs expected to obtain monopoly powers and earn considerable rents in return for these partnerships. This can be verified by examining the enterprises in Table 5.1. Almost all the enterprises in which the PCSC held equity were monopolies or oligopolies and therefore enjoyed considerable market power. But if the creation of monopolies induced new investment by the private sector in risky infrastructure projects, then we would argue that the rents were not necessarily socially damaging. It is more than likely that the creation of these monopolies had a positive effect on private sector investment in infrastructure projects simply on the grounds that 'normal' profits would be unlikely to attract significant private capital into a conflict zone. The Progress Report does not show investments by other PNA institutions such as Al-Bahar, PNCED, the Petroleum Public Commission, the Radio and Television Commission, and others, so it is difficult to assess the scope of this strategy.

However we have to consider seriously the possibility that PNA shareholdings in these private sector companies was a form of extortion. It may be that private investors were 'willing' to be partners with PNA institutions because they had no choice, if they wanted to enter or remain in rent-generating businesses (e.g. gas stations). In a World Bank Business Environment Survey (WBES) 11 per cent of respondents claimed that a government agency or government official had asked for part ownership of their firm as a condition to allow them to operate. This result does not mean that the PNA itself had put forward such conditions but as the WBES report argues, it is possible that senior public officials were involved.

But we need to ask a more general question. Why would the PNA want to be a partner in private enterprises? After all, individuals within the PNA could have extracted rents in the form of bribes without such elaborate arrangements. The partnership and shareholding strategy (reminiscent of the Kuomintang's ownership of shares in Taiwanese companies in the 1950s, see Chapter 2 by Hilal and Khan) clearly requires a more specific explanation. Part of the answer may lie in the specific political and economic constraints facing the PNA, and the need for off-budget sources of revenue to cover essential political expenditures. As MacIntyre (2000: 250) explains, there may be a variety of constraints on the use of the official public budget for large-scale rent transfers. In addition there may be specific constraints that prevent political leaders retaining discretion over budgetary funds.

In the Palestinian case, there were serious constraints imposed by the agreements with Israel (as part of the Oslo Accords) and the Israeli policies and measures that followed. Approximately 60 per cent of the PNA's annual revenues came from or through Israel. The concern that Israel may use these revenues as a political weapon to exert pressure on the PNA to get political concessions was real and Israel's willingness and ability to do this was demonstrated on various occasions. The comprehensive and complete closure of the WBGS during the Second *Intifada* and the withholding of PNA money by Israel was final confirmation of these concerns. Furthermore, the official public budget was subject to the scrutiny of many groups, including the PLC, donor countries and Israel. All of this constrained the flexibility of the PNA in the use of these funds, especially for purposes of political stabilization through patron–client expenditures.

In such a context, the PNA's strategy of collecting rents in a systematic and semi-formalized manner through partnerships and shareholdings to finance off-budget activities did have systematic factors driving it. The political logic behind this is no secret, and in fact the National Economic Dialogue Conference organized by the emerging private sector (Paltrade 2000: 51) also concluded that one of the main reasons behind the emergence of PNA monopolies and investments was the resource requirement of the PNA and the PLO to cover expenses inside and outside Palestine. The Israelis too were well aware of this, despite accusations of non-transparency and corruption. For example, the Israeli newspaper *Ha'aretz* (4 April 1997) argued that the revenues of PNA monopolies provided resources for financing PNA activities that donor countries refused to finance.

There is little information about the magnitude or breakdown of the PNA's off-budget revenues and expenditures. However, the PNA announced that it earned approximately $77 million of net profits on its investments through PCSC operations in 1999 (PNA 2000). The revenues earned from other PNA institutions are unknown, as is the total size of the PNA's off-budget revenues. It is claimed that part of these revenues was reinvested in business operations while a part was deposited in unofficial accounts. Khaled Salam, economic advisor of President Arafat, has consistently refused to confirm or deny the existence of such accounts. He argues that each country has the right not to disclose its financial capabilities, especially when a 'large part of your body is under occupation' (*Al-Ayyam* Newspaper, 6 November 1997).

This interpretation supports our claim that the creation of private monopolies was at least partly motivated by economic concerns to accelerate large-scale infrastructural investments. The evidence suggests that private monopolies were not entirely sustained by corruption whereby individual private investors protected their monopoly rents by bribing individuals in the state. To a large extent, the PNA claimed a share of these monopoly rents in a more organized and deliberate way through share ownerships. This suggests that the creation of some of these monopolies at least was a deliberate political decision and that the PNA had a long-term stake in the economic success of these enterprises. But equally, given the secrecy of off-budget accounts, it is also more than likely that the PNA strategy included areas of inefficiency where corruption and clientelism were likely to have played a role in protecting specific monopoly rents. In particular, this would be very likely where private monopolies were owned (or managed) by high-ranking officials. The Council on Foreign Relations Report (Rocard *et al.* 1999: 19) attributed the emergence of private firms owned or managed by public officials to the lack of a regulatory framework, which led 'to undisclosed commercial dealings by public servants and to privileged access for private actors to the award of contracts, licences and exclusive dealerships'. The PLC Special Committee (1997: 57) cited many examples of high-ranking officials using their position to generate or protect monopoly rents for relatives or special groups and recommended that 'PNA officials should not be allowed to participate in establishing companies, accept membership of the Board of Directors, or do any commercial activities that may lead or give the impression of conflict of interest or use of official influence'. This recommendation has been repeated by the NTDC (Paltrade 2000: 55) and the Council on Foreign Relations (Rocard *et al.* 1999: 20) which both recommended that all public servants and elected officials should be required to disclose, and if necessary divest, private commercial interests. These recommendations are entirely appropriate, and they are also compatible with our analysis. The challenge for the PNA or its successor is to make explicit the economic goals of the state and to devise a regulatory structure that can monitor and discipline firms that are receiving rents as part of such a strategy.

**Public monopolies**

Table 5.1 shows that the PNA not only owned shares in primarily private sector companies like Paltel, but also effectively owned a number of companies through majority or exclusive shareholdings. These companies were by definition 'public monopolies', and like the cement monopoly, they were mainly import monopolies. The PNA's ownership of shares and of import-monopolies in particular has been widely criticized for many reasons. First, while private monopolies in infrastructure can be justified on economic grounds, import monopolies appear to be inconsistent with the free-market strategy the PNA claimed to support. Many, if not all, of these activities could have been undertaken by the private sector. If so, the PNA was only crowding out private investment. Second, many of the PCSC's holdings were in commercial enterprises distributing Israeli imports. This was inconsistent with the Palestinian strategy of trying to end, or at least to reduce significantly, dependence on Israel. Third, many of these goods could be imported from other countries at lower cost, which meant that a large part of the monopoly rent collected in Palestine was going to Israelis at the expense of Palestinian businesses and consumers. Fourth, the revenues from these monopolies were put into accounts that were not part of the official budget or under the Ministry of Finance, which was supposedly in charge of supervising state revenues. Fifth, there have been concerns about the lack of transparency with respect to the methods through which the PNA obtained equity holdings in all these companies. Sixth, there have also been concerns about possible monopoly powers obtained by enterprises in which PNA investment took place (Sewell 2001: 9).

Khaled Salam, economic advisor to President Arafat claimed (CPRS 1998: 41) that the PNA import monopolies were limited to only two cases, namely petroleum and cement. According to him, the PNA had been 'working hard on formulating appropriate mechanisms to handle them and transfer them to the private sector.' This was not the first time the PNA promised to privatize state monopolies but, as noted by the report of the Council on Foreign Relations (Rocard *et al.* 1999: 19), 'pledges made by PNA to privatize monopolies have not yet been fulfilled, and their revenues have not been consolidated under the Ministry of Finance as promised'. This applies to both the PNA shareholdings and its import monopolies.

With regard to the Cement Company monopoly, as shown in Table 5.1, the PCSC owned the entire equity of the company, which controlled almost all the cement imported from Israel and Jordan.[3] The monopoly was sustained with the collusion of Israeli border and security forces. There were reports that cement imported by private traders from Egypt (as allowed in theory by the Paris Economic Protocol) was subjected to intrusive inspection by the Israeli customs authority 'for security reasons' that led to many bags being torn open. The PNA cement monopoly has been criticized not only because it eliminated competition and raised costs for the vital construction sector, but also because it created a powerful coalition against the development of a Palestinian cement industry. Under these arrangements, it is likely that Israeli suppliers of cement, especially the Nesher Company, would have powerful Palestinian allies to prevent efforts to establish a cement industry in the WBGS.

Another state import monopoly was the fuel monopoly. It was not included in the PCSC equity holdings (Table 5.1) because petroleum was imported through the Palestinian Petroleum Commission. Although the Paris Protocol allowed the PNA to sell gasoline at a price up to 15 per cent lower than the Israeli price, the PNA sold petroleum at Israeli prices, if not higher. According to the Legislative Council member Mu'awiya Al Masri, the PNA took advantage of the fact that it was the sole party in control of the fuel sector to raise prices and make huge profits. He claimed that security officers who guarded the gas conveyor trucks en route from Israel confiscated any fuel that did not come via the Palestinian Petroleum Commission, so that the Commission remained the sole supplier of the commodity. According to Al-Masri, this monopoly was harmful to major sectors in the economy, mainly the farmers who consumed millions of litres of fuel, especially during the dry season.

Some economists, like Samir Abdullah of Paltrade, did not see a problem with the PNA monopoly in the fuel sector. For Abdullah a problem would only arise if 'the Petroleum Commission goes beyond its role in importing and monitoring fuel prices and gets involved in distribution [by holding equity in some gas stations]. Here it enters into a competition with the private sector.' Others believe state monopolies were seriously harmful for the standard economic reasons (CPRS 1998: 22–7).

For a proper analysis, we have to go beyond the standard economic analysis and take into account the political and security environment in which these monopolies were established. The Palestinian economy was at this time in a transition period, constrained by political agreements with Israel, and subject to Israeli policies and measures. In particular, Joseph Saba points to the restrictions imposed by the Paris Economic Protocol and argues that it created a 'discouraging bureaucratic environment' in which only large firms or firms with PNA participation or support could operate (CPRC 1998: 54–59). Although the Protocol allowed the Palestinians to import specific quantities of a limited range of goods from countries other than Israel, in practice Israel was able to limit Palestinian direct imports and to retain its control over the Palestinian market. According to Saba (CPRC 1998: 58), Israel did so in three main ways: enforcing limits on Palestinian direct imports, controlling external market access and controlling all import tax remittances. Thus, although the Palestinians were theoretically free to import from abroad, in practice it was cheaper and safer to import from Israel.

This context had profound implications for trade. Let us consider cement, which was imported mainly from Israel, although it could be purchased directly from abroad according to the Paris Protocol. In fact, small quantities were indeed imported from Jordan, Egypt and Turkey, but they did not exceed 10–15 per cent of the total. The Israeli control of borders, the restrictions on the movement of Palestinian individuals and vehicles and various Israeli obstacles (including delays at borders and checkpoints, excessive inspections, destroying bags for alleged security reasons, and so on) provided a massive advantage to Israeli producers. Saba concludes: 'the Palestinian direct importer finds that he cannot import and sell for less than the Israeli price, while his ability to move goods to delivery is always uncertain. Thus, Israeli suppliers and middlemen can offer equal or more attractive terms and quick delivery (and often finance) to Palestinian buyers' (CPRS 1998: 56).

But why would the PNA import cement (or fuel) by itself? Why did it not allow Palestinian importers to purchase cement from any source, including Israeli suppliers? Sewell argues that it is significant that under the Oslo Accords (and the Paris Economic Protocol), the bulk of petroleum imports into the WBGS effectively have to come from a single source, namely Israel.

'Given that the PNA cannot do much about this provision in the Oslo Accords, a monopsony (or single buyer) in WBG may represent the best method of limiting the resulting monopoly rents' (Sewell: 2001: 9). This is further explained by Saba who points out that

> high PA income tax, the complications of licensing, and the procedures of the 'clearance bills' of direct purchases from Israel discourage private Palestinian business from delivering the clearance bills to the Palestinian Ministry of Finance. This in turn encourages the PA to deal with a few businesses, which will do it. These few Palestinian firms are also the same firms which can cut the deals with Israeli suppliers and assure movement with the security administration.
>
> (CPRS 1998: 56)

The National Trade Dialogue Conference reached the same conclusion when it pointed out that a major reason behind the emergence of state monopolies was to prevent a leakage of Palestinian taxes and customs duties to the Israeli treasury (Paltrade 2000: 51). To see why, we have to examine the Paris Protocol once again. Article VI of the Protocol specifies the conditions and procedures of VAT revenue clearance between Israel and the PNA. These procedures involve submitting special-form bills (invoices) to the representatives of each side for tax rebates. Failure to submit these bills by one party meant that this party would not be able to collect the tax rebates on these bills. Many businesses would fail to deliver bills to the PNA Ministry of Finance for various reasons (such as to conceal revenue and profit figures and hence minimize income taxes, or to avoid the complexity of clearance procedures). In the Palestinian case, non-delivery of clearance bills by importers from or through Israel cost the PNA treasury millions of dollars every year. From the PNA's point of view, the best way to minimize these losses and to ensure delivery of clearance bills to the Ministry of Finance was to control the entire import of cement (or petroleum) from Israel, which could be done by organizing all of these imports through the PCSC (or Petroleum Public Commission). PCSC also directly imported most of the cement permitted by the Paris Protocol and sold it at the Israeli price, collecting much of the associated monopoly rents for itself.

Of course, the PNA could have granted a licence to just one private firm to import all the cement from Israel or from other countries as permitted by the Paris Protocol, and then have taxed this private company to extract all the rents. It could also have ensured that the clearance bills were delivered to the Ministry of Finance since there would be a single firm to deal with. But apart from the obvious problem of finding a private entrepreneur who would agree to run a monopoly and have all the profits taxed, this solution was also problematic from the PNA's perspective because all the tax revenues in this case would have to go through the official budget. Given the intensely conflictual situation and the PNA's desire to have some revenues in off-budget accounts, we can understand why *public* import monopolies were not only rational but also almost unavoidable.

## Conclusions

There has been widespread recognition of some of the damaging effects of private and public monopolies in Palestine. There has been far less recognition of the fact that some monopolies may have played a positive role in promoting private-sector investments in certain sectors, especially in infrastructure and services, *in a context of extreme conflict and uncertainty about the future*. Similarly, there has been little recognition that many of the public import monopolies could have been rational responses on the part of the PNA in a context where its trade and fiscal opportunities were seriously constrained by the Paris Economic Protocol, and where its needs for off-budget financing were critical for its political survival.

Such an analysis has important implications for any process of reform. While it is undoubtedly true that many monopolies have immediate costs for society in the form of higher prices, economic inefficiency, and the associated rent-seeking and corruption, it is important to distinguish between different types of monopolies and the motivations behind them. Any process of viable reform has to distinguish between types of monopoly, identify the reasons why they emerged, and identify the implications of trying to operate without them. Even without the peculiar restrictions of the Paris Protocol, the economic and political conditions in Palestine are likely to remain sufficiently uncertain for some time. Is it likely that any Palestinian authority in the near future can attract foreign or Palestinian expatriate capital in critical infrastructure projects without being able to offer temporary rents? Is it likely that without Palestinian trading monopolies, the monopoly rents on critical commodities purchased by Palestinians within an Israeli-controlled customs union can be captured even partly by a Palestinian political authority? Can the resource base of a Palestinian political entity be rapidly improved in the short-run to make unnecessary the contingency funds and accounts that its leadership has had to rely on? Reform within the Palestinian Authority to make its regulatory structure more accountable is important, but if these reforms undermine its ability to respond to the critical questions we have identified, the viability of the Authority is likely to *decline* rather than improve.

The tendency towards monopolization coming from the peculiar restrictions of the Paris Protocol needs to be addressed by re-visiting the terms of the interim economic agreements between Israel and the Palestinians. Clearly, the unequal terms of this Protocol and the control that the Protocol gave to the Israelis over Palestinian trade and the fiscal base of its authority were unworkable. One of the lessons of the PNA experience is that these arrangements made contingency funds critical. Clearly, the political demand from Palestinian society is that these funds have to be accounted for, even if the details are not immediately publicly divulged. But reform has to recognize that without addressing these fundamental causes, putting pressure on the Palestinian Authority to give up its limited sources of autonomy is likely either to be ignored or to result in the Authority becoming even less viable.

A peace agreement between the Palestinians and Israel that gives substantial sovereignty to a Palestinian state would in itself significantly contribute to reduce the motivations for state-led monopolization. In such a context, it would be more feasible to persuade the PNA or its successor to adopt an alternative incentive approach to promote investment. This is not to say that rent-seeking, clientelism and corruption will end, rather the need for particular types of rent-creation and rent-seeking to overcome political constraints will diminish.

## Notes

1 If we assume that consumers are less wealthy than owners of the firm and that income is subject to diminishing marginal utility, we may conclude that the aggregate social welfare is reduced by the redistribution of income from consumers to shareholders.
2 See, for example, *Middle East Newsline*, vol. 2 no. 463 of 29 November 2000 and the Israeli newspaper, *Ha'aretz*, of 4 April 1997.
3 Some 10–15 per cent of cement was imported by other companies from Egypt and Turkey (Sewell 2001: 9).

## References

Baunsgeard, T. (1998) 'Development Under Adversity: The Palestinian Economy in Transition', in Development Studies Program *Funding Palestinian Development*, Ramallah: Birzeit University and Ministry of Planning and International Cooperation.

CPRS (Center for Palestine Research and Studies) (1998) *Palestinian Economic System: Planned or Market Oriented?* Seminar Report Series, No. 7, Nablus.

Colander, D. C. 1984. (ed.) *Neoclassical Political Economy: The Analysis of Rent-Seeking and DUP Activities*, Cambridge MA: Ballinger Publishing Co.

Comanor, W. S. and Smiley, R. H. (1975) 'Monopoly and the Distribution of Wealth', *Quarterly Journal of Economics* 89 (2): 177–94.

Cowling, K. and Mueller, D. C. (1978) 'The Social Costs of Monopoly Power', *Economic Journal*, 88: 727–48.

Crandall, R. W. (1983) *Controlling Industrial Pollution: The Economics and Politics of Clean Air*, Washington, DC: The Brookings Institution.

Demsetz, H. (1968) 'Why Regulate Utilities', *Journal of Law and Economics*, 11: 55–65.

Harberger, A. C. (1954) 'Monopoly and Resource Allocation', *American Economic Review*, 44 (2): 77–87.

Henderson, D. R. (ed) (1993) *The Fortune Encyclopedia of Economics*, New York: Warner Books.

IMF (International Monetary Fund) (2003) *West Bank and Gaza: Economic Performance and Reform Under Conflict Conditions*, Washington: IMF.

Kamerschen, D. (1966) 'An Estimation of the "Welfare Losses" in the American Economy', *Western Economic Journal* 4 (3): 221–36.

Khan, M. H. (2000) 'Rents, Efficiency and Growth', in Khan, M. H. and Jomo, K. S. (eds) *Rents, Rent-Seeking and Economic Development: Theory and the Asian Evidence*, Cambridge: Cambridge University Press.

Krueger, A. O. (1974) 'The Political Economy of the Rent-Seeking Society', *American Economic Review*, 64 (3): 291–303.

Leibenstein, H. (1966) 'Allocative Efficiency vs. X-Efficiency', *American Economic Review* 56 (3): 392–415.

Leibenstein, H. (1978) 'X-Inefficiency Exists – Reply to an Xorcist', *American Economic Review*, 68 (1): 203–11.

MacIntyre, A. (2000) 'Funny Money: Fiscal Policy, Rent-Seeking and Economic Performance in Indonesia', in Khan, M. and Jomo, K. S. (eds) *Rents, Rent-Seeking and Economic Development: Theory and Evidence in Asia*, Cambridge: Cambridge University Press.

Maloney, M. T. McCormick, R. E. (1982) 'A Positive Theory of Environmental Quality Regulation', *Journal of Law and Economics* 25 (1): 99–123.

MAS (Palestine Economic Policy Research Institute) (1997) *Economic Monitor* Issue 1. Jerusalem and Ramallah.

Nasr, M. (1986) *The Differential Impacts of Regulation: Empirical Evidence from the Chemical Industry*, Unpublished Ph.D. Dissertation, Ohio State University.

—— (1994) 'Small Scale Industry and Commerce', paper presented at the *Conference on the Contribution of Turkey for the Construction and Development of Palestine*, Ankara: Friedrich Naumann Foundation and Ankara University.

Palestinian Authority in collaboration with the International Monetary Fund (2000) *Progress Report on the Economic Policy Framework*, May 31.

Paltel (1998) *Annual Report 1998*, Ramallah: Paltel.

—— (1999) *Annual Report 1999*, Ramallah: Paltel.

Pashigian, P. (1984) 'The Effect of Environmental Regulation on Optimal Plant Size and Factor Shares', *Journal Of Law and Economics* 27: 1–28.

PCBS (Palestinian Central Bureau of Statistics) (1998) *The Establishments Report – 1997: Final Results*, Ramallah.

PLC (Palestinian Legislative Council) (1997) *Special Committee Report*.

PNA (Palestinian National Authority) (1996) 'Palestinian Development Strategy', presented to the *Conference on the Assistance to the Palestinian People*, Paris, 9 January.

Paltrade (Palestine Trade Center) (2000) 'Conference Conclusions and Private Sector Recommendations', *National Economic Dialogue Conference*, Ramallah.

PLO Economic Department (1991) *The Palestinian Economic Development Program: 1994–2000*, Tunisia.

Posner, R. A. (1975) 'The Social Costs of Monopoly and Regulation', *Journal of Political Economy*, 83 (4): 807–27.

Primeaux, W. J. (1977) 'An Assessment of X-Efficiency Gained through Competition', *Review of Economics and Statistics*, 59 (1): 105–8.

Rocard, M., Siegman, H., Sayigh, Y., and Shikaki, K. (1999) *Strengthening Palestinian Public Institutions, Executive Summary*, Report of an Independent Task Force. Sponsored by the Council on Foreign Relations.

Ross, T. W. (1984) 'Winners and Losers Under the Robinson–Patman Act', *Journal of Law and Economics*, 27 (2): 243–71.

Scherer, F. M. and Ross, D. (1990) *Industrial Market Structure and Performance*, 3rd edn, Boston: Houghton Mifflin Co.

Sewell, D. (2001) *Governance and the Business Environment in West Bank/Gaza*, Middle East and North Africa Working Paper Series No. 23, Washington: The World Bank.

Shepherd, W. G. (1997) *The Economics of Industrial Organization*, 4th edn, New Jersey: Prentice Hall.

Stigler, G. J. (1968) *The Organization of Industry*, Chicago: The University of Chicago Press.

—— (1971) 'The Theory of Economic Regulation', *Bell Journal of Economics and Management Science* 2 (1): 3–21.

Tullock, G. (1967) 'The Welfare Costs of Tariffs, Monopolies, and Theft', *Western Economic Journal*, 5: 224–232.

UNSCO (United Nations Special Coordinator's Office) (1998) *The West Bank and Gaza Strip Private Economy: Conditions and Prospects. Special Report*, Gaza: Office of the United Nations Special Coordinator in the Occupied Territories.

The World Bank (1993) *Developing the Occupied Territories: An Investment in Peace. Vols 1–6*, Washington DC: The World Bank.

—— (2000) *West Bank and Gaza Update*, December, Washington: World Bank.

# 6    Taxation and state formation in Palestine 1994–2000

*Odd-Helge Fjeldstad and Adel Zagha*[1]

In contrast to the European experience of state formation in the context of conflict and war, the Palestinian state-formation process during the period 1994–2000 did not witness a corresponding increase in state tax collection or a rapid growth in the accountability of the state to the electorate. In comparing the European process of taxation and state formation that occurred over centuries with the Palestinian experience that spanned little over five years we do not intend to suggest that exact parallels can be drawn. Nevertheless, an examination of taxation can provide some useful insights about the nature of the constraints facing the Palestinian quasi-state over this period.

This chapter analyses the evolution of the tax system in the territories governed by the Palestinian National Authority over the period 1994–2000. The relevance of the tax system lies in the fact that tax revenues are central to (i) building state capacity and service delivery (ii) shaping state–society relations and (iii) determining the sustainability of aid. Furthermore, based on historical evidence from the West, the way a state tackles the issue of domestic revenue mobilization significantly influences its potential for economic growth and democratic consolidation (Tilly 1992). In the Palestinian context, we examine the impact of and changes in four main constraints to revenue mobilization emanating from (a) the socio-economic structures of Palestine, (b) the nature and capacity of the political and administrative institutions of government, (c) the PNA's bargaining position vis-à-vis various groups of citizens, and (d) the international context, here defined as the external actors and institutions that affected the PNA's economic policies. Of particular relevance are the Israeli–Palestinian linkages and the role of foreign aid.

The first section of this chapter describes the Palestinian tax system over the period 1994–2000. The second section discusses a number of theoretical approaches to analysing the constraints facing a state's revenue policies. The third section provides an analysis of these constraints in Palestine over our study period. A concluding section points to possible lessons for the tax system of a future Palestine state.

## Economic structure and the tax system

With a gross domestic product (GDP) per capita of US$ 1387 (in 1998), Palestine could be classified as a middle-income country (PCBS 1999).[2] The PNA was committed to a liberal economic policy regime, emphasizing incentives for private investments and a stable macroeconomic environment. At the same time, political imperatives meant that the public sector expanded rapidly. Total public expenditures accounted for more than 27 per cent of GDP in 1999, compared to 14.7 per cent when the PNA was established (Fischer *et al.* 2001: 256). This expansion was mainly due to an almost four-fold increase in public sector employees, including security forces (from 31,140 in 1994 to approximately 110,000 in mid 2000), and an expansion of social services in health and education. The PNA also used public office as a reward for political and personal loyalty, using the mechanism of incorporation to stabilize the regime (Chapter 2, Hilal and Khan). Despite the growth-oriented policies during the period 1994–2000 private sector job creation remained disappointing, and as a result the tax base did not expand significantly. This meant that public sector employment growth had to slow down considerably by the end of the 1990s, and growing criticism of inefficient and overstaffed government departments supported the slow-down. Nevertheless, the public sector was by far the largest employer in the areas controlled by the PNA. By the end of 1999, about 19 per cent of all employed persons in the West Bank Gaza Strip (WBGS) (approximately 110,000 people) were on the PNA's payroll (including education, health and security forces).[3] In the private sector, small, family-owned firms dominated the economy. According to UNSCO (1998), 76 per cent of the firms in the WBGS were sole ownerships, and almost 60 per cent of the people working in these companies were owners and unpaid family members. Furthermore, in the industrial sector more than 90 per cent of the companies had less than 10 employees (PCBS 1999).

It is clear that that the WBGS's economic performance was substantially hampered by the 'siege and closure' policies of Israel since the establishment of the PNA (Chapter 3 by Zagha and Zomlot). The policy of closure was particularly damaging because it was often totally unpredictable (Kanafani 2001: 289). Closures were declared for different lengths of time and were imposed on various categories of workers, according to age, sex, marital status and so on (Arnon and Weinblatt 2001: 298). All existing permits were suspended as long as a closure was in effect. Consequently, political uncertainty was perceived to be the main obstacle for investments. In a survey of the business environment in WBGS, 77 per cent of the respondents from the private business sector cited instability and uncertainty as the major constraints for their operations and expansion (Sewell 2001). Moreover, in a survey of small- and medium-scale enterprises, 76.5 per cent of the respondents in the WB and 84 per cent in the GS said that political instability was a major problem for their businesses.[4] Furthermore, three decades of Israeli occupation had imposed huge constraints on the development of the domestic market by neglecting improvements of physical and administrative infrastructure, and restraining trade and access to financial resources (Nasr 1994).

## Tax collection

The ratio of Palestinian fiscal revenue to GDP was estimated at 23.4 per cent in 1999, which compares well with countries at a similar level of development (Fischer *et al.* 2001: 272).[5] Table 6.1 provides an overview of the composition of fiscal revenues in Palestine during the period 1995–99. The major tax bases were personal and corporate income taxes (8.2 per cent of total tax revenues in 1999), indirect taxes on domestic goods and services (47.7 per cent) and taxes on international transactions (30.3 per cent). Furthermore, various types of fees and charges were collected. While VAT and other indirect taxes on domestic goods and services still accounted for almost half of total tax revenues, their share dropped substantially during the late 1990s. In 1995, they had accounted for about 66 per cent of total revenues. During the same period, revenues from customs duties and taxes

*Table 6.1* Composition of Palestinian fiscal revenues: 1995–2000
(as % of total fiscal revenues)

| Revenue sources | 1995 | 1996 | 1997 | 1998 | 1999 | 2000 |
|---|---|---|---|---|---|---|
| Income taxes | 11.6 | 8.3 | 8.6 | 9.0 | 8.2 | 8.3 |
| Indirect taxes on domestic goods and services | 66.0 | 61.2 | 54.6 | 51.0 | 47.7 | n.a. |
| Indirect taxes on international transactions | 6.2 | 16.0 | 20.0 | 26.7 | 30.3 | n.a. |
| Property taxes | 0.16 | 0.14 | 0.07 | 0.06 | 0.15 | n.a. |
| Non-tax revenues (fees and charges) | 15.8 | 14.3 | 16.7 | 13.3 | 13.6 | n.a. |

Source: Palestinian National Authority (2000) and World Bank (2001)

on imported goods increased from about 6 per cent of total revenues in 1995 to approximately 30 per cent in 1999. Income tax revenues remained fairly stable between 8–9 per cent of total fiscal revenues during the period 1996–99.

The PNA's fiscal operations in the period 1994–2000 were to a large extent governed by the principles of the Paris Economic Protocol (PEP), signed in 1994 (see Chapter 3 by Zagha and Zomlot). The share of Palestinian fiscal revenues collected by Israel through the clearing system remained fairly stable in the period 1995–99, and accounted for around 63 per cent of the PNA's fiscal revenues in 1999 (Fischer *et al.* 2001: 267). However, for individual revenue bases some changes were observed during this period. For instance, in 1995 Israel collected 80.2 per cent of indirect taxes on domestic goods and services, compared to 70.8 per cent in 1999. The opposite trend was observed for indirect taxes on international transactions where Israel collected 72.1 per cent in 1995, compared to 87.9 per cent in 1999 (see Table 6.2).[6]

These figures demonstrate the heavy dependence – and vulnerability – of the Palestinian economy on Israel with respect to foreign trade, employment and tax revenues. However, they also indicate that during the first years of

*Table 6.2* Palestinian fiscal revenues collected by Israel through the clearance system: 1995–99
(as % of total revenues in the specific revenue base)

| Revenue sources | 1995 | 1996 | 1997 | 1998 | 1999 |
|---|---|---|---|---|---|
| Income taxes | 10.1 | 7.2 | 9.1 | 13.5 | 8.4 |
| Indirect taxes on domestic goods and services | 80.2 | 75.6 | 72.8 | 70.2 | 70.8 |
| Indirect taxes on international transactions | 72.1 | 79.1 | 86.7 | 89.5 | 87.9 |
| Non-tax revenues (fees and charges) | 25.4 | 12.4 | 14.3 | 15.6 | 15.2 |

*Source*: Palestinian National Authority (2000) and World Bank (2001)

operation, the unified invoice system seemed to function fairly well, and probably better than most other arrangements between the PNA and Israel. But it is clear that Israel's narrow interpretation of the clause of 'place of final destination' of imports led to substantial revenue losses. Goods imported to the WBGS via the Israeli market were not considered by Israel as being 'proper imports' and thus not eligible for reclaim of customs duties by the PNA (see Chapter 3 by Zagha and Zomlot).

## Tax administration

In the areas controlled by the PNA, there were four central government agencies authorized to collect taxes: (1) The Customs Department collected customs on goods imported directly from Jordan and Egypt or through these countries; (2) The VAT and Excise Taxes Department collected VAT and purchase tax on domestic goods and services; (3) The Income Tax Department (ITD) collected personal income taxes through a withholding system, as well as corporate profit taxes from registered companies based on self-assessment albeit subject to negotiations with taxpayers in virtually all cases; and (4) The Fiscal Department collected the property taxes. There were 12 offices for each of these departments in the main towns in the WBGS. Health, insurance, transportation fees, and other charges were collected through different offices on an annual basis.

With respect to local government taxes, the taxing power of local authorities was limited. Fiscal decentralization – including increased local tax autonomy – was discussed during the late 1990s, but the implementation of such policies moved very slowly. However, in January 2001, the responsibility for collecting property taxes was transferred from the Ministry of Finance to local authorities in the WB. In addition, various forms of 'user charges' were major revenue sources for local authorities. However, due to the uncertain political situation and the PNA's well-founded fear of increased fractionalization of the country, there continued to be a highly centralized taxing authority.

In the period 1995–2000, there were few and limited changes in the tax structure, mainly simplifications of the rate structures and the reduction of some rates. The most important changes were related to the granting of tax exemptions which we discuss later. The limited number of changes is not surprising since the PEP placed substantial restrictions on how and what revisions could be made. Thus, due to the compelling need to raise revenue quickly, the PNA focused on improving tax administration, including the revenue clearance system with Israel, rather than revising the existing tax structure. The increased domestic revenue generation during the period was, therefore, mainly due to administrative measures such as the implementation of a tax arrears settlement programme, improvements in enforcement provisions in the legislation, and a campaign for tax registration. Additional measures to improve the tax administration included the creation of a large taxpayer unit, a delinquent taxpayer unit, and the establishment of a tax court.[7] These measures enabled the PNA to establish a potentially well functioning central government tax administration within a fairly short period of time.

Despite the progress made in improving the tax administration, substantial weaknesses remained. First, the tax base was eroded due to generous tax exemptions. In particular larger companies, foreign investors, professionals and the agricultural sector benefited from exemptions. Second, some procedures facilitated tax evasion and corruption. These included:[8]

- the absence of consistent audit and enforcement procedures and techniques;
- a practice of 'negotiating' income tax assessments;
- insufficient resources allocated to the large taxpayers unit; and
- inadequate training of staff.

According to the Director of the ITD of the West Bank, there were only 10 employees in this department in 2000. On average each of these income tax officers handled some 65 files in the West Bank.[9] Tax assessments by the Palestinian Revenue Authority (PRA) found that in 90 to 95 per cent of the cases incomes were underreported. But, in spite of the existence of a tax court only two to three cases were filed per year. Most of the cases found a compromise through negotiations between the taxpayer or his representative and the income tax official.

## Taxation and state-formation: theoretical perspectives

Before we discuss the constraints that may have been preventing improvements in the Palestinian tax system, we will look at some general theoretical approaches that have been used to explain the relationship between the tax system and the state. In this section four such analytical approaches are outlined.

First, the structure of a country's economy may be important in determining both the level of taxation and the characteristics of the tax system (Tanzi 2000). It is, for example, administratively easier and cheaper to tax major industrial activities compared to peasant agriculture.[10] Literature on tax structure maintains that economic development creates new tax bases that can be exploited, and, thereby, raises the 'taxable' capacity of the country (Hinrichs 1966; Musgrave 1969). Thus Tanzi (2000: 224) argues that the 'increasing importance of taxes on personal income in many countries is closely related with the increase in the share of wages and salaries in national income as well as the expansion of incomes from interest, rent and dividends, as compared with incomes of independent contractors including farmers'.

Second, political institutions also matter (Brennan and Buchanan 1980; Levi 1988; and Steinmo 1993).[11] According to Steinmo (1993), differences in tax systems and tax burdens between countries are due to different political institutions, and not differences in citizens' attitudes to service delivery or willingness to pay taxes.[12] Domestic political institutions must in turn be understood in the context of the broader social, economic and political setting in which they are embedded. Political institutions provide the context in which individuals, groups and classes interpret their self-interest and thereby define their policy preferences. Political institutions affect the distribution of power between participants, and influence how different groups develop their policy preferences.

Steinmo (1993) points out that individual interests are often confused (for example wanting better public services and at the same time lower taxes). Sometimes citizens also oppose outright what the government must do, for instance raising taxes to achieve macroeconomic balance. If all citizens were in agreement about what policy should be, the mechanisms through which these opinions were discovered would have little effect on determining the final policy. But when public opinion is unclear, divided or subject to different interpretations, political institutions become important in determining the final policy decisions including those relevant for tax. Such institutions also shape the trade-off between the autonomy of the ruling elite and its responsiveness to the public's ambiguous tax/spending preferences. Thus Steinmo (1993) argues that institutions rather than ideology are significant in shaping tax systems.

Third, the interests of individuals also matter. Levi (1988) adds the perspective of individual actors to her analysis of revenue generation and tax compliance.[13] She assumes that actors are self-interested in the way that they calculate costs and benefits of proposed actions and they choose actions that are most consistent with their preferences. She also assumes (Levi 1988: 10) that rulers are predatory because they need state revenues to pursue their personal objectives of staying in power.

Levi's main proposition is that 'rulers maximise revenue to the state but not as they please' due to various constraints: transaction costs in tax enforcement, their own time preference, and their relative bargaining power vis-à-vis agents and constituents (Levi 1988: 10). These constraints determine the choice of revenue system, since rulers do not possess unlimited power, nor do constituents pay taxes voluntarily. Even with extensive power and effective monitoring of taxpayers, a ruler cannot achieve full compliance. Consequently, a ruler attempts to improve compliance at minimum cost, while taxpayers try to avoid and evade taxes (Levi 1988: 49). A 'balance' between these conflicting interests is achieved through bargaining between the ruler and various groups making up the polity. This results in a 'fiscal constitution' for a polity (Therkildsen 2001: 104).

Once a 'fiscal constitution' is negotiated, the contract between rulers and constituents comes under pressure due to free-rider problems, imperfections in the specification of the contract, and changes in the relative bargaining power between rulers and constituencies. For instance, various interest groups may negotiate favourable new deals for themselves, or people may find new ways to evade taxes. Moreover, state functions may change in scope and character. Such factors will all influence people's perceptions of the costs and benefits of a given revenue system. Most taxpayers are of course unable to assess the exact value of what they receive in return from the government for taxes paid. However, it can be argued that the taxpayer has some general impressions concerning his own and others' terms of trade with the government (Fjeldstad 2001). If this is the case, then it is reasonable to assume that a taxpayer's behaviour is affected by his satisfaction or lack of satisfaction with his terms of trade with the government. Thus, if the system of taxes is perceived to be unjust, tax resistance may, at least partly, be considered as an attempt by the taxpayer to adjust his terms of trade with the government.

Fourth and last, the domestic tax system may be affected by the international context. In Palestine, the Israeli occupation undoubtedly affected the economy and institutional and political developments. Many of the institutional forms set up by Israel were transferred to the PNA directly. Moreover, the Oslo Accord and the Paris Protocol limited the PNA's room for manoeuvring its own policies (see Chapter 3 by Zagha and Zomlot). Furthermore, foreign aid was an important revenue source for the PNA.

Moore (1998) provides an innovative contribution to this debate by emphasizing the international context as a factor determining a government's tax policy.[14] According to Moore, successful state formation in Europe came about through two main processes.[15] First, through inter-state military competition, and, second, through an intra-state process of resource mobilization for war that stimulated the creation of state–society linkages, markets, bureaucracies, tax systems, and so on. In this process, states lost despotic power (i.e., direct arbitrary control over subjects) but gained 'infrastructural' power (i.e., the capacity to penetrate society, to extract resources from it and to cooperate with social classes to achieve collective goals). Consequently, there is considerable historical evidence to suggest that the emergence of a representative government and, more loosely, of reciprocity and mutual accountability between states and citizens is more likely when states face incentives to increase income through bargaining with citizens.

The process discussed above, however, did not take root everywhere. It was most pronounced where capital was mobile, that is in the form of financial and trading assets. Here the mutual advantages of cooperation between rulers and citizens were greatest (Therkildsen 2001: 114). Cooperation protected owners of capital from arbitrary and exploitative tax enforcement. It also gave owners of capital direct and legitimate influence over military and diplomatic policies and operations. This was useful when competing with other trading nations. Rulers on the other hand could gain greater tax compliance from cooperation by retaining owners of mobile capital within their jurisdiction and by attracting capitalists from other states. But, such processes are not likely to operate when the state is fiscally *independent* of its population because its revenues are obtained from owners of fixed property, or from a few specific internal natural sources (such as oil and minerals), or from foreign aid.

Thus, Moore's key proposition is that the more a state 'earns' its tax income from its domestic population, the more it needs to enter into reciprocal arrangements with citizens about the provision of services and political representation.[16] In other words, the greater the share of 'earned' tax incomes in total revenues, the more likely it is that state-society relations will be characterized by accountability, responsiveness and democracy. But, aid dependency may thwart these processes. A relevant question is therefore whether foreign aid, so substantial in relation to other income sources, made the PNA relatively dependent on external political and material support, and relatively independent of its own citizens in the WBGS?

## Tax policy in Palestine

How was the socio-economic structure of Palestine reflected in the politics and administration of taxation during the period 1994–2000? To what extent were the interests of particular groups reflected in the tax system? Had any interest group any significant impact on the tax system? To what degree did the nature and capacity of the administrative and political institutions in Palestine represent a constraint for the PNA in implementing tax policy? Moreover, to what extent was the influence of Israel reflected in the tax system? And what impacts on tax policy had foreign aid since the establishment of the PNA? The theoretical frameworks discussed above may all offer some insights into these questions, and, together, they suggest that the PNA faced four major constraints in terms of revenue mobilization.[17] These constraints were:

- the socio-economic structure;
- the nature and capacity of administrative and political institutions;
- the bargaining powers of interest groups; and
- the influence of external actors, that is the international context.

In the remaining part of this section, these four factors are discussed as potential constraints on the efforts of the PNA to raise revenues, and thus on state-formation attempts in Palestine and related rent-seeking activities.

### The socio-economic structure

It can be argued that if a sector of society controls major economic interests, the ability of the state to tax these interests is challenged (Levi 1988). Likewise, but inverting the argument, Moore (1998) questions the willingness of a government to abide by democratic rules if the same government controls major economic resources through state ownership and rents (see Rakner 2001: 137). In Palestine during the period 1994–2002, the economy was dominated by small, family-owned farms and enterprises, and peasant agriculture. However, many of the larger private firms, including some monopolies, were owned or managed by high-ranking public officials (PLC 1997; CPRS 1998). Moreover, some of the larger companies were fully or partially owned by the PNA. These included, for instance, the Petroleum Public Commission, the Tobacco Commission, the Radio and Television Commission, and the Palestinian National Company for Economic Development (see Chapter 5 by Nasr).

To what extent did this ownership structure affect economic policy and the tax system? Following the Oslo Accord between the PLO and Israel, the PNA's principal challenges were to promote economic development and alleviate poverty. But, the PNA faced major constraints in pursuing these objectives: lack of control over borders, limited control over land, water and other natural resources, poor physical infrastructure, weak institutions, limited financial and human capital, and a high degree of political and economic uncertainty. In this setting, the PNA was faced with a choice between either a policy of drastic redistribution that might have resulted in the better-off pulling out of Palestine altogether and creating an uninviting climate for new foreign investments, or alternatively, a policy of encouraging foreign and domestic investments and private enterprise at the expense of postponing some welfare policies. The PNA chose the second line, assuming that investor-friendly policies would further economic growth (see Chapter 5 by Nasr and Chapter 3 by Hilal and Khan).

The important role played by the international community in setting up the peace agreement with Israel and the financial assistance from donor countries, made the World Bank and the International Monetary Fund (IMF) very influential in pushing for an export-oriented, private-sector-led market economy (PNA 1996). Thus, since 1994 the PNA implemented an economic policy that benefited large firms which had close linkages to (and were sometimes partly owned by) the political and administrative elite or owned by foreign investors.

To some extent small-scale agriculture also benefited. Since most agricultural activities were located in either the B-designated areas where security was joint between the PNA and Israel or in the C-designated areas where security was totally under Israeli control, both the PNA and foreign donors were reluctant to give aid to agricultural activities due to the uncertain political situation. The sector was partly compensated by various economic concessions, including tax exemptions. In the West Bank, but not in Gaza, all agricultural incomes were exempted from income tax. The differences between the West Bank and Gaza in this respect is partly historical. Under the Jordanian tax codes that were in force in the WB during the period of 1951–67 and onwards until the establishment of the

PNA, farmers and the agricultural sector were exempted from income taxes. In the GS, however, the tax codes were influenced by the Egyptian codes, which did not exempt farmers from taxation. The PNA did not show any willingness to change these codes under the pretext that agricultural income in the WB was more subject to weather fluctuations since it depended heavily on olive production. But, the fact that farmers, peasants and village dwellers in general played an important role in the national movement in the WB, most likely also had an impact on the tax policy adopted toward these groups.

### Institutional constraints

As emphasized by Rakner (2001), one obvious weakness of much of the current theoretical literature on revenue mobilization is the implicit assumption that, once decided on, policies will be implemented. In a developing country context, a major obstacle is the government's *capacity* to carry out policies (Therkildsen 2000). The institutional constraints on policy change were substantial in Palestine after Oslo. The extreme political uncertainty added to these institutional constraints. Thus, factors beyond the control of the PNA had a significant impact on both policy formulation and implementation. Much of the PNA's fiscal operations were governed by the Paris Protocol, which only gave the PNA a limited role in designing its own fiscal and trade regimes. Thus, with respect to tax policy, the best the PNA could do was to strengthen the domestic tax administration and establish the revenue clearance system with Israel.

A tax system is potentially an instrument for political control based on information about citizens and a network of tax collectors (Moore 1998). With little bureaucratic presence and limited information about what goes on at the grassroot level, the tax administration of a state can be vulnerable to organized predators in the form of local mafias. Moreover, in the absence of strong institutions states may have to rely more on patrimonial and personal linkages in enforcing decisions of the government. These observations may contribute to explain why the PNA put so much effort into establishing the new tax administrations. It may also explain why several revenue administrations were set up, thereby not risking that one central revenue authority should be at risk of failing.

A centralized revenue administration may have taken more effort to set up and require higher institutional capacity to run than several smaller ones. Moreover, the set-up of the tax administrations in the WBGS was heavily influenced by the IMF and the World Bank. Several IMF missions in the mid and late 1990s resided with the Ministry of Finance, offering technical assistance and policy advice on taxation and administration. In particular, the International Finance Institutions focused on building institutional capacity within the PNA, emphasizing 'transparency' in government operations.[18]

However, the administrative structure that was established with several tax administrations put severe burdens on senior officials within the Ministry of Finance. For instance, they had to intervene to settle disputes on tax assessment especially when influential taxpayers were involved. 'Give a discount or a tax exemption' was the approach often used to solve problems. The integrity of the tax officers was under heavy pressure due to social obligations and political interventions, which reduced the arm's length relations between taxpayers and enforcers.

Furthermore, low wages in the public sector in general and in the tax administration in particular, left no option but to accept the employment of less qualified graduates with limited skills in accounting. The best graduates were usually recruited to more attractive jobs in private accounting companies. Moreover, some of those who were recruited to the tax administration exploited their positions to supplement their meagre salaries by extracting rents through the informal system of settling accounts. For instance, in our survey of small- and medium-sized firms,[19] 41 per cent of the respondents in the WB said that their own tax assessment differed from that of the PRA. Businesspeople interviewed gave various reasons to explain the differences in tax assessment, including 'the PRA officials do not trust the books', and 'some expenses are not recognised by the tax officers'. Some 35 per cent of the respondents in the WB said the differences were solved through negotiation with the tax officers. Dishonest tax collectors were perceived to be a problem by 38 per cent of the respondents in the WB and by 30 per cent in Gaza.[20] According to an official interviewed in the ITD in Ramallah, very few corrupt tax collectors were detected. However, the few who were caught were asked to resign to maintain their dignity instead of being brought to court.

### Interest groups and the role of civil society

Within pluralist systems of rule, voluntary associations operating independently of state structures can be expected to play a major role in shaping and implementing tax policies. Thus, we might expect that the introduction of competitive electoral policies would bring new stakeholders into the debates over the politics of taxation. The establishment of the PNA does not support this expectation.

The PNA inaugurated a liberal 'constitution'. The general election in 1996, which was largely conducted in a free and democratic way, gave this emerging state system the necessary legitimacy (see Chapter 2 by Hilal and Khan ). However, the executive controlled the security apparatus. Moreover, most of the members of the 'Palestinian leadership' (i.e., the Speaker of the PLC, the Speaker of the PNC, heads of the main security forces, ministers, executive committee members, and so on) owed their position to Arafat personally (see Amundsen and Ezbidi, Chapter 4). Furthermore, the political 'leadership' did not have representatives from the private business community or the opposition or civil organizations. These features led to a situation where the PNA managed to centralize power. The 1996 election campaign produced a variety of political programmes of different political organizations. But neither Fateh nor the opposition made any reference to taxation. Therefore, the PNA did not face any major challenges from its political opponents with respect to revenue policies.

The increasing influence of executive power in Palestine during the period 1994–2000 is partly due to the weakness of interest groups (see Chapter 2 by Hilal and Khan ). Few of the economic interest groups in Palestine had the capacity, in respect of membership density, finances and organizational resources, to engage in an active dialogue with the regime on issues of taxation and, more generally, on economic development. Fateh dominated most of the professional associations, including those of lawyers, doctors and engineers (see Chapter 2 by Hilal and Khan ). The relationship between professionals and Fateh may have allowed important channels of rent-seeking and influence. For instance, many professionals stayed outside the tax net. The ITD was tolerant towards them on the ground that 'it was enough that they paid VAT'.[21] This was so even though the tax authorities assumed that many professionals underreported their sales to evade taxes, and it was very difficult to check their true turnover. Thus, the lion's share of personal income tax revenues was generated from wage employees where taxes were deducted at source.[22]

In contrast to local capital that was dominated by small-scale family capital, expatriate capital was represented by larger businesses. Following the Oslo Agreement, a number of large expatriate businesspeople were offered a 'partnership' with the PLO to develop Palestine economically. In return, the PNA granted expatriate capital selective monopolies (see Chapter 5 by Nasr) and tax exemptions.

The PNA established 'investor-friendly taxes' with relatively low corporate taxes and no capital gains taxes. The 'Investment Promotion Law', which was passed in 1995 and modified in 1998, aimed to provide incentives to local and foreign private entrepreneurs (Ministry of Economy and Trade 1998: 18–19).[23] In 1997 and 1998, 144 projects applied for tax exemptions (74 in 1997 and 70 in 1998).[24] The Palestinian Investment Promotion Agency (PIPA) approved 125 projects. Of these only 52 projects were implemented in 1997 and 1998, representing a total investment of US$ 97.5 million (i.e. 28.4 per cent of the projected investment). The remaining either existed before the Law or were not implemented. In 1998, 22 'existing' projects benefited from the tax exemptions (almost one third of those approved in 1998) with a total value of more than US$ 20 million.

Almost two-thirds of the projects that were granted tax exemptions were classified as 'industrial' while the rest were in the service sector, including tourism and health. However, many projects classified as 'industrial', were actually hotels and private medical services. Moreover, most of these projects were large projects of which the capital investment exceeded one million US dollars. Due to fairly generous exemptions and tax holidays benefiting larger companies, some critics argued that the law was biased towards large firms, thus promoting monopolies and rents for politically influential groups. Moreover, it was argued that the 'Investment Promotion Law' ignored small-scale businesses that represented the majority of Palestinian enterprises.

This argument is supported by survey-data. According to Sewell (2001), perceptions of the tax system and regulations differed between firms according to firm size. Almost 65 per cent of small firms sampled (with fewer than 10 full-time employees) and 57 per cent of medium-size firms (with 10 to 50 full-time employees) considered taxes and regulations to be major or moderate constraints to business. In contrast, less than 35 per cent of the larger firms gave this answer. With respect to taxation, 74 per cent of small firms and 61 per cent of medium-sized firms but only 26 per cent of large firms considered high taxes to be a moderate or major constraint to their businesses. Moreover, in contrast to smaller and medium-sized firms, a majority of large firms (58 per cent) said that they or their trade associations were frequently, mostly or always consulted about changes in regulations or policies.

The tax concessions given to larger investors could partly reflect the substantial bargaining power of owners of mobile capital vis-à-vis the PNA, in contrast to the bargaining power of small-scale businesses whose major capital was in the form of fixed property (see Moore 1998; and Tilly 1992). But, given the extreme political instability in the Palestinian territories, and the fact that the PNA during this period was a 'government' that lacked many of the formal powers of a national government, these achievements of attracting large-scale investors were not trivial. Here the mutual cooperation between rulers and capitalists was highest. Thus, these activities indicate that the PNA managed to take a longer-term perspective for developing Palestine. Yet, the PNA faced substantial institutional constraints in terms of both extracting more revenues from the business sector and widening its tax base.

### The influence of Israel and the foreign donors

The Paris Protocol of Economic Relations limited the role of the PNA in designing its own fiscal and trade regimes. Moreover, the interpretation by Israel of the terms of the Protocol resulted in the loss of significant revenues for the Palestinian quasi-state (Chapter 3 by Zagha and Zomlot). There have been several attempts to estimate these lost revenues (Kanafani 2001: 286). According to Sahban and Jawhary (1995: xxxiii), the revenue lost on imports coming through Israel was about 6 per cent to 7 per cent of GDP. The PNA estimated the 'fiscal leakage' at US$ 380 million annually (PNA 1998).[25] Dumas (1999), however, concluded that the lost revenues amounted to US$ 90–140 million in 1997, equivalent to 2.6 to 4.2 per cent of the GDP of the WBGS. According to estimates made by the IMF resident mission in the

WBGS, the annual loss in revenues through these unequal arrangements corresponded to 77 per cent of the amount actually refunded in 1997.

It is clear that the way certain aspects of the Paris Protocol were designed and implemented led to continuous conflicts of interest between the contracting parties. It also raises the question of why Palestinian negotiators initially accepted such terms. However, it is clear that the Palestinian negotiators tried to acquire as many attributes of sovereignty as possible, while the Israelis wanted to postpone as many decisions as possible to the negotiations over the final status of the Palestinian territories (Arnon and Weinblatt 2001: 296). The Palestinians aspired to set their own priorities, without Israeli interference, including the formation of a new Palestinian trade policy. The Israeli negotiators, however, proposed to continue the existing de facto (partial) customs union, which did not require the creation of trade borders between the two economies. They succeeded in convincing the Palestinians that a more protectionist policy would reduce the Palestinians' chances of building a prosperous economy. Clearly the Paris Protocol reflects the uneven balance of power between the two parties and the transitional nature of the agreements (Arnon and Weinblatt, 2001: 301).

The dependency on Israel left the PNA extremely vulnerable and gave Israel a political weapon to exert pressure on the PNA. On several occasions during the 1997–2000 period, Israel withheld tax revenues in prima facie violation of the Paris Protocol (Chapter 5 by Nasr; Arnon and Weinblatt 2001: 302). To reduce its vulnerability, the PNA undertook various types of off-budget (and by definition unregulated) activities and established 'secret' accounts. Little information exists on the sources and scope of these off-budget accounts, or how these funds were used.[26] Nevertheless, there have been repeated accusations of non-transparency and manipulations of the secret accounts controlled by the PNA. Given the unstable political situation and the fact that Israel on several occasions stopped transferring tax revenues collected to the PNA, it seems both legitimate and rational that the PNA operated with such accounts as a buffer to meet urgent needs and commitments.

To what extent did the inflow of foreign aid to Palestine provide a disincentive for the PNA in terms of its tax-collection effort? During the period 1994–2000, the PNA had significant, although declining, 'unearned' incomes in the form of foreign aid (Table 6.3). We could, therefore expect international aid organisations to have a substantial influence in shaping economic policies – including the tax policies – of the PNA. Moore's (1998) approach may offer important insights into the question whether pressures for accountability and transparency came from internal or external actors.[27]

Annual disbursements to the PNA – in the forms of loans and grants – averaged US$ 600 million per year in the period 1994–99, corresponding to almost 14 per cent of gross national income (GNI) per annum over the six years (see Table 6.3). Almost 90 per cent of the aid in this period was provided in the form of grants. Moreover, more than half of the aid was for

*Table 6.3*  PNA revenues cleared by Israel and from foreign aid 1994 –1999 (million
US$, figures in brackets are percentages of gross national income)

| | 1994 | 1995 | 1996 | 1997 | 1998 | 1999 | 1994-99 |
|---|---|---|---|---|---|---|---|
| Revenue clearance (from Israel) | 25 (0.06) | 266 (6.4) | 420 (10.3) | 496 (11.1) | 542 (11.4) | 626 (12.2) | 2,375 (9.0) |
| Total foreign aid disbursements | 612 (15.4) | 547 (13.2) | 647 (15.8) | 654 (14.7) | 553 (11.6) | 609 (11.9) | 3,622 (13.8) |

Source: Fischer *et al.* (2001: Table 1) and Arnon and Weinblatt (2001: Table 4)

current spending, including job creation and technical assistance, and the
rest was devoted to investments projects (Fischer *et al.* 2001: 258). In 1999
foreign aid funded all Palestinian public investments, around 5 per cent of
GDP (including investments undertaken by United Nations Relief and
Works Agency). Still, the ratio of fiscal revenue to GDP was about 23 per
cent in 1999, compared to an aid to GDP ratio of around 10 per cent.
However, when excluding the revenues collected by Israel through the
clearing system, the 'domestic' fiscal revenue to GDP ratio was approximately 9 per cent. Furthermore, foreign aid amounted to almost US$ 175
per capita, making the West Bank and Gaza one of the largest recipients of
aid in the world on a per capita basis, together with Bosnia Herzegovina and
Israel where non-military foreign assistance represented approximately US$
200 and US$ 247 per capita, respectively (DAC 1997). This level of assis-
tance reflects the great importance that donors placed on supporting the
Middle East peace process. Donor support for current expenditures
declined, however, over the period in question. Overall, foreign aid fell from
18 per cent of GDP in 1994 to around 10 per cent in 1999.

Based on the available data, it is not possible to provide a clear answer to
the question raised above on the possible impact of foreign aid on domestic
revenue generation. With respect to taxation, the scope for influencing tax
policy was also limited. First, the PNA inherited a fairly developed tax
system, including VAT, because of the Israeli occupation since 1967. Second,
after 1994 the tax system, especially for indirect taxes, was to a large extent
regulated by the principles of the Paris Protocol.

But, there can be no doubt that donor assistance had a substantial effect
on the Palestinian domestic economy in the period 1994 to 2000. Most
immediately, the inflow of foreign aid stimulated local economic activity and
contributed to household incomes. Moreover, until the Israeli demolition of
the administrative and physical infrastructure on the West Bank in April

2002, aid also enhanced the productive potential of the economy by supporting investments that expanded the underlying economic productive capacity.

The World Bank (2000: 26–7) estimated that the production capacity of the Palestinian economy was 6–7 per cent higher than it would have been without donor-financed investments. Thus, foreign aid contributed to offset parts of the cumulative negative effects of the Israeli policy of border closure and other restrictions against the Palestinian people. In particular, the initially high degree of budget support provided by donors helped the PNA to establish operations and avoid potentially destabilizing fiscal deficits at a critical stage. However, recurrent budget support also facilitated an expansion of public sector employment that led to overstaffing and probably undermined the administrative efficiency of the PNA.

On several occasions the donors criticized the PNA for lack of transparency in its financial operations, including the off-budget fiscal activities and weak technical decisions in its handling of public finances. But, the donors' focus was on keeping the peace process alive. Thus, generally, foreign donors' seemed to turn a blind eye to issues such as transparency and accountability in the PNA's fiscal affairs. Given the political instability and the contagious effects of the escalating violence in the area, this position may seem to have been justified. However, by making the PNA relatively dependent on external political and material support, and relatively independent of its own citizens on the WBGS, this approach may in the long-term have contributed to undermining the development of state–society relationships based on responsiveness and accountability.

To summarize, we have looked at the socio-economic structure, the nature of government institutions, the bargaining powers of interest groups, and international actors as potential constraining factors on the efforts of the PNA to raise revenues. First, and not very surprisingly, the socio-economic structure mattered. Poverty and the dominance of small-scale farming and small, family owned enterprises meant that taxable capacity of the economy was limited. This partly explains why the most productive tax revenue was income taxes on public sector employees and taxes on international trade. Second, the administrative and political institutions in Palestine during the period in question were to a large extent controlled by the executive, but nevertheless, institutional capacity was weak and had to be built up from scratch. Third, various interest groups, particularly foreign-based capital owners (the Palestinian Diaspora) and to some extent professionals, constrained the PNA's revenue mobilization efforts. The tax exemptions given to larger investors could reflect the substantial bargaining power of owners of mobile capital vis-à-vis the PNA, but it could also be interpreted as a part of the more general PNA policy of relying on the large-scale sector for generating rapid economic development. Finally, the international context was a factor that substantially influenced the revenue-collection efforts. More than any other factor, Israel represented a constraint on the

PNA's tax policies and revenue collection. Moreover, the dependency on external assistance both for investments and to cover running expenses may have had an impact on the PNA's incentives to enter into reciprocal and accountable arrangements with citizens about provision of services and representation in return for tax contributions.

The state formation process in Palestine during the period 1994–2000, in contrast to the European experience, was not related to inter-state war but to insurgency against, or negotiation with, Israeli occupation. This conflict did not contribute to increased tax-extracting capacity of the PNA as wars did in the West. Although the conflict changed the relations between the new rulers and the ruled, relations of accountability between the PNA and citizens remained weak – perhaps because the government depended only partly on its citizens to mobilize revenues. The authority relied more on foreign aid and taxes on international trade.

In terms of its achievements, within its room for manoeuvre, the PNA raised significant domestic revenues subject to the constraint of consolidating and maintaining its power. The PNA also used the tax system as a means of enhancing rents for industries and sectors which the leadership believed were important for development, and to grant generous tax exemptions to politically important stakeholders such as professionals. In contrast, few tax concessions were given to employees in the formal sector. At the same time, during the first four years after its inauguration, the PNA was able to maintain macroeconomic orthodoxy while providing generous tax incentives for important groups in society as well as fairly progressive social policies paid for with the revenue windfall from foreign aid and the monopolies. The PNA also made real progress, with generous external assistance, in establishing a functioning economic administration and in developing the physical and institutional infrastructure of the economy. This secured widespread internal legitimacy among the Palestinian population, which also was reflected in the 1996 election that helped the PNA to consolidate and centralize power.

On the other hand, a major problem for the PNA was that the limitations on political accountability meant that the delivery of these results could not be *politically* assessed by a broad range of representatives. As a result, the PNA leadership often suffered criticisms for its lack of accountability to political representatives. The deteriorating security situation in the late 1990s and declining social welfare raised citizens' perceptions of exploitation from an unequal contract with the government. Perceptions of fairly extensive corruption contributed to undermine popular confidence in the PNA as a trustworthy force in the struggle against the Israeli occupation. The Al-Aqsa *Intifada* marks the end of the first phase of state-formation in Palestine. Revenue in the form of general tax and incomes from monopolies dried up with the escalation of the conflict. From October 2000 Israel stopped transferring revenues collected on behalf of the PNA and the central state organs in Palestine became cash strapped.

This led to long delays in payment of salaries to ministerial staff and the maintenance of infrastructure came to a standstill. Foreign aid did not manage to compensate for this revenue shortfall.

These factors, combined with Israel's re-occupation of large parts of the West Bank towns in April 2002 and the destruction of administrative and physical infrastructure that followed, eroded the centralized power of the PNA. Nevertheless, the establishment of a developmental Palestinian state, with a strong central authority, remains the only guarantee for a lasting peace. While the long-term viability of any state must depend on the emergence of a viable and transparent social contract between citizens and the state, we have also seen that in the Palestinian case a precondition for any progress is a more balanced structure of economic relations between Israel and Palestine.

## Notes

1   A draft version of this chapter was presented at the *Bergen Seminar in Development Economics*, March 2002. We are grateful to the workshop participants for useful comments. We have also received valuable comments from Inge Amundsen, Carmenza Gallo, Mushtaq Khan and Aslak Orre.
2   This average excludes East Jerusalem with a population of more than 210,000 (in 1997). The figure also hides substantial differences between the West Bank and the Gaza Strip.
3   According to Nasr (Chapter 5), the public sector wage bill amounted to more than 12 per cent of GDP in 1999.
4   The last survey was carried out in 2001 as part of our study and covered 34 firms in the WB (Ramallah and Nablus) and 50 firms in Gaza.
5   The figure is, however, higher than the average for Arab countries. In 1995, tax revenue as a percentage of GNP for Egypt was 26.3%, Yemen 13%, Morocco 23%, Syria 17.8%, Jordan 20.4%, Tunisia 21%, Lebanon 10.8%. All these countries had lower GDP figures than the PNA due to their dependence on migrant remittances (World Bank 1997: 258–9).
6   These figures include income taxes, indirect taxes on domestic goods and services (VAT and excises), taxes on international transactions, and non-tax revenues. However, property taxes and local government taxes and charges are excluded.
7   No tax disputes seem to have been solved by bringing them to court. Disputes have been solved either by forwarding them to the Chairman of the PNA (President Arafat), or by negotiations and compromises between the taxpayers and tax officials.
8   Personal interview with an international public finance expert who resided at the Ministry of Finance for a period while on an IMF mission (11 January 2001). The person preferred to be anonymous.
9   Only 650 private companies were registered and had files at the ITD in 2000. In addition, there were some 30 partnerships registered with files in the department. Public companies did not file. Registration procedures were based on the registration at the Ministry of Economy and Trade, which provided a licence number accompanied with the internal by-laws and contract of establishment. Procedures for tax assessment were based on officially audited statements according to the companies and the tax code. The Director of the ITD was not able to provide corresponding data from Gaza.
10   In a study of tax shares (tax to GDP ratios) in sub-Saharan Africa, Stotsky and WoldeMariam (1997) estimate a tax share for each country based on the struc-

ture of its economy. As expected, tax shares are negatively related to agriculture's proportion of the economy, and positively correlated with export share and per capita income.

11 Therkildsen (2001) provides an excellent critical review of this literature.

12 Steinmo (1993) analyses the development of the tax systems in Britain, Sweden and the USA within a historical institutional framework.

13 Levi, working within the tradition of rational choice institutionalism, is inspired by Machiavelli and theories of collective action. She uses case-studies from republican Rome, medieval England and France, Britain in the eighteenth century, and Australia in the twentieth century.

14 This discussion builds on the review by Therkildsen (2001).

15 Moore builds here on Tilly (1992) who explores the evolution of European states. Tilly's main argument is that in Europe over the past two centuries taxation and disputes over the use of revenues stimulated the development of greater citizen rights and privileges, with democratic institutions enforcing accountability and greater transparency in expenditures.

16 Moore (1998: 94) argues that the use of the concept 'earned' is a logical extension from the term 'rentier', since rentier is 'unearned' in the language of classical political economy.

17 This framework follows the analytical approach suggested by Rakner (2001).

18 In April 2000, however, the PNA consolidated all tax revenue under the Ministry of Finance. According to Fischer *et al.* (2001: 271), the PNA took this step to 'make its own financial operations more transparent'.

19 This survey was carried out in 2001 as part of our study and covered 34 firms in the WB (Ramallah and Nablus) and 50 firms in Gaza.

20 Some respondents mentioned that certain tax collectors gave them a 'secret account number' where deposits could be made to settle a tax assessment differential. Others said that they had to pay in the form of a gift (usually electrical devices).

21 Personal communications with staff at the ITD (21 June 2001, Ramallah).

22 To further illustrate this point, there were only 650 files of registered companies in the West Bank, and no company was registered in Gaza Strip. This implies that on average a company in the West Bank paid less than US$ 18,000 in corporate taxes on an annual basis. This supports the argument that the Palestinian income tax during the period 1994–2000 was mainly imposed on individual wage earners and, to some extent, on smaller firms with limited opportunities for evading.

23 The *General Department of Investment* at the Ministry of Economy and Trade provided internal reports (in Arabic) on investment projects that benefited from the law. The information in this paragraph is based on the reports for 1997 (before the law was passed by the PLC) and 1998.

24 These projects represented total investments of US$ 343 million. Fully domestically owned projects, represented about 57 per cent of this capital, while pure foreign owned investments represented less than 5 per cent of the capital. Joint-ventures between foreign and domestic investors, contributed with the remaining 38 per cent.

25 In comparison, the total donor funding to the WBGS in 1998 was US$ 553 million (see Table 6.3).

26 According to Fischer *et al.* (2001: 258), a large part of this money went to finance investments in commercial operations through the Palestinian Commercial Services Company (PCSC). But it is still not known how much has been used on current expenditures.

27 Brautigam and Botchwey (1999) suggest that many 'aid dependent' governments face more organized and effective pressures for accountability and transparency

from the international community and donor agencies than from their own citizens and parliaments.

## References

Arnon, A. and Weinblatt, J. (2001) 'Sovereignty and Economic Development: The Case of Israel and Palestine', *The Economic Journal*, 111 (472): 291–308.

Brautigam, D. and Botchwey, K. (1999) 'The Institutional Impacts of Aid Dependence on Recipients in Africa, *CMI Working Paper* (WP 1: 99) Bergen: Chr. Michelsen Institute.

Brennan, G. and Buchanan, J. M. (1980) *The Power to Tax: Analytical Foundations of a Fiscal Constitution*, Cambridge: Cambridge University Press.

Butenschøn, N. A. (1998) 'The Oslo Agreement: From the White House to Jabala Abu Ghneim', in Lønning, D. and Giacaman, G. (eds) *After Oslo: New Realities, Old Problems*, London/Chicago: Pluto Press.

CPRS (Center for Palestine Research Studies) (1998) 'The Palestinian Economic System: Planned or Market Oriented', *Seminar Report Series*, No. 7, Nablus.

DAC (Development Assistance Committee) (1997) *DAC Guidelines on Conflict, Peace and Development Cooperation*, Paris: Organization for Economic Cooperation and Development.

Dumas, J.-P. (1999) *Fiscal Leakage in the West Bank and Gaza Strip*, MEDA Team, MEDA Programme, EU Directorate General 1B.

Fischer, S., Alonso-Gamo, P. and Erickson von Allmen, U. (2001) 'Economic Developments in the West Bank and Gaza since Oslo', *The Economic Journal*, 111 (472): 254–75.

Fjeldstad, O.-H. (2001) 'Taxation, Coercion and Donors: Local Government Tax Enforcement in Tanzania', *The Journal of Modern African Studies* 39 (2): 289–306.

Fjeldstad, O.-H. and Semboja, J. (2000) 'Dilemmas of Fiscal Decentralisation: A Study of Local Government Taxation in Tanzania', *Forum for Development Studies*, 27 (1): 7–41.

Hinrichs, H. H. (1966) *A General Theory of Tax Structure Change During Economic Development*, Cambridge, MA: The Law School of Harvard University.

Kanafani, N. (2001) 'Trade – A Catalyst for Peace?' *The Economic Journal*, 111 (472): 276–90.

Levi, M. (1988) *Of Rule and Revenue*, Berkeley: University of California Press.

Local Aid Co-ordination Committee Co-chairs (LACC) (2002) 'Damage to Civilian Infrastructure and Institutions in the West Bank Estimated at US$ 361 million', *Press Release* LACC, Jerusalem (15 May 2002).

Ministry of Economy and Trade (1998) *Investment Encouragement Law*, Article 23, Ramallah.

Moore, M. (1998) 'Death Without Taxes: Democracy, State Capacity and Aid Dependence in the Fourth World', in Robinson, M. and White, G. (eds) *The Democratic Developmental State: Politics and Institutional Design*, Oxford: Oxford University Press.

Musgrave, R. (1969) *Fiscal Systems*, New Haven: Yale University Press.

Nasr, M. (1994) 'Small Scale Industry and Commerce', Paper presented at the *Conference on the Contribution of Turkey for the Construction and Development of Palestine*, Friedrich Neumann Stiftung and University of Ankara, Turkey.

PCBS (Palestinian Central Bureau of Statistics) (1999) *Population, Housing and Establishment Census – 1997*, Final results report – Palestinian Territory, First part, Ramallah.

Palestinian Economic Policy Research Institute (PEPRI/MAS) (1997) *Economic Monitor*, Issue 1. Jerusalem and Ramallah.

—— (2000) *Economic Monitor*, Issue 7 (December), Jerusalem and Ramallah.

Palestinian Legislative Council (PLC) (1997) *Special Committee Report*, Ramallah.

—— (2000) *Second Reading of the New Income Tax Law*, Ramallah.

PNA (Palestinian National Authority) (1996) *Palestinian Development Strategy*, Presented at the 'Conference on the assistance to the Palestinian People', Paris (January).

—— (1997) *Income Tax Guide: Identifying Your Rights and Duties*, Ministry of Finance, Income Tax General Directorate, Issue No. 1, Ramallah.

—— (1998) 'Financial Losses', a letter from the Palestinian Ministry of Finance to the JEC's Palestinian coordinator, the Deputy Minister's Office (15 March), Ramallah.

—— (2000) *Events, West Bank and Gaza: Economic Policy Framework*, Progress Report (31 May, p. 12) Ramallah.

Palestinian NGO Emergency Initiative in Jerusalem (PNEIJ) (2002) *Report on the Destruction to Palestinian Governmental Institutions in Ramallah Caused by the IDF forces between March 29 and April 21, 2002*. Available online <http://electronicintifada.net/features/destruction/reports/ramallahgov.pdf> (accessed 29 April 2002),Ramallah.

Rakner, L. (2001) 'The Politics of Revenue Mobilisation: Explaining Continuity in Namibian Tax Policies', *Forum for Development Studies*, 28 (1): 125–45.

Shaban, R. and Jawhary, M. (1995) *The Palestinian-Israeli Trade Arrangements: Searching for Fair Revenue Sharing*, MAS: Jerusalem.

Sewell, D. (2001) 'Governance and the Business Environment in West Bank/Gaza', *Middle East and North Africa Working Paper Series* No. 23, Washington DC: World Bank.

Steinmo, S. (1993) *Taxation and Democracy: Swedish, British and American Approaches to Financing the Modern State*, New Haven: Yale University Press.

Stotsky, J. G. and WoldeMariam, A. (1997) 'Tax Effort in Sub-Saharan Africa', *IMF Working Paper*, WP/97/107 (September). Available online at <http://www.imf.org/external/pubs/ft/wp/wp97107.pdf>' (accessed 15 February 2004).

Tanzi, V. (2000) 'Taxation and Economic Structure', in Perry, Whalley and McMahon (eds) *Fiscal Reform and Structural Change in Developing Countries, Vol. 2*, London: Macmillan Press.

Therkildsen, O. (2000) 'Efficiency, Accountability and Implementation: Public Sector Reform in East and Southern Africa', UNRISD *Democracy, Governance and Human Rights Programme Series*, no. 3. Geneva: United Nations Research Institute for Social Development.

—— (2001) 'Understanding Taxation in Poor African Countries: A Critical Review of Selected Perspectives', *Forum for Development Studies*, 28 (1): 99–123.

Tilly, C. (1992) *Coercion, Capital and European States, AD 990–1990, Cambridge, MA: Blackwell.*

UNSCO (United Nations Special Coordinator's Office) (1998) *The West Bank and the Gaza Strip Private Economy: Conditions and Prospects*, Special Report, Office of the Special Coordinator in the Occupied Territories. Gaza (February).

—— (2000) *Report on the Palestinian Economy*, Office of the Special Coordinator in the Occupied Territories, Gaza. Available online at < www.arts.mcgill.ca /mepp/unsco/spring00> (accessed September 2000).

—— (2001) *Report on the Palestinian Economy*, Office of the Special Coordinator in the Occupied Territories, Gaza.

World Bank (1997) *World Development Report: The State in a Changing World* (Arabic Version), Washington DC: The World Bank.

—— (1999) *West Bank and Gaza: Strengthening Public Sector Management*, Washington DC: The World Bank.

—— (2000) *Aid Effectiveness in the West Bank and Gaza*, Washington DC: The World Bank.

—— (2001) *West Bank and Gaza Update*, Washington DC: The World Bank.

# 7 Donor assistance, rent-seeking and elite formation

*Sari Hanafi and Linda Tabar*

With the commencement of the Oslo interim period in 1993, the international donor community pledged $2.4 billion for the reconstruction of Palestinian society as part of its effort to promote the peace process. Additional contributions raised the total pledged to $3.4 billion (Khadr 1999). Significantly, during this period of political transition the Israeli occupation was not fully removed but was replaced by a complex system consisting of three players: the Israelis, the Palestinian National Authority (PNA) and Western donors of international aid (Beck 2000).

In this chapter, we will examine the role played by Western donors in state building from 1994 until the eruption of the Second *Intifada* in 2000 and assess their impact on rent-seeking in the territory as they attempted to reconstruct Palestinian social and political structures. Undoubtedly, aid contributed to the consolidation of the PNA, with donors providing both initial start-up costs and recurrent budget expenses. Aid also reinvigorated the declining Palestinian non-governmental organizations (NGOs). However, there were concerns underlying this relationship, especially those concerning administrative and political corruption within the PNA and questions about the quality of monitoring and whether better practices could have been promoted. There were also other issues such as the stated aims of donors to promote civil society and democracy and the changes taking place on the ground. While donors sought to empower Palestinian society, the outcome was that society, already weakened by the occupation, became even more fragmented during this period.

We identify a number of factors that are important for explaining these outcomes. First, donor agenda, commitments, and organizational constraints were important and should be looked at carefully. Second, with the restructuring of the aid industry, NGOs also underwent changes, with a new emphasis on professionalization and 'scaling up' that produced very large NGOs. And finally, the circulation of knowledge within aid channels and the emergence of a 'development discourse' created new terms of legitimacy for local NGOs. Despite the language of participation and empowerment, only a narrow educated elite could effectively participate in this discourse and thereby control resources. We refer to this group as a 'globalized elite' and we observe that they dominated the Palestinian NGO (PNGO) sector before the collapse of PNA institutions during the Israeli re-occupation which began in 2000. The fragmentation of Palestinian society is analysed in the light of these difficulties and challenges facing the NGO sector.

## Globalization, the restructuring of aid and supra-national donors

The peace-building assistance provided by the international community to the Palestinian people must be understood against the changes that had taken place in Western development assistance over the last two decades. Over this period, the scope of Development aid had expanded, with the emergence of new development partners and new policy agendas. Since the end of the Cold War, Western governments had increased their involvement in conflict areas, either as part of short-term humanitarian relief operations during conflicts, or as part of reconstruction efforts after the cessation of hostilities. This meant that a growing share of bilateral aid was directed towards short-term relief. At the same time, as Brynen explains, new peace-building efforts had been devised which not only entailed diplomacy and military peacekeeping, 'but also a variety of social and economic objectives and instrumentalities, underpinned by substantial commitments of financial support' (Brynen 2000: 6–7). As the Palestinian case revealed, donor involvement in 'post-conflict' reconstruction projects fused developmentally oriented initiatives with overarching political objectives. Donor support for the Palestinian–Israeli peace process and their concern for political stability in the region buttressed a wide range of interventions, including supporting the start-up costs of the PNA, infrastructure projects and a range of social as well as economic initiatives.

In addition to this, since the 1980s there had been an *increase in the number of professional development actors* and a change in the way *aid had been disbursed.* In the past, Southern grassroots organizations had a more informal relationship with their funding agencies and received financial assistance and solidarity support from a number of different private voluntary organizations in the West. Over time, this relationship underwent a change as Northern NGOs (NNGOs) became more dependent on government funding and took on greater responsibilities in distributing bilateral aid. Moreover, Western governments started entering into their own bilateral relations with organizations and governments in the South. As a consequence, aid recipients in non-Western societies were able to apply directly for funding from a range of NNGO and Government organizations grant bodies, which brought with it increased reporting requirements, new relations of accountability, and a greater professionalization and rationalization of the distribution of Western development assistance.

In addition to the changes set out above, there were also other changes in the attitude of Western donor agencies. For instance, there was an increased emphasis on economic and political liberalization. These changes in the pattern of Western development assistance corresponded with and were reinforced by an overall transformation in the international system following the end of the Cold War. The impact of *globalization* on relations between states, international organizations and capital also played its part. The effects of these changes could be seen in the new, overlapping forms of development cooperation between Southern and Northern organizations that cut across borders.

This then raises the question of whether aid, like any other public resource, could be misused in the absence of proper regulations (Maipose 2000). Did the new relations adequately address the question of transparent and accountable governance? This is a common problem faced by all types of supra-national aid. In Europe, a debate has been waging about the problem of allocation of funds by supra-national institutions such as the European Union (EU). Usually the capacity of the EU to monitor the actual usage of funds by recipients is limited. Moreover, the ability of the national government to oversee the activities and monitor the finances of aid recipients is also limited, nor does it have the same incentive to monitor the use of money coming from outside. Even in an advanced country like France, crises have frequently erupted, with critics charging the French state with a failure to monitor and control projects funded by the European Union. Some have gone so far as to suggest that this supra-national institution inadvertently supports and favours an elite that is not necessarily elected by the people nor sufficiently embedded in accountability mechanisms that allow public oversight. This example clearly suggests that the way in which aid is being distributed today raises new questions about 'responsibility' and 'accountability'. Whose responsibility is it to monitor the practices of aid recipients: the donor, the national authority or the public? What mechanisms are donors using to promote transparent practices among recipients at either the governmental or non-governmental level and what factors constrain donors from developing and using effective monitoring systems?

This brings us to one of the central issues of the paper. What is the relationship between aid and rent-seeking: both in the manner that aid structures the opportunity for rent-seeking behaviour, and in the way donor programmes can support efforts to inhibit and restrict corruption? During the Cold War, donors were disinclined to raise or tackle the issue of corruption among aid recipients. But since the 1990s, instances of corruption in Western Europe, Latin America and Africa, as well as the concern for organized crime in Eastern Europe and the former Soviet Union have dislodged donor reluctance to address this issue. Today, all bilateral donors and international organizations have developed policies on corruption. However, as some have suggested, a coherent strategy and clear enforcement mechanism to prevent corruption is still a long way off. Both the UN Global Programme Against Corruption and the World

Bank Anti-Corruption Action Plan are still at an incipient stage (Amundsen 1999: 23). In order to elucidate the issues at stake in the relationship between aid and rent-seeking it is essential to turn to the debate on conditionality.

## Donor assistance, rent-seeking and conditionality

Donors have a variety of means available to them to respond to corrupt behaviour among aid recipients. The debate on conditionality is interesting because it illustrates the interrelated set of factors that have a bearing on the capacity of donors to shape recipient practices. Of importance here is that analysts have critically commented on the way conditionality has been used by donors. They have argued that conditionality has been ineffective in inducing policy reforms because generally donors *do not provide significant rewards* or *punishments* to promote a change in performance (Gwin and Nelson 1997). The implicit message underlying this argument is that aid is not a single transaction, but a complex relationship embedded in and shaped by multiple, overlapping interests, agenda, and practical considerations.

This being the case, we suggest that there are three main issues that determine the way donors endeavour to promote reform among aid recipients:

1   What are the donor's interests and commitments? Can the donor withdraw the aid?
2   What instruments are available to provide incentives for reform or to impose punishment for poor performance?
3   What monitoring mechanisms is the donor using?

### Donor interests and commitments

One of the central reasons why donors often failed to provide sufficient incentives for reform was that donors can be motivated by larger interests and commitments. This has been the case historically, for instance, in Africa, Western donors and institutions continued to provide foreign aid, grants and concessional loans to Zaire, whilst being fully aware of the extreme forms of corruption engaged in by its leader, Mobutu. In this instance, donors' actions were motivated by political concerns (Maipose 2000: 94). Similarly, multilateral institutions have sometimes avoided using conditionality due to internal considerations and the fear that such action will cause the recipient to default on their loans. In the Palestinian case, the donors' commitment to the peace process was the anchor that shaped the way the donors intervened in the society. This inevitably had an impact on the incentives or penalties that the donors could provide to encourage better conduct among Palestinian recipients.

## Instruments to reward or punish

At times, however, it was not a matter of interests or donor commitments, but whether instruments were available enabling the donor to affect the recipient's performance. Our research suggests that donors could have spent time and effort in identifying corruption among aid recipients, but were constrained by their own incapacity to punish. The case of one of the Palestinian NGOs provides a good example: information emerged about the mismanagement of funds and the corruption of the leader of this NGO who was implementing a project with the support of USAID. The agency suspended the project, investigated the organization with a local audit and then sent an investigator from Washington. When evidence of dishonest practices was discovered, USAID declared that it was not able to go on any further and stopped the project. While the process of investigation continued over three years, a USAID officer informed us that it was difficult to take the measures enacted against this NGO seriously. Generally, donors and international organizations do not have adequate mechanisms to verify recipient practices as presented on paper, and the local governing authorities find it hard to oversee practices among organizations like NGOs without seeming to exert an authoritarian hand.

## Monitoring mechanisms

It was also the case that the donors' own organizational constraints, including strict timetables and pressures to move money, made adherence to rigorous monitoring mechanisms difficult. As Amundsen (1999: 24) points out, 'some international aid and donor agencies have their particular concerns, agendas and timetables, and are willing to pay for their (swift) implementation'. Each of these factors help to explain the specific effects of aid on rent-seeking in particular contexts.

## Donor assistance to the PNA

In Palestine as elsewhere, the aid industry had often served to create rents that could be captured by well-placed NGOs and state bureaucrats. In the case of donor assistance to Palestine, it was evident that aid was often not given judiciously or in a targeted manner. Moreover, in the Palestinian case, aid was part of a broader set of obligations and objectives, and an important element in the political agenda of peace-building. Donor assistance to the Palestinians thus had two broader objectives:

1  To allow the PNA to expand its bureaucracy and its patronage network as a way of stabilizing the regime.
2  To maintain and extend the space for Palestinian NGOs by reconstituting the structure of rents these NGOs could capture.

With respect to the support provided to the PNA, while the donors tried to reduce the opportunities for rent-seeking, this had at best a moderating affect, due to the priority given to peace-building assistance, practical considerations and the donors' own overlapping interests. To begin with, donor assistance to the Palestinians arrived at a very critical moment. State institutions were being set up for the first time. One cannot ignore that this was also an extremely complicated and difficult period. The Palestinians were faced with the challenge of building state agencies *from scratch*, and were confronted with a flood of new tasks from the most rudimentary ones of acquiring office equipment to the complex matter of delineating bureaucratic responsibilities.

The donors played a vital role in this regard by providing financial and technical assistance. Initial plans for the sequence and disbursement of aid were based on long-term development schemes but were modified in practice to take into account immediate political and economic requirements, and in particular, the start-up costs of the PNA.

In 1994, 40 per cent of total disbursements went to cover the PNA's budget and its set-up expenses (Frisch and Hofnung 1997: 1250). In the same year, the Holst Fund was established under the World Bank to support the PNA's recurrent budget expenses over the short-term. Viewed as short-term measures, the direct funding of the Authority was not expected to be required beyond 1994. However, donor funding became a sizable source of external rent, upon which the Authority came to depend from the very beginning of the state-building project. Even in 1996, 30 per cent of the Authority's budget was provided by external rents, in the form of direct transfers from the donors (Beck 2000: 53).

What were the implications of this influx of external rents for state building, and what were the effects on the state formation process? It could be argued that the Authority's reliance on external rents had a negative impact on political developments that left a long-term legacy. Rents provided a particular type of income that gave the quasi-state power without responsibility (Beck 2000: 52). A steady inflow of external rents enhanced the autonomy of the political elite, and increased the propensity for regime consolidation through a dispensation of patronage. This not only created problems of rent-seeking and corruption, but also led to a system where social forces were subordinated to the emerging state through a strategy of co-optation. Overall, society was weakened and this reduced the prospects for the development of democratic structures that could hold the political elite accountable to society.

Allegations of 'misuse' of aid were significant in light of other allegations of administrative and political corruption (see Chapter 2 by Hilal and Khan). The question we have to address is whether the donors could have made the granting of political rents conditional on the development of democratic norms and good governance (Beck 2000). The uncertainties of political transitions, the weakness of institutions and the reconstitution of elite roles all created opportunities and incentives for corrupt practices, which makes any analysis of whether a donor could *determine* the conduct of the recipient much more complex. Furthermore, as Nasr and other contributors in this book have argued, some of the rent-seeking practices of the PNA, in particular the creation of monopolies, were strategies to overcome the constraints imposed by Israel. With this in mind, let us turn to examine the role of the donors.

## The commitments to peace-building

It is generally recognized that institutional capacity-building is one area where donors can intervene to promote better government performance. Efficient and well-organized state structures, supported by meritocratic recruitment, are necessary for creating state agencies that can develop and implement effective policies. However, institution-building is often hampered by patronage, public sector job-creation to absorb the unemployed middle class and politicized appointments to technocratic posts. All of these processes were going on in the PNA. As a result, observers argued that since donors had supported the Authority to centralize its power, it was also necessary for them to support institutional capacity-building and to promote government accountability (Frisch and Hofnung 1997).[1]

The donors were of course aware of the importance of institutional capacity-building. But this issue was complicated in the Palestinian case because the expansion of the PNA's bureaucracy was a function of regime consolidation and seen as part of an attempt to ease unemployment under the impact of Israeli closure policies and restrictions on the Palestinian economy. In April 1995, a Tripartite Action Plan (TAP) was negotiated between the donors, the PNA and Israel. It contained a commitment by the PNA that it would improve revenue collection, reduce civil service hiring and clarify the division of responsibilities between its institutions. It also contained a commitment from Israel that it would allow a safe passage of goods between the West Bank and Gaza and from both to the outside world by effectively lifting the closures (Brynen *et al.* 2000). Another TAP was negotiated in January 1996. However, many of the commitments made by both sides were not fulfilled. An important component of the problem here was that the donors lacked the ability or the willingness to exercise leverage on the Israelis and Palestinians. In particular, with the decline of the Palestinian economy the donors did not want to stop the aid for fear of the implications this would have on the peace process (Brynen *et al.* 2000). Neither were donors willing to impose sanctions on Israel for its violations of agreements and Israel continued to be a major aid recipient of the donors. Therefore, whilst the TAPs were meant to enhance the performance of the PNA, the donors did not provide sufficient incentives or penalties to alter the behaviour of either the PNA or the Israelis.

This brings us to the central concern of this chapter, namely the ways in which donor commitments shaped rent-seeking behaviour. This issue is quite well explained in the World Bank report on aid effectiveness. This report explains that the aid provided to the Palestinians had the 'fundamental political purpose' of consolidating the peace process (World Bank 1999: 2). In other words, donor assistance operated within the horizon of the interim arrangement and all of its constraints, and its aim was the furtherance of peace-building. The practical implication of this was that political and socio-economic agendas were *connected* but not always *complementary.* At times peace-building went hand in hand with long-term development. 'At other times, however, they may be in tension; programs that promote immediate improvements in living conditions, for example, may be of greater political utility than those that foster long term improvements' (World Bank 1999: 5).

In the context of the restrictions on the Palestinian economy and the harsh effects of the closure policy, donors found themselves supporting employment-generation schemes and providing assistance to keep the PNA afloat, as part of their effort to address immediate political and economic priorities (Khadr 1999: 149). The growth of the PNA's bureaucracy, police and security forces provided most of these jobs (Brynen 1996: 81–2). In this regard, the short-term political concerns for regime stability and the overarching concern to show peace dividends to the public converged. The result was that donor assistance unwittingly allowed for the bloating of the bureaucracy and the formation of mechanisms that created opportunities for rent-seeking and patronage.

### Strategic interests, organizational constraints and monitoring mechanisms

Apart from the constraints of peace-building, a number of other factors affected the ways in which donors distributed aid. These include donors' strategic interests, their organizational constraints and the types of monitoring mechanisms used. Each will be considered briefly in turn.

With regard to strategic interests, it was clear that political considerations and foreign policy agendas played a role in the way donors intervene. In particular, there were tensions between the political objectives of supporting the peace process (and specifically the concern for a strong authority capable of clamping down on opposition) and donor willingness to use conditionality to promote transparency. This is supported by a number of observations. During the elections to the Palestinian legislative council (PLC), the head of the European Observers sent by the European Commission received an order not to report publicly any infractions committed by the PNA. Moreover, reviewing donor support for civil society in Palestine and Egypt, Brouwer argues that Western donor countries had more compelling objectives than simply promoting civil society and democracy. The priorities of the USA, the EU, and most European governments in his opinion, were the security of Israel, ensuring Palestinian support for the peace process, providing a solution acceptable to the majority of Palestinians, and further economic liberalization (Brouwer 2000: 29). These strategic interests therefore had an impact on how aid was channelled.

Concerning organizational constraints, a number of factors were relevant. First, an insufficient knowledge of the local context and a lack of understanding of the political roots of some forms of corruption often prevented donors from identifying problems correctly. Furthermore, the pressure to move money quickly often affected the quality of outcomes. Thus, while it was true that donors generally followed lengthy project assessment and procurement procedures, there was no consistent follow up and there were times when oversight of projects was lacking. For example, one of the Palestinian Ministries received a grant from the German Government with the supervision of the German Technical Cooperation to set up a computer network in its offices. A contract evaluated at $1 million was allocated to a local computer company without a bidding process. Ironically, this would have been impossible if the money had come from the Palestinian treasury.

Finally, turning to limitations in the monitoring of aid, two observations can be made. First, some donors, in particular the World Bank, approached rent-seeking and political corruption solely through the lens of liberal economics. According to this approach, liberalization would reduce the need to develop the state's monitoring capacity since the state would be doing less and therefore there would be less to monitor. As a result, the World Bank and the IMF called upon the PNA to close down monopolies, withdraw from its involvement in the private sector, privatize the public sector, and focus on strengthening the PNA's fiscal management. The limitations of such an approach have been examined in other chapters (in particular Chapter 2 by Hilal and Khan). Figures from the World Bank show that even towards the end of this period, donors were still not allocating funds to develop state administrative capacity (World Bank 1999: 178, 185; World Bank 2000: 17–18).

Second, it is evident that instead of using conditionality and linking aid to improvements in performance, donors formed their own linkages with PNA ministries. This was reinforced by an initial period of competition between the ministries to approach the donors separately. Some donors arranged projects with the ministries that were most amenable to them. This inevitably meant that, if that ministry was inefficient or there were problems of corruption, donors were often unwilling to cooperate with investigations (Brynen *et al.* 2000). Thus, in the absence of a proper system to monitor and promote transparency, an ad-hoc system emerged, with donors committing their assistance to the more competent institutions. This however reinforced a pattern of uneven institutional development.

## NGO leadership as an emerging elite

In this section, we will study the type of elites reinforced by foreign assistance, and the manner in which external assistance unwittingly reinforced the fragmentation of Palestinian society. In the Palestinian case, the structure of rents available to the NGO sector was not used to re-consolidate an old elite, as in the case of Lebanon (Kingston 2001), but served to strengthen a new emerging elite. The advent of this elite can be traced back to the First *Intifada* and the rise of new middle-class leaders who led the party structures of the national movement in the West Bank and Gaza.

In the 1970s, during the period of direct Israeli military rule, a new generation of Palestinian activists emerged. Characterized by some as new middle-class actors, these individuals were educated in local universities and found new opportunities for their upward mobility through the channels of the political parties. By creating a new infrastructure of mass organizations through the national movement, this generation of activists extended the existing array of social organizations, including the voluntary charitable societies – the oldest types of NGO in Palestine. Popular organizations were formed, including women's committees, labour unions, student organizations and voluntary initiatives. This was followed by the creation of developmental NGOs providing services in areas like health and agriculture (Barghouthi 1994). These Palestinian grassroots committees and mass organizations performed two pivotal functions: first, they established an alternative system of service provision to that of the Israeli occupier. But Second, they also mobilized the grassroots under the banner of the national movement, forming an institutional network that enabled resistance against Israeli rule and sustained the First *Intifada* for its first two years.

Over time, the national movement and the Palestinian society as a whole was weakened by harsh Israeli crackdowns and counter-insurgency measures. The Palestinian Left also suffered its own crisis after the demise of the former Soviet Union. Within this context, many Palestinian organizations took on a more narrowly defined developmental role, evolving into professionalized institutions. However, despite the shift in emphasis, these organizations continued to have former political activists and in particular leftist leaders in their midst. Rema Hammami describes how, with the retreat of the nationalist movement, political activists began to withdraw from the public sphere at a moment in which the only remaining edifice of the national movement were nascent NGO formations that had evolved out of earlier organizing initiatives. She states:

> mass popular organizing ceased to exist and all that remained in most cases were the leadership structures and the standing projects or professional staff (such as day-care centres, offices and clinics). Many of these professionalized development centres became the sole political base for the intellectuals and activists from the left parties.
>
> (Hammami 1995: 58)

The evolution of Palestinian NGOs into their contemporary form was shaped by this local context. Equally important, however, was the arrival of new forms of international support buttressed by an aid paradigm that recognized the importance of the role of NGOs in development processes. With the increased availability of Western donor funding, a new type of elite began to emerge in Palestinian society. Thus, a process of competition for organizational continuance began, in which the middle class intelligentsia and former political actors were overturning the old elite of voluntary charitable societies.

The historical evolution of PNGOs must be understood against a backdrop of shifting funding patterns. Initially, funds available to political factions through the PLO in the mid-1980s enabled a nascent institution-building process that was led by these political committees. Interestingly, even at this early stage PNGOs followed different funding patterns. For instance, the Communist Party was not a member of the PLO, and was oriented towards Western sources of funding much earlier than the other factions. They were pioneers in searching for funding, focusing primarily but not exclusively on France and Germany. In this regard, organizations like the Medical Relief Committees, Palestinian Agricultural Relief Committee and LAW not only accumulated experience in fundraising but also formed long-term relationships with international NGOs (INGOs). Not surprisingly, INGOs, which were mainly solidarity groups with leftist backgrounds, provided most of the support to leftist local organizations. At the same time, Islamist NGOs, were also emerging in the 1980s.They raised most of their funds locally, while also drawing on their own external networks, with funding being provided by the Palestinian Diaspora, as well as foreign, primarily Arab states.

In general, one can chart the trajectory of funding available to NGOs as follows. During the First *Intifada*, in addition to the funding available from the PLO, significant aid began to be provided by Arab and Western sources. One can characterize the period up to the first Iraq war of 1991 as one in which there was a diversity of funding sources. At the Baghdad summit of the Arab League in 1979, Arab support was pledged at $150 million per year (Brynen 2000: 47). The actual support provided by Arab states was estimated at having been approximately $30–100 million annually until 1991 (Clark and Balaj 1996). At the same time, the *zakat* organizations and charitable societies were mobilizing approximately $30 million locally (Clark and Balaj 1996). Some trace Western aid to PNGOs as far back as the 1970s (Brynen 2000: 44). But it is necessary to qualify this. During the first few years of the First *Intifada* PNGOs received a significant amount of solidarity funding from leftist oriented INGOs. Over time, solidarity funds were supplanted by formal development assistance, which was organized according to thematic areas of concern and was underpinned by the conceptual and theoretical vision of the donor.

After the first Iraq war of 1991, Arab funding dropped substantially, and PLO funding steadily declined. At the same time, Western donor funding continued and after the 1990s, this became the main source of assistance for PNGOs. Overall, this amounted to a decline in funding and from the early 1990s onwards to the present, funding to PNGOs has been cut in half. While receiving $170–240 million yearly in the early 1990s, (Brynen 2000: 187) it was estimated that in the late 1990s, PNGOs received approximately $60–90 million per annum (Hanafi 1999). This was clearly due to the effects of the first Gulf war on Palestinian–Arab relations, and the establishment of the PNA. The latter took on greater responsibility for many services, as well as large-scale development projects that were not easily implemented by NGOs. Finally, the peace process and the Oslo Accords ushered in a new funding trend, with very large and significant amounts of aid being channelled into the Palestinian territories as part of donor peace-building efforts. For instance, Finnish aid increased ten times, and Japan began to provide assistance to the Palestinian territories.

This brief review reveals that in the period following the first Iraq war there was a quantitative shift in the types of funding available to PNGOs. This had important effects on the organization of PNGOs. First, Western donor assistance induced PNGOs to become independent of political parties. This was reflected in donor discourses as well as in donor condition-alities (Shawa 2003). Second, charitable societies and non-professionalized committees lost most of their own sources of funding, especially those that were dependant on funding from other Arab countries. Third, Western donor funding criteria established a hierarchy of organizations, which meant that certain societies and committees became marginalized in terms of access to funding. Clark and Balaj summarized these processes and noted that since the 1991 Iraq war, the charitable societies' external support had halved, and the committees lost even more funding. Furthermore, they note, 'in spite of the large number of NGOs it is estimated that 30–40 of them receive up to 70 per cent or 80 of total NGO funding' (Clark and Balaj 1996: 3). In other words, there was an overall contraction in the funding of the NGO sphere, a large number of organizations became marginalized and a minority began to acquire a larger share of the funding. These trends illustrated a new type of competition within the NGO sphere that centred on organizational survival. New middle-class actors began overturning the old elite of the voluntary charitable societies and began to represent an emerging social force.

### PNA–PNGO relations

In 1994, when the PNA was set-up, the PNGO sector consisted of a network of institutions and service providers that could have been one of the building blocks of the emerging state. The PNGO sector was responsible for 60 per cent of primary healthcare, 49 per cent of secondary and tertiary

*Table 7.1* Donor assistance to the PNA and to Palestinian NGOs ($ million)

| Total contribution | 1996 | 1997 |
| --- | --- | --- |
| Donor aid to the PNA and NGOs from government agencies | 549.414 | 432.259 |
| MOPIC's Report: Donor aid to NGOs from government agencies | 58.069 | 45.995 |
| Percentage to NGOs (MOPIC) | 10% | 11% |
| Welfare Survey: Donor aid to PNGOs from governments and INGOs | 54.804 | 76.897 |
| Percentage to NGOs (welfare survey) | 10% | 18% |

Source: MOPIC is the Palestinian Ministry of Planning and International Cooperation, the Welfare Survey was carried out by Hanafi (1999). For more on both sources see Hanafi (1999)

care, and 100 per cent of day-care services (Barghouthi 1994). However, the PNA did not use this infrastructure and chose to create its own separate ministries and institutions, declaring itself the 'only legitimate development authority' and asking donors to channel funds to its ministries (Abdul Hadi 1999). This not only created tensions between the two sectors, but also fuelled distrust at a time when the responsibilities of each sphere needed to be addressed and clearly delineated. Subsequently, antagonism gave way to cooperation in the delivery of services, particularly in the health and education sectors. Nevertheless, an element of competition remained a feature of the relationship between the PNA and PNGOs. The amount of funding that PNGOs received made them competitors with the state elite. The donor community contributed more than $62 million to the NGO sector annually, and $248 million during the four years 1995–98.[2] Table 7.1 shows that this was estimated to be 10–20 per cent of the total international assistance dispensed to the Palestinian people. Table 7.2 shows the distribution of NGO activities by sectors.

Since the establishment of the PNA, the donor community effectively participated in empowering the NGOs to perform two roles: to complement service delivery by the state and to increase the accountability of the state. However, this may have contributed to a more fragmented relationship between state and society since from the formation of the PNA, we can identify three different spheres of institutional operation and rents. First, there was of course the Fateh-dominated PNA, then a predominantly leftist NGO sphere, and finally the Islamists, with their network of grassroots

*Table 7.1* Distribution of NGO expenditures by sector ($ ,000 and percentages)

| Sector | Funding in 1995 | % 1995 | Funding in 1996 | % 1996 | Funding in 1997 | % 1997 | Funding in 1998 | % 1998 | Total | Total percentage |
|---|---|---|---|---|---|---|---|---|---|---|
| Agriculture | 3936.2 | 6.5% | 5717.8 | 10.5% | 4603.8 | 5.9% | 3843.7 | 6.7% | 18101.5 | 7.4% |
| Culture | 2899.4 | 4.8% | 3074.4 | 5.7% | 7054.3 | 9.0% | 7579.9 | 13.2% | 20608.0 | 8.2% |
| Democracy | 331.0 | 0.5% | 146.0 | 0.3% | 1741.0 | 2.2% | 1800.0 | 3.1% | 4018.0 | 1.5% |
| Education | 12206.2 | 20.2% | 14321.0 | 26.4% | 16771.4 | 21.5% | 14340.8 | 25.0% | 57639.5 | 23.3% |
| Environment | 653.9 | 1.1% | 2035.6 | 3.8% | 2367.6 | 3.0% | 2138.4 | 3.7% | 7195.5 | 2.9% |
| Health | 9710.6 | 16.1% | 10621.6 | 19.6% | 18230.2 | 23.4% | 11202.1 | 19.5% | 49764.5 | 19.6% |
| Human rights | 301.9 | 0.5% | 537.4 | 1.0% | 2891.9 | 3.7% | 3682.8 | 6.4% | 7414.0 | 2.9% |
| Infrastructure (except water) | 2000.0 | 3.3% | 2106.0 | 3.9% | 2937.0 | 3.8% | 193.3 | 0.3% | 7236.3 | 2.8% |
| Institution building | 6527.5 | 10.8% | 3343.5 | 6.2% | 1796.5 | 2.3% | 1838.0 | 3.2% | 13505.5 | 5.6% |
| Micro credit | 3389.2 | 5.6% | 1960.5 | 3.6% | 2402.5 | 3.1% | 1817.0 | 3.2% | 9569.2 | 3.9% |
| Multi-sectoral | 12446.9 | 20.6% | 533.9 | 1.0% | 567.7 | 0.7% | 1156.0 | 2.0% | 14704.5 | 6.1% |

| | | | | | | | | | | |
|---|---|---|---|---|---|---|---|---|---|---|
| Relief | 352.3 | 0.6% | 352.3 | 0.6% | 1066.0 | 1.4% | 699.0 | 1.2% | 2469.7 | 1.0% |
| Research | 661.5 | 1.1% | 923.8 | 1.7% | 1338.6 | 1.7% | 1685.1 | 2.9% | 4609.0 | 1.9% |
| Social services | 2324.8 | 3.8% | 4826.4 | 8.9% | 8390.9 | 10.7% | 3700.4 | 6.4% | 19242.5 | 7.5% |
| Tourism | 33.0 | 0.1% | 60.0 | 0.1% | 67.0 | 0.1% | 880.0 | 1.5% | 1040.0 | 0.4% |
| Trade & industry | 1813.0 | 3.0% | 1820.0 | 3.4% | 4197.0 | 5.4% | 235.4 | 0.4% | 8065.4 | 3.0% |
| Vocational/ technical training | 868.8 | 1.4% | 1898.8 | 3.5% | 1634.5 | 2.1% | 656.8 | 1.1% | 5059.0 | 2.0% |
| Grand Total | 60456.3 | 100.0 | 54279.1 | 100.0 | 78057.9 | 100.0 | 57448.7 | 100.0 | 250242.0 | 100.0 |

*Source*: (Hanafi, 1999). These figures are from the Welfare Survey reported in Table 7.1

social services. But these three sets of institutions tended to operate largely in their own spheres. The NGOs were particularly unwilling to challenge the PNA or to hold it accountable.

A number of important factors may help to explain this. First, donor assistance reinforced the emergence of a so-called *'progressive' elite* within the NGO sector, particularly at the leadership level which had considerable influence. These were middle-class individuals and included former political activists and intellectuals. Compared to other Arab countries and even other regions, PNGOs were relatively strong. Most of the PNGOs were vibrant independent institutions, run by charismatic and politically skilled individuals. To appreciate the significance of this one only has to look at other post-conflict cases. For instance, in post-war Vietnam there were many restrictions and controls on setting up NGOs. Here, to set up an NGO, individuals required strong government contacts and the state determined who gained access to external resources. Moreover, although Vietnamese NGOs were set up since 1990, there is still no formal law governing the operation of these groups (Gray 1999: 698). In comparison, PNGOs were much more independent, and were able to negotiate a legal framework within which they could work with the PNA. Second, within aid channels, there has been a growing emphasis on 'scaling up', which produced very large, professionally run NGOs. This created a niche for influential members of indigenous progressive elites. Finally, a new development discourse has also developed within the aid industry, which has created new terms on which the legitimacy of NGOs is based, requiring in turn a re-negotiation of local sources of support. Legitimacy increasingly comes from efficient service delivery and not from political engagement. All of these factors contributed to the NGO sector de-linking itself from the state formation process.

## Monopolistic mega-NGOs

The fragmentation of Palestinian society and the role of PNGOs in this context cannot be analysed without paying attention to the emphasis within the aid system on 'scaling up' and the effect this has on local organizations. In Palestine, donor aid policies had pushed and supported the creation of mega-NGOs, such as the Palestinian Medical Relief Committee, Palestinian Agricultural Relief Committee and the Palestinian human rights organization LAW. This was an international phenomenon and was not restricted to Palestine alone. The rise of colossal NGOs was driven primarily by the aid system's emphasis on efficiency. In addition to this, scarcity of resources and competition between NGOs meant that only the fittest survived. The impact that these large NGOs had on society was not necessarily beneficial. They created inequalities between civil society organizations and a monopolization of resources by a few entities. In Bangladesh, for instance, these processes resulted in the creation of a two-tier NGO sector, with about 30 NGOs receiving about 80 per cent of all funding (INTRAC 1998: 18–27).

Together with the emphasis on efficiency and competent service delivery, the rise of very large NGOs was also led by a drive for increased profession-alization. This led to situations such as that in Kenya where donors over-funded a small group of credible NGOs because of the weak capacity of alternative organizations (INTRAC 1998: 69). Personal contacts between NGOs and donors also play an important role. Donors often admit that the reputation of the leader of an NGO is a significant factor in the funding decision. All of this meant that donors often ended up supporting pro-state or elitist NGOs.

In the Palestinian case, donors became very strict about dispersing funds to organizations that did not have sufficiently developed administrative capacity. This marginalized many organizations. ANERA, an American NGO that received much of its funding from USAID, used to have consider-able freedom in determining its projects, including whom to disperse funds to. According to the Women's Charitable Society of Hebron, in the past ANERA provided it with 70,000 Jordanian Dinars (about $80,000) to purchase land and build a day-care centre. Later, the same Palestinian orga-nization was unable to acquire further funding from ANERA. One USAID officer whom we interviewed acknowledged that grassroots organizations (GROs) in Palestine were being marginalized but suggested that the GROs themselves were simply unable to keep up because of weak administrative capacity.

Writers such as Salamon (1993) have suggested that NGOs have a role in meeting the diversity of social demands. Modern society does not enjoy a consensus about public expenditure priorities and this made the monopo-listic position of mega-NGOs difficult to justify. There are also a number of other concerns about this trend. According to Bebbington and Riddell (1997: 125), one function of NGOs was to challenge the state to promote social justice. This goal could be diluted if the NGO sector was reduced to a few big organizations working closely with the state. This was clearly happening in the case of some PNGOs. For instance, in the health sector in the West Bank and Gaza, it was widely acknowledged that the development of a health insurance system was vital for the future sustainability of the healthcare system. But this was not supported by the large NGOs in the health sector who did not wish to play an advocacy role, even though they recognized the importance of the insurance issue.

## New bases of legitimacy and rent-seeking in the NGO sector

Since NGO leaders and employees have access to incomes that they would not otherwise have had, they are effectively capturing rents, and to seek and maintain these rents, we would expect them to engage in both legal and illegal rent-seeking. To begin with, it is necessary to highlight two aspects of NGO financing that have implications for NGO rent-seeking. First, NGOs are incapable of procuring funds independently of the donors. The absence

of endowment funds often results in over-budgeting in order to secure organizational resources for the future. Some of the PNGOs we spoke to
admitted to using fake receipts for expenditures for almost the entire budget
in the initial proposal. This money was usually used for other activities and
was not necessarily appropriated by the directors/officers of the NGO.
Second, NGO leaders and employees usually paid themselves relatively high
salaries. This type of highly paid employment was a significant factor in the
emergence of new elites. The donors obviously play a role in sustaining this
process. Donors, especially USAID, insisted on high employee wages, and
often doubled the salaries of directors of PNGOs. Such high salaries
inevitably created incentives for rent-seeking activities as the new elite
competed to capture these positions.

There are two ways of conceptualizing rent-seeking in the NGO sector.
The first approach builds on Sogge and Zadek's notion of 'margin', which
viewed rent-seeking in the NGO sector as an attempt to capture money
that was not officially accounted for. Sogge and Zadek, explained the
concept of 'margin' as the difference between the income that an NGO
received and the expenditures of a project. They suggested that the margin
could be used to fund recurring or discretionary expenses or even for
personal gain. The authors argue that 'the drive to gain wide margins
resembles rent-seeking, in that revenues gained through margins are independent of the quality or effectiveness of the activity' (Sogge and Zadek
1996: 88). The first type of rent-seeking then focuses on the conscious
intention of the actors involved. Actors within NGOs, facing structural
constraints may consciously manipulate budgets by using 'creative
accounting' to manage their ongoing costs. In some cases, donors were
aware of the over-budgeting but did not react to it and continued to
support the organization for political and pragmatic reasons.

A second conceptualization of rent-seeking draws on political economy
approaches. These focus on the outcomes of rent-seeking and emphasize
differences in the political, economic and organizational abilities and powers
of groups to explain different types of rent capture and their economic and
social implications (Khan and Jomo 2000: 5; Robinson 1998: 5). The
outcomes of this broader conceptualization of rent-seeking are open. The
rent-seeking involved could be legal or illegal, and more importantly, the
rents captured may vary widely and have very different implications for
development. This broader approach can be used to examine how rent-
seeking changes the behaviour of individuals in ways that are *sanctioned* by
the norms of the rent-givers. This can be very significant because the ability
to play this game may be unevenly distributed, meaning that some elites
rather than others will benefit. The social and economic outcome will
depend on the identity of this elite, the rents they want, and the effects of
this rent-seeking for social organization more widely. Observers have recognized the self-selection that NGO rent-seeking involves. Thus Carapico
points out that

some activists decline subsidies from Western or Arab sources entirely, pointing to a new kind of dependency: *NGO rent-seeking*. These critics call attention to the class dimension of criteria for qualifying for international loans, grants or programs – such as preferences for those who speak English, understand spreadsheets, or dress in appropriate business attire.

(2000: 14)

Other behaviour that is often sanctioned by donors includes the exercise of personal power inside the NGO, strong informal relations with donors that keep the lines of patronage open and accessible, as well as the manipulation of margins and personal aggrandizement. Thus, NGO rent-seeking was not just about manipulating margins for profit, but also about the practices and behaviours that were approved by donors in the process of competing for and maintaining rents.

## The emergence of NGO-leaders as a new globalized elite

In line with the political economy approach, our focus is on the dynamics of power and agency rather than individual self-interest. We concur with those who have suggested (Scott 1999) that at times the impact of corruption was a counter-hegemonic one insofar as it promoted the entry of new forces into the social arena. Certainly, the aid industry promoted this counter-hegemonic influence by reinforcing NGO actors as a new and emerging elite. With regard to Palestinian NGO actors, they constituted a new elite by virtue of their *strategic institutions,* and by implication their influence and decision-making authority in social, economic and political circles. In this context, an elite can be defined as a group that holds strategic positions in powerful organizations, and which has the ability to affect national political outcomes regularly and significantly (Dogan and Higley 1998: 15). There is also the possibility of a 'shadow elite' which occupies prominent institutions and is able to influence political decisions intermittently (Dogan and Higley 1998: 15). Based on these definitions, it is evident that the PNGO leaders constituted an emerging elite, or at the very least a 'shadow elite', by virtue of their decision-making sway in national or municipal levels in a range of sectors. It is also important to reiterate that the NGOs in Palestinian territories were taken over by disenfranchised and leftist sections of the middle classes. This not only provided them with room to affect social development but also gave them status and influence over decision-making.

Sogge and Zadek (1996) identify the central dynamic that underpins NGO survival and organizational continuity in the modern aid industry. They suggest that NGOs are engaged in an ongoing process of *anticipating and responding* to new policy concerns, new development themes and trends, and are continuously expanding the 'oeuvre' of knowledge and concepts. The NGO 'economy' is a non-productive economy that depends on the inflow of external aid. A central part of this process is the circulation of knowledge and a development discourse upon which cooperation between NGOs and donors often depends. The appropriation and use of this system by local actors enables them to participate in this system of rent distribution. In the case of PNGOs, it was clear that what started as material power, led to symbolic power and ultimately to the emergence of a local 'globalized elite' (Hanafi and Tabar 2002). This new elite overturned older elites (including the leaders of older voluntary charitable societies or in some cases the elite in the rural areas) through a process of competition for resources. In the remainder of this paper we will suggest that having entered the aid system, PNGOs acquired a new basis of power but then faced challenges in re-negotiating their local sources of support and legitimacy.

The term globalized elite refers to the self perception of these actors and not their objective position in a globalized political economy. In the Palestinian context, despite the adoption of a leftist discourse, the emerging elite was often parochial, factionalized and conservative, and sought to maintain its rents. In contrast to its leftist discourse and claims of promoting democracy and civil society, it was in large part an inward-oriented elite, and in the main only interested in entering into accommodation politics with the PNA. Moreover, this elite was not only a tiny fraction of society; but also small compared to traditional Palestinian elites.

A number of characteristics of this elite are relevant for understanding the implications of this pattern of rent-seeking in the Palestinian context. First, this elite often found itself closer to the INGOs and their Northern allies than to their own society. By describing them as a globalized elite, we are trying to highlight that these actors were *informed by global agendas* and were closely aligned with internationally endorsed development paradigms. They moved within the space occupied by donors and INGOs, attending global conferences and forming their own relations with international organizations. Thus, referring to a globalized elite does not mean that these individuals were really part of a global elite but that their power derived from their access to global actors, mainly international NGOs and donors. Second, by its very nature, this access was personalized and based on command of a specific language and discourse. This in turn meant that PNGOs were led by strong personalities who commanded this access, and the pattern of clientelism and privilege was reproduced within the organization.

A third feature of the globalized elite is particular to the Palestinian context; this elite was distinguished by its position on the peace process. *It supported the peace process* or at least believed in the importance of giving this process and the PNA sufficient time without exercising violence against the Israeli occupation. In this regard, this elite was strikingly different from the Nationalist-Islamist leaders, and this explains why it had a comparative advantage in engaging in the globalized discourse on the 'peace process'.

Finally, it was a *professionalized elite*: PNGO actors were no longer the activists of the First *Intifada*, they were either former activists with technical knowledge, or technocrats who never had a connection with the national movement.

It is not surprising that the allocation of resources to NGOs was likely to reflect the location and interests of the NGO leaders and their command over the dominant discourses. When we look at the geographical distribution of funding for NGO projects, we see an imbalance between centre and periphery, between urban and rural areas, and between cities with high and low population densities. Many districts with a high population density received a small percentage of funding. According to Hanafi (1999), the distribution of projects was found to be extremely lopsided between the Gaza Strip and West Bank, with $26.4 million for Gaza (only 19 per cent) and $111.5 million for the West Bank (81 per cent). This was disproportionate both in terms of population and in terms of needs. According to the 1997 census figures, the population of the Gaza Strip was 35 per cent of the Palestinian population and it had far higher poverty and unemployment rates than the West Bank. This imbalance in funding could be explained partly by the historical weakness of the PNGO sector in Gaza compared to that of the West Bank.[3] But it could partly be explained by the concentration of the leftist middle class in the West Bank who played leadership roles in PNGOs. Jerusalem and Ramallah alone accounted for 45 per cent of the Palestinian NGOs (208 and 130 NGOs respectively). This percentage increases to 57 per cent if Bethlehem is added (with more than 90 NGOs).[4]

Finally, as we have already seen, while individuals who supported the peace process generally led the NGOs, these individuals were increasingly marginal in terms of contemporary Palestinian politics. Those who came from leftist political backgrounds had long since lost their local political constituencies and had not managed to cultivate a new political base for themselves. Therefore, if aid contributed to the peace process, it was primarily through the job creation that was achieved by the PNA. This was further assisted by the service-delivery achieved by the NGOs. But the empowerment of ex-leftist NGO leaders had little to do with the peace process or political stabilization. If anything, the absence of any political constituency for these leaders and their growing competition for rents resulted in a political fragmentation of civil society together with a recognition on the part of the NGOs that their best political strategy was to work with the PNA and to desist from too many overt criticisms of PNA performance.

In conclusion, the relationship between donors and PNGOs on the one hand, and between PNGOs and the state formation process on the other did not result in political pressure on the PNA for more inclusive politics, and did not contribute to a deepening of political stabilization through the empowerment of critical constituencies. PNGOs did have an effect on stabilization indirectly through providing services, and their efficiency is likely to have improved through professionalization. After 2000, Palestinian state formation began to be pushed back with an Israeli re-occupation, and attacks on PNA institutions. In this context, the role of NGOs is likely to take a back seat. Large professional service-delivery PNGOs are likely to play a secondary role in the survival strategies of an encircled and besieged population. Donors have responded to the humanitarian crisis in a number of different ways. The most significant has been employment generation schemes. In April 2001, the United Nations Development Programme set aside $22 million for employment generating projects throughout the West Bank, targeting skilled and semi-skilled workers denied entry to the Israel labour market. They received a third of their former daily wage while working in temporary projects in the West Bank. If the setback is long-lasting, the NGO sector will have to play a role in sustaining service-delivery. But the important task of mobilizing the Palestinian masses for a new phase of resistance is unlikely to be carried out by this sector.

## Notes

1   The Declaration of Principles following Oslo stipulated that there should be a strong Palestinian police force that could maintain 'public order' and 'internal security', and it was agreed that this would be partially financed by the donors (Milton-Edwards 1998: 96). In 1994, the donors disbursed $40.9 million to fund the establishment of the Palestinian police force and have provided subsequent financial and technical support.
2   This amount is based on Welfare Association survey conducted by Sari Hanafi (Hanafi 1999). The survey gathered information from about 100 organizations.
3   PNGOs were legally recognized in Gaza only after 1967. Previously, the Egyptian military authorities banned the formation and registration of local organizations and unions, with the exception of the Lawyers' Union. According to the Welfare Association survey, 25 per cent of Palestinian NGOs (186 NGOs) were located in the GS.
4   This percentage figure does not increase much when one factors in the Northern region of the West Bank, which includes Nablus, Tulkarem and Jenin, therefore revealing the unbalanced distribution of the NGOs between centres and peripheral areas (see Hanafi 1999: Table 7). It is also true, however, that some donors held the view that the PNA invests proportionately more in Gaza than in the West Bank (although this is not verified by statistics on funding), and chose to compensate for this by directing more funding to NGOs in the West Bank.

## References

Abdul Hadi, M. (1999) 'NGO Action and the Question of Palestine: Sharing Experiences, Developing New Strategies', in Abdul Hadi, M. (ed.) *Dialogue on Palestinian State-Building and Identity, PASSIA Meetings and Lectures 1995–1998*, Jerusalem: PASSIA.

Amundsen, I. (1999) *Political Corruption: An Introduction to the Issues*, Norway: Chr. Michelsen Institute.

Barghouthi, M. (1994) *Palestinian NGOs and Their Role in Building a Civil Society*, Jerusalem: Union of Palestinian Medical Relief Committees.

Bebbington, A. and Riddell, R. (1997) 'Heavy Hands, Hidden Hands, Holding Hands? Donors, Intermediary NGOs and Civil Society Organizations', in Hulme, D. and Edwards, M. (eds) *NGOs. States and Donors. Too close for comfort?* New York: MacMillan Press.

Beck, M. (2000) 'The External Dimensions of Authoritarian Rule in Palestine', *Journal of International Relations and Development*, 3 (1): 47–66.

Brouwer, I. (2000) *US Civil-Society Assistance to the Arab World: The Cases of Egypt and Palestine*, EUI Working Paper no 2000/5, Florence: European University Institute.

Brynen, R. (1996) 'Buying Peace? Critical Assessment of International Aid to the West Bank and Gaza', *Journal of Palestine Studies*, 25 (3): 79–92.

—— *A Very Political Economy: Peacebuilding and Foreign Aid in the West Bank and Gaza*, Washington: United States Institute of Peace Studies.

Brynen, R., Awartani, H. and Woodcraft C. (2000) 'The Palestinian Territories', in Forman, S. and Patrick S. (eds) *Good Intentions: Pledges of Aid for Postconflict Recovery*, Boulder: Lynne Rienner Publishers.

Carapico, S. (2000) 'NGOs, INGOs, GO-NGOs and DO-NGOs: Making Sense of Non-Governmental Organizations', *Middle East Report*, No. 214, 30 (1): 12–15. Available online at <http://www.merip.org/mer/mer214/214_carapico.html> (accessed 15 February 2004).

Clark, J. and Balaj, B. (1996) *NGOs in the West Bank and Gaza*, Washington: World Bank.

Collier, P. (1997) 'The Failure of Conditionality', in Gwin, C. and Nelson, J. (eds) *Perspectives on Aid and Development*, Washington: Overseas Development Council.

Dogan, M. and Higley, J. (1998) (eds) *Elites, Crisis and the Origins of Regimes*, Oxford: Rowman and Littlefield.

Frisch, H. and Hofnung, M. (1997) 'State Formation and International Aid: the Emergence of the Palestinian Authority', *World Development* 25 (8): 1243–55.

Gray, M. L. (1999) 'Creating Civil Society? The Emergence of NGOs in Vietnam', *Development and Change*, 30 (4): 693–713.

Gwin, C. and Nelson, J. M. (1997) 'Development and Aid: New Evidence and New Issues', in Gwin, C. and Nelson J. M. (eds) *Perspectives on Aid and Development*, Washington: Overseas Development Council.

Hammami, R. (1995) 'NGOs: the Professionalisation of Politics', *Race & Class* 37 (2): 51–63.

Hanafi, S. (1999) *Profile of Donors Assistance to Palestinian NGOs: Survey and Database*, Report submitted to the Welfare Association, Jerusalem.

Hanafi, S. and Tabar, L. (2002) 'Donors, International NGOs and Local NGOs: The Emergence of a Palestinian Globalized Elite' (Mimeo in English and in Arabic).

INTRAC (1998) *Direct Funding From a Southern Perspective: Strengthening Civil Society?* Oxford: The International NGO Training and Research Centre.

Khadr, A. (1999) 'Donor Assistance', in Diwan, I. and Shaban, R. A. (eds) *Development Under Diversity: The Palestinian Economy in Transition*, Washington: International Bank for Reconstruction and Development, World Bank Group.

Khan, M. H. (1996) 'A Typology of Corrupt Transactions in Developing Countries', *IDS Bulletin* 27 (2): 12–21.

Khan, M. H. and Jomo, K. S. (2000) 'Introduction', in Khan, M. H. and Jomo, K. S. (eds) *Rents, Rent-Seeking and Economic Development: Theory and Evidence in Asia*, Cambridge: Cambridge University Press.

Kingston, P. (2001) 'Patrons, Clients and Civil Society: A Case Study of Environmental Politics in Postwar Lebanon', *Arab Studies Quarterly* 23 (1): 55–72.

Maipose, G. S. (2000) 'Aid Abuse and Mismanagement in Africa: Problems of Accountability, Transparency and Ethical Leadership', in Hope, K. R. and Chikulo, B. C. (eds) *Corruption and Development in Africa: Lessons from Country Case-Studies*, Hampshire: Macmillan.

Milton-Edwards, B. (1998) 'Palestinian State-Building: Police and Citizens as Tests of Democracy', *British Journal of Middle East Studies* 25 (1): 95–120.

Riley, S. P. (1999) 'Western Policies and African Realities: the New Anti-Corruption Agenda', in Hope, K. R. and Chikulo, B. C. (eds) *Corruption and Development in Africa: Lessons from Country Case-Studies*, Hampshire: Macmillan.

Robinson, M. (1998) 'Corruption and Development: An Introduction', in Robinson, M. (ed.) *Corruption and Development*, London: Frank Cass Publishers.

Salamon, L. M. (1993) *The Global Associational Revolution: the Rise of the Third Sector on the World Scene*, Occasional Papers, no. 15, Baltimore: Institute for Policy Studies, Johns Hopkins University.

Schild, V. (1998) 'New Subjects of Rights? Women's Movements and the Construction of Citizenship in the "New Democracies"', in Alvarez, S. E., Dagnino E. and Escobar A. (eds) *Cultures of Politics, Politics of Cultures, Re-visioning Latin American Social Movements*, Colorado: Westview Press.

Scott, D. (1999) *Refashioning Futures: Criticism After Postcoloniality*, Princeton: Princeton University Press.

Shawa, S. (2003) 'NGOs and Civil Society in Palestine: a Comparative Analysis of Four Organizations', in Benefissa, Hanafi, Milani and Abdel Fatah (eds) *The NGOs and Governance in the Arabic World*, UNESCO.

Sogge, D. and Zadek, S. (1996) '"Laws" of the Market', in Sogge, D., Biekart, K. and Saxby J. (eds) *Compassion and Calculation: the Business of Private Foreign Aid*, London: Pluto Press.

World Bank (1999) *The World Bank Annual Report 1999*, Washington: World Bank.

—— (2000) *Aid Effectiveness in the West Bank and Gaza*, Washington: World Bank and the Government of Japan.

—— (2001) *Palestinian Economic Assistance and Cooperation Expansion (PEACE) Faculty*, News Release. Available online at <http://www.worldbank.org> (West Bank and Gaza country page accessed December 2001).

# Index